The St John Ambulance Brigade Ilford
Its Beginnings, Its Founders and Its Members

Copyright © 2023 Brian Leonard Porter

All rights reserved.

Cover and Book design by Brian Leonard Porter No part of this book can be reproduced in any form or by written, electronic or mechanical, including photocopying, recording, or by any information retrieval system without written permission in writing by the author. Published by Brian Leonard Porter

Printed by Book Printing UK www.bookprintinguk.com Remus House, Coltsfoot Drive, Peterborough, PE2 9BF

Printed in Great Britain

Although every precaution has been taken in the preparation of this book, the publisher and author assume no responsibility for errors or omissions. Neither is any liability assumed for damages resulting from the use of information contained herein.

ISBN   978-1-9196468-0-0

A RESEARCH PAPER No 2/2022

By Brian L Porter OStJ. Heritage Lead
East London District St John Ambulance

Dr Edmund King Houchin c 1897 (photographer unknown)

President of *The United Kingdom Police Surgeons' Association 1897*
First St John Ambulance Brigade, Divisional Surgeon, Ilford Division

William Robert Magnus – Photograph Credit: *The Great Eastern Railway Magazine*

Railway Challenge Shield - National Competition Winner
Great Eastern Railway 1897 and 1898
First St John Ambulance Brigade, Divisional Superintendent, Ilford Division
President of The Hospitallers' Club 1921

FORWARD

The Worshipful the Mayor 2022/23
Councillor Thavathuray Jeyaranjan

Mayor's Office
Town Hall
High Road
Ilford IG1 1DD

Telephone: 020 8708 2297
Email: mayorsoffice@redbridge.gov.uk

March 2023

This book outlines the long association between what was the Borough of Ilford and now the London Borough of Redbridge and St John Ambulance, the United Kingdom's premier First Aid Volunteer and First Aid Training organisation.

This book highlights and mirrors the history of growth in the Borough through the early years and that history held by St John Ambulance and the LB of Redbridge Heritage Teams.

The history starts with the introduction of First Aid Training in the Railways that ran through the Borough. This training became more widespread with other Railway companies and lead to the formation of First Aid Competitions in London and Nationally in which the Ilford based teams took part. The story also covers the First World War, when the St John Ambulance Brigade Divisions in Ilford provided service at home and abroad. This included service with the Royal Army Medical Corps and support to the Voluntary Aid Detachments (VAD) that were prominent in assisting with the running of the Ilford Emergency Hospital, Valentines Mansion Hospital and Oakwood Hospital.

Such actions still put Ilford, now Redbridge at the forefront of community life in London, as was the case during the COVID19 pandemic.

On behalf of the borough, I wish to thank Mr Brain Porter, District Heritage Lead for East London District, St John Ambulance for his work in compiling this book, a very worthwhile read.

Cllr Thavathuray Jeyaranjan
Mayor of Redbridge
2022/23

Introduction

This is a story of the early years and formation of the St John Ambulance Brigade in Ilford. It shows the much wider social impact that the organization had on town and beyond.

An overview of Ilford, from the year 1830 became a separate ecclesiastical parish with the building of St Mary's church in the High Road. In 1870 -1878, *John Marius Imperial Gazetteer of England and Wales* described Ilford (Great), like this -

> "a small town, as chapelry, a ward in the Barking Parish, Essex. The town stands near the river Roding and on the Eastern Counties Railway (Later Great Eastern Railway), near Epping Forest, 3 ½ Miles ENE of Stratford; It is within the jurisdiction of the central criminal court and the Metropolitan Court; and has a station of the name of Ilford (opened in 1839)."

Ilford did not have municipal responsibilities until 1888 when it elected its own council. Essentially Ilford was a small town with small hamlets and farms, but with some grand houses. London as this time was expanding eastwards, into what was then regarded at the County of Essex.

The population of Ilford in 1891 was 10,711, but ten years later it had grown to 41,235 as there was a major house building boom and population influx of new families. By 1931 the population had grown to 131,061 people.

This story examines the key roles undertaken by Dr Edmund King Houchin and Willian Robert Magnus. As a Police Surgeon and a Coroner Dr King Houchin had already played a distinguished role in the life of East London, before moving to Ilford. He joined St John Ambulance after he had moved from Stepney and like William R. Magnus he joined No 15 East Ham Ambulance Division with the intention of establishing a new St John Ambulance Brigade Division in Ilford.

William Magnus was a very able man who grew to become a key member of the Great Eastern Railway (GER) management team and also the GER St John Ambulance Corps. He was also an early member of No. 4 Leyton and Leytonstone Ambulance Division.

This paper covers the initial approaches to the St John Ambulance Brigade by the Ilford community and the period when Edmund King Houchin and William Magnus joined No.15 East Ham Ambulance Division and started a section of that division and established a St John Ambulance presence in Ilford. It also covers William's wife Maud, who supported her husband's efforts and then went on to be a force in her own right forming a Nursing Division.

It goes on to give a vivid picture of the Coronation duty in 1911 and a little-known fact that the Division had two members on duty for the Investiture of the Prince of Wales in Caernarfon Castle on 13 July 1911. It also covers the 1912 Royal Review of St John Ambulance by King George V in Windsor.

The story continues with the unfolding events of WWI and the movement establishing a hospital in Ilford and the role of the Voluntary Aid Detachments in supporting the war effort.

I look at William Magnus's life after Ilford. This story is one of leadership, in St John terms, from 1900s to the 1920s and beyond. It shows the professional roles, of Magnus and Houchin up to and including WWI, and the effort of Mrs Magnus with the Voluntary Aid Detachments.
It also offers a glimpse into the social history of hospitals in the early twentieth century, during WWI and long before the days of the National Health Service.

Newspaper reports are frequently used in this research. As a result, St John Ambulance is often quoted as St John's Ambulance in these.

This research displays the character of this local triumvirate and the success they achieved, over a thirty-year period at the turn of the twentieth century.

Acknowledgement

Firstly, I would like to thank Squadron Leader Alan R D Clark MBE(Mil) MStJ., St John Ambulance Area President (London Borough of Redbridge) for his encouragement when I first took on the role of Heritage Lead in East London. Secondly, Alan Sharkey has been very supportive especially with material on the Great Eastern Railway (GER), which has been useful with this paper, with so many of the key people having roots in the GER from where much of St John Ambulance, in East London was conceived. Special thanks are due to Malcolm Knight OStJ and Arwyn Evans both of whom have spent many hours assisting me with this manuscript. The assistance of the Anna Mason and Sophie Denman at The Museum of the Order of St John and Paris Sydes Heritage Assistant at Redbridge Museum and Heritage Centre has been invaluable, along with advice from Gary Coker. However, much of the information used comes from newspaper reports complied by reporters of various publications, to these unknown folk I owe my thanks.

In conclusion I, Brian L Porter confirm that the work presented in this document is my own. Where information has been derived from other sources, I confirm that this has been indicated in this research paper. The right of Brian L Porter to be identified as the author of this work except where specified and acknowledged has been asserted by in accordance with the Copyright and Patents Act 1988.

Where possible I have acknowledged the source of the material used. Some, where still under copyright, it may no longer be feasible to trace the original copyright holder. I acknowledge and am grateful for use of images and material to enhance this work. Some are available for use under Creative Commons Licence, this is stated where applicable. However, I apologise for any copyright infringement which I am happy to correct in future editions of this research paper, if advised. I am confident that, in line with advice from the British Library all the material quoted may be used for research and educational purposes.

Content

Copyright		Page	3
Research		Page	4
Forward		Page	6
Introduction		Page	7
Acknowledgements		Page	8
Content Index		Page	10
Chapter One	Dr Edmund King Houchin	Page	12
Chapter Two	Mr William Robert Magnus	Page	16
Chapter Three	Approach to St John Ambulance	Page	27
Chapter Four	The Beginning of St John in Ilford	Page	30
Chapter Five	1911 Coronation Year and 1912 Royal Review	Page	44
Chapter Six	1914 and The Start of WWI	Page	54
Chapter Seven	The Ilford New Year's Day Train Crash	Page	59
Chapter Eight	WWI Gathering Momentum	Page	66
Chapter Nine	The Gallantry of William Stephen Chevalier MSM	Page	78
Chapter Ten	The War Years 1917 -1918	Page	94
Chapter Eleven	VAD Records and Post War Events	Page	107
Chapter Twelve	Ilford Emergency Hospital	Page	111
Chapter Thirteen	Time to Move On	Page	124
Chapter Fourteen	Dr Wynne Baxter – Dr King Houchin's Boss	Page	137
Chapter Fifteen	Ilford Division and the Upminster Section	Page	139
Chapter Sixteen	William Magnus MBE - The LNER Ambulance Corps	Page	146
Chapter Seventeen	Superintendent A. A. Atkins Retirement	Page	150
Chapter Eighteen	The Death of William Magnus MBE	Page	152
Chapter Nineteen	A. A. Atkins and Dr King Houchin Pass Away	Page	154
Chapter Twenty	Mrs Maud B Magnus	Page	155
Appendix No 1	The Cases of Dr Edmund King Houchin	Page	158
Appendix No 2	The Rymer Family - A new life in Canada	Page	163
Appendix No 3	A Fine Romance	Page	165
Appendix No 4	Ilford VAD Members	Page	176
Appendix No 5	VAD Record for Ilford Members	Page	177
Appendix No 6	County Directors and VAD Working Parties in Ilford	Page	192
Appendix No 7	Royal Red Cross – Ilford	Page	193
Appendix No 8	'B' Mention in Dispatches for Ilford	Page	194
Appendix No 9	Silver War Badges – Ilford	Page	195
Appendix No10	Valentines Mansion	Page	196
Appendix No 11	Miss Alice White – 1880 -1962 A Founder Member	Page	201
Appendix No 12	Joseph Charles Raith 1894 -1984	Page	201
Bibliography		Page	203

Chapter One – Dr Edmund King Houchin

Dr King Houchin was destined to become the first Divisional Surgeon of the Ilford Division of St John Ambulance. It may be useful to look at Dr King Houchin and his early career in the lead up to his involvement with the Brigade in the early twentieth century.

Edmund King Houchin was born in April 1847 in Colchester, Essex. He was the youngest son of John Cooper Houchin of Stambourne, who was 27 and his mother, Sarah, was 34. His two brothers were the Reverends J. W. Houchin of Ingatestone and E. M. Houchin of Felstead.

17 December 1875 The Chelmsford Chronicle noted he passed his examination in the science and practice of medicine and received a certificate to practise from Apothecaries Hall in December 1875, these details being noted on 11 December 1875 in the *London Evening Standard*. It further showed he was living at 112 High Street, Stepney and was working at the London Hospital.

Edmund King Houchin married Amy Elizabeth Pattison on 28 March 1878 at Trinity Church in Stepney. Amy's father, John was a Master Mariner. Edmund was eleven years her senior.

The Marriage Certificate of Edmund King Houchin and Amy Elizabeth Pattison 28 March 1878

Edmund and Amy were destined to have three children. Victor born 1881, Violet born 1886 and finally Olive born in 1892.

Police Surgeon

Many cases Dr Houchin was involved in, as a Police Surgeon and subsequently as a Deputy Coroner, were reported in the press. In writing this research I have taken the opportunity, in brief, to give a feel for his work in both roles. These stories are not directly related to his role with St John Ambulance, but provide an informative background to his work in the East End and Ilford. These accounts can be found separately in Appendix One.

Houchin's Operation

On 5 August 1893, Dr Houchin required an operation and he placed the following notice in the *East London Observer*.

> Notice Dr E. K. Houchin begs to state that he has been obliged to relinquish his professional duties at his Surgery, High Street, Stepney, for a time, in order to undergo a critical operation, which was successfully performed on Wednesday, and should no further complication arise, he expects to resume work in about six weeks' time.

Houchin - Deputy Coroner

On 10 March 1894, the *East London Advertiser* stated that

> Dr Houchin, of Stepney, will be nominated by Mr Wynne E. Baxter as the deputy coroner for the North-east division of the County of London, in succession to the Mr George Collier.

This was confirmed in the Advertiser of Somerset on 22 March 1894,

> Dr Edmund King Houchin has been selected as deputy coroner, subject to the approval of the London County Council.

President of the United Kingdom Police Surgeons' Association

On 21 August 1897 the *British Medical Journal* reported on the annual general meeting of the United Kingdom Police Surgeons' Association for 1897, it was held on 28 July. Over 200 copies of the report were to be printed and distributed to police surgeons. A resolution congratulating the retiring President (Sir J. J. Littlejohn) on his appointment as Professor of Forensic Medicine in the University of Edinburgh was unanimously adopted, and Dr Edmund King Houchin, Metropolitan Police Surgeon and Deputy Coroner for East London, was elected his successor.

Dr Edmund King Houchin c 1897 President of the Police Surgeons' Association (photographer unknown)

Census 1901.

By 1901, Dr Houchin's household was recorded in the Census as living at 'Ravensworth' Cranbrook Road, Ilford. It lists four member of the family and also three domestic servants which was normal for the time.

Ilford Census Return for Dr Houchin's Family

1903 The Hot Summer

1903 proved to be a very hot summer and resulted in increased work for St John Ambulance and indeed the Coroner, Dr Houchin.

Subsequent to these events' Dr King Houchin became a Divisional Surgeon with the St John Ambulance Brigade for Ilford.

On 17 July 1903 in the *Leominster News,* reported on Edmund King Houchin -

> Death from the Heat. – The heat in London on Saturday was again abnormal, the thermometer at one o'clock registering 84deg in the shade and 124deg. in the sun. Several cases of heat stroke occurred at quite an early hour this morning, and were treated at the station of the St John Ambulance Association and various of the Metropolitan hospitals. Two deaths were reported as a result of the exceptional heat. At South Kensington an elderly gentleman was discovered in a railway carriage in a state of collapse, and he died shortly afterwards. A van driver fell from his seat in Wandsworth Road, and expired almost immediately. In the City the heat was painfully felt, and in Cheapside two ladies and a gentleman fell to the pavement completely prostrated half an hour before midday.
> At Whitechapel infirmary, on Saturday, Dr King-Houchin held an inquest on the body of James Dixon, aged about fifty-five, occupation unknown. Dr Herbert Larder, Medical Superintendent, deposed that the man was admitted on Friday. He said he had no home and no friends. He had walked from Stratford and was hungry and dead tired. He was put to bed and died soon afterward from the heat acting on a weak heart. The jury returned a verdict accordingly.

The High Court Action

In 1903 Dr Houchin brought a case in the High Court for money owed from the sale of his Stepney practice. was heard before Mr Justice Lawrence and was widely reported. The following report is taken from the *Evening Post* of 31 July, 1903.

> Doctors' Differences Settled. – The Price of the Practice Caused the Trouble. The hearing of the action taken by Dr E. K. Houchin, of Ilford, against Dr Fred Marshall, of Coatbridge, to recover £987, the unpaid balance of the purchase price of £2,000 which the defendant had agreed to pay the plaintiff for his medical practice in Stepney, was concluded in the King's Bench Division of the High Court yesterday.

The defendant had admitted the amount was due, but said he was induced to purchase the practice by the fraudulent misrepresentation of the plaintiff that the receipts averaged over £2000 a year, and that the district was an improving one.

When the case was called yesterday there was a consultation between parties, and eventually Mr Gregory, for the defendant, stated that his Lordship would not be further troubled with the case, as parties had arranged terms. Dr Houchin had made a very handsome allowance to the defendant, and the defendant, on his side, would withdraw all charges of fraud against the plaintiff.

His Lordship said that was a very proper ending to the case, and the jury, he might say, had long since told him they thought it was a case that ought to be settled.

Dr Houchin's Resignation

The Shipping Gazette and Lloyds List on 23 March 1907 reported-

> Dr James Godding, of East India Dock Road has been appointed deputy to Mr Wynne Baxter, the East London Coroner, in succession to Dr King Houchin, who has resigned after 13 years' service. Dr Godding is medical office to Trinity Corporation and London and India Docks Company.

The Berks and Oxon Advertiser on 31 May 1907 reported-

> At Stepney Coroner's Court, Dr King Houchin, late deputy-coroner, was presented with a silver set of entrée dishes and a double silver inkstand by the medical men of the district.

The St John Ambulance Brigade Ilford

Chapter Two – Mr William Robert Magnus

William Robert Magnus (1877 – 1934) and Maud Beatrice Magnus (1878 – 1962)

William R Magnus was born in December 1877 to Ann Marie Magnus (née Shrive) and Robert J Magnus[1] a Railway Guard, and he was baptised on 20 January 1878 at Chipping N. Witham, his birthplace.

At the time of the 1891 Census William, aged 13, was living with his family at 66 Westdown Road, Lower Leyton, Essex. This address being located near the Stratford Works of the Great Eastern Railway, probably where his father, being a train guard, was based.

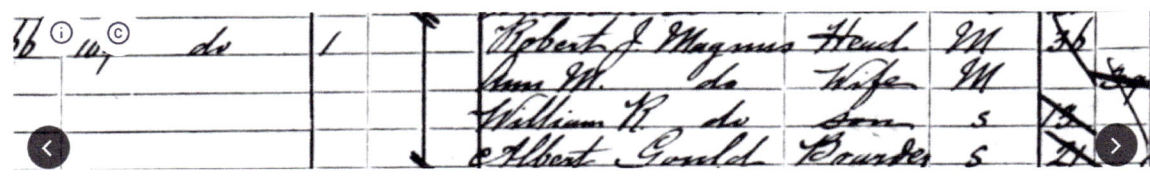

Census of 1891

1892 William joins the Great Eastern Railway

William first entered the Superintendent's Office of The Great Eastern Railway, at Liverpool Street on 31 October 1892.

After establishing himself and gaining considerable experience, he was eventually appointed to control of the Superintendent's Train Delay Section known as the "Punctuality Department". An article in the *Great Eastern Railway Magazine*[2] described him thus

> But, like Cromwell Mr W. R. Magnus, chief of section, is "not a man scrupulous about words or names or such things": what he wants are results.

Early in his railway service William obtained his first ambulance certificate in May, 1895, aged 17 years.

---

[1] Robert J Magnus. William's father Robert J Magnus worked for Great Eastern Railways. He had been a loyal servant of the company for many years. He also had the distinction of serving on the Royal Train. The following was announced in a local newspapers, the *Essex Herald* on the 11 July 1893. *"Honour to a Witham Man. – Robert Magnus, of Witham, was selected from a number to act as one of two guards in charge of the royal special train from Liverpool-street to Sandringham"*. The "Royal Special Train" referred to was to take Prince George, Duke of York, and Princess Mary of Teck, (later George V and Queen Mary) to Sandringham, this followed their wedding which took place on 6 July 1893 at the Chapel Royal, St James's Palace in London. One newspaper, The Forres, *Elgin and Nairn Gazette* of July 12, 1893, gave a few more details on the Royal Train. *"The Royal pair proceeded on their way to Liverpool Street, where they were conducted to a special train, consisting of a saloon with a composite carriage and brake at each end. The saloon was upholstered in blue, and its interior tastefully furnished. The engine was garlanded, and bore a modelled gilt and velvet crown. The train left the station amid ringing cheers"*.

[2] *Great Eastern Railway Magazine Volume 3 September 1913 No. 33*

It is clear that William had joined both the Great Eastern Railway Ambulance Corps and also the London Metropolitan Corps. His home Division, for the GER Ambulance Corps was Liverpool Street, which by the time he joined had separated from the Metropolitan Corps of which it had been part until 1893.

Shortly after obtaining his "First Aid to the Injured" Certificate William also joined No 4 Leyton and Leytonstone Division of the St John Ambulance Brigade, London Metropolitan Corps.

Back to William Magnus. One of William's early public duties with Leyton and Leytonstone Division was discovered thanks to an article in the *"Herald"* on 8 August 1896. It gives a full account of a public duty covered by the division on Wanstead Flats. It read:-

> Ambulance Brigade and Bank Holiday.
>
> Ambulance duty on Monday on Wanstead Flats was undertaken by the following: Supt. J. J. Olley, acting-sergeant H. Slack, honorary secretary, H. Marston, Bugler A. Burland, Privates W. Shinglar, C. J. Fitch, W. Sayers, W. Magnus, W. Wallis (Leyton and Leytonstone Division), Nursing Sisters Collier and Cornell (Barking Division), assisted by Misses Hetty and Ada Olley, also Mr Lynch and Mr F. W. Cox. The number of cases treated during the day was twelve, as follows: 2 contusions, 1 slight concussion, 4 fainting fits, 1 epilepsy, 1 bruised wrist, 1 spasmodic asthma, 2 lacerated wounds. One case was taken to West Ham Hospital.
>
> During the day great assistance was given by the police, both officers and men, and by the Forest Rangers, to all of whom the superintendent returns sincere thanks on behalf of the Division.

1897 GER Ambulance Corps Competitions

As a member of the GER. Ambulance Corps, William was part of the Liverpool Street First Aid Competition team in which he competed for the Inter-Railway Ambulance Shield in 1897. The Corp had a history of first aid competition work going back to its formation. Various unit, which originated through the suggestion of John Furley in 1879, were amalgamated as the Great Eastern Ambulance Corps of the Brigade in 1892. In 1893 the Great Eastern Railway inaugurated its Annual Challenge Cup Ambulance Competition and other companies followed[3]. The first winners, in 1893 were Norwich Thorpe, followed in 1894 by the team from Liverpool Street the Competition being held in a Waggon Shop at the Stratford Works[4].

Fast forward to William's involvement. Like most competitions there were preliminary rounds, these occurred in April 1897 and were reported in several local newspapers. *The Tower Hamlets Independent and East End Local Advertiser* edition of 10 April 1897, carried the following

> AMBULANCE COMPETITION. The annual competition in ambulance work between the Great Eastern Railway Ambulance Corps took place on Saturday afternoon at the Conference

---

[3] *Annals of the Ambulance Department,* by N. Corbet Fletcher, Second Edition 1947
[4] *The Thetford and Watton Times*, 10 November 1894.

The St John Ambulance Brigade Ilford

Hall[5], Stratford, Lord Claud Hamilton[6], the chairman of the company, presiding, when the prizes were awarded by the Duchess of Abercorn.

The Principal item was the stretcher drill competition, in which corps representing Ipswich, Norwich, Liverpool- street, Stratford, Bethnal Green and Cambridge divisions took part.

Each detachment had to march out and treat an apparently wounded man according to the label attached to his clothing, place him on a stretcher, and convey him to a fixed point.

The judges placed the teams in the following order of merit: First, Liverpool-street, 245 marks; second Cambridge, 217; third, Norwich, 215; fourth, Stratford, 214; fifth, Bethnal Green, 206; and sixth, Ipswich, 184. The winning team was composed of Messrs. W. Magnus, J. Peck, R. Stiff, G. Keary, and S Ashton. The prize was a splendid challenge-cup, given by the directors of the company, and each man received an electro plated inkstand. For individual Competition in bandaging, the prize, an electro plated cup, was awarded to Mr F. Wolveridge. The judges were the Hon. Surgeon Heaton C. Howard, Hon Surgeon W. J. Hunter, and Brigade Chief Superintendent. W. J. Church Brasier.

The Conference Hall, West Ham Lane.

---

5 The Conference Hall, West Ham Lane was destroyed by fire-bombs on May 10-11, 1941. Built in 1884, it had a large hall seating 1,600, and smaller halls. The land was owned by the Methodist Church who sold the plot to the Metropolitan Police for £7,000. The site was then redeveloped. A new Police Station was opened, at 18 West Ham Lane in 1969, at a cost of £165,000. (Behind the Blue Lamp by P. Kennsion & D. Swinden Published by Coppermill Press 2003 ISBN 0-9546534-0-8) Photograph accessed 21/1/2022. https://www.eastlondonhistory.co.uk/west-ham-conference-centre-ww2-photos/

6 Lord Claud Hamilton was a Member of Parliament for Londonderry between 1865 and 1868. He held the office of a Lord of the Treasury in 1868. He then held the office of Member of Parliament for King's Lynn between 1869 and 1880. and the Liverpool between 1880 and 1888. He held the office of Aide-de-Camp to HM Queen Victoria between 1887 and 1897. Between 1910 and 1918 he was Member of Parliament for South Kensington. He was invested as a Knight of Justice, Order of St John of Jerusalem and was appointed to the Privy Council in 1917. He died in 1925, aged 81. However, his principal contribution to British public life was as a director of the Great Eastern Railway from 1872, becoming vice-chairman in 1874, and chairman in 1893, continuing as chairman until 1922. (Internet accessed on 30 January 2022. www.geni.com/people/Lord-Claud-John-Hamilton/6000000003714066802)

Another article on the same event appeared in the *West Ham and South Essex Mail* 10 April 1897.

It gave more details of the guests.

> Great Eastern Railway Corps, Annual Competition. The Annual competition of the Great Eastern Railway Corps of the St John's Ambulance Brigade. Took place on Saturday afternoon. The competition, which attracts a good deal of public attention, lost none of its interest by being held in the Conference Hall, instead of the usual place – Stratford Town Hall. About 500 people attended to witness it. During the first part of the afternoon the Mayor of West Ham (Alderman A. Govier. J.P.) presided; later on, Lord Claud Hamilton took the chair. There were also present on the platform Lady Hamilton, the Duchess of Abercorn, Colonel W. T Makins, Messrs J. Farley, J. F. H. Reed, Alderman Fielder, and others.

The article then gave full details of all the teams, William Magnus's team is detailed above, however the Bethnal Green team, which came fifth, is worth a passing mention as it included A. A. Atkins. Atkins would, in 1901, become Superintendent of No15 East Ham Ambulance Division, which William would later join from No4 Leyton and Leytonstone Ambulance Division, and would go on to form Ilford Section, under Superintendent Atkins guidance.

1897 The Queen Victoria Jubilee First Aid Competitions

Having won the Great Eastern Railway Corps Ambulance Competition, the team moved on to the major event, a national competition to mark Queen Victoria's Diamond Jubilee.

The Essex Herald edition dated 18 May 1897 reported, as follows, on the competition

> The St John Ambulance Brigade. The Great Eastern Railway Company's team in competition with the principal railways of the kingdom, won the magnificent shield given by the Prince of Wales as Grand Prior of the Order of St John of Jerusalem in England Ambulance Association. The winning team comprised; - 1 Magnus, 2 Peck, 3 Stiff, 4 Keary (captain); and 5 Ashton. The shield was presented by H.R.H. the Princess Christian is a new design by Elkington. It is to be placed on exhibition on the main line platform at Liverpool-street. The same team are holders of the Silver Challenge Cup given by the Great Eastern Railway Company.

More recognition followed their outstanding success. On 29 May 1897, *The Herald* reported G.E.R. SHIELD WINNER. It continued

> The members of the G.E.R. team who won the ambulance shield at Crystal Palace, met Lord Claud Hamilton in his private room at Liverpool- street station. His lordship highly complimented the men on their success, and presented each with a portrait of himself and his daughter, framed in fancy leather, with the words "G.E.R., victory, Ambulance Competition, 1897", in gold, and his lordship's autograph.

The Great Eastern Railway then held a further event, which was reported in the *Essex County Chronicle* on 4 June 1897.

> The G.E.R. AMBULANCE CORPS. In celebration of their recent successes, the G.E.R. Company's London Ambulance team were on Wednesday entertained at the Liverpool- street Hotel to a complimentary tea and concert. About 150 were present. Mr H. G Drury (Superintendent of the Line) occupied the chair, and was supported by Mr R. P. Ellis

(assistant superintendent of the line), Mr C. Randall (district superintendent Liverpool-street), and others. The evening was well spent, much honour being done to the ambulance team, which consists of Messrs. Keary, Stiff, Magnus, Peck and Ashton.

Magnus is mentioned in Alan Sharkey's book on the Great Eastern Railway (GER), the names of the members of the GER competition team are shown on the plaque commemorating the 1897 Challenge Shield for the Railway Competition.

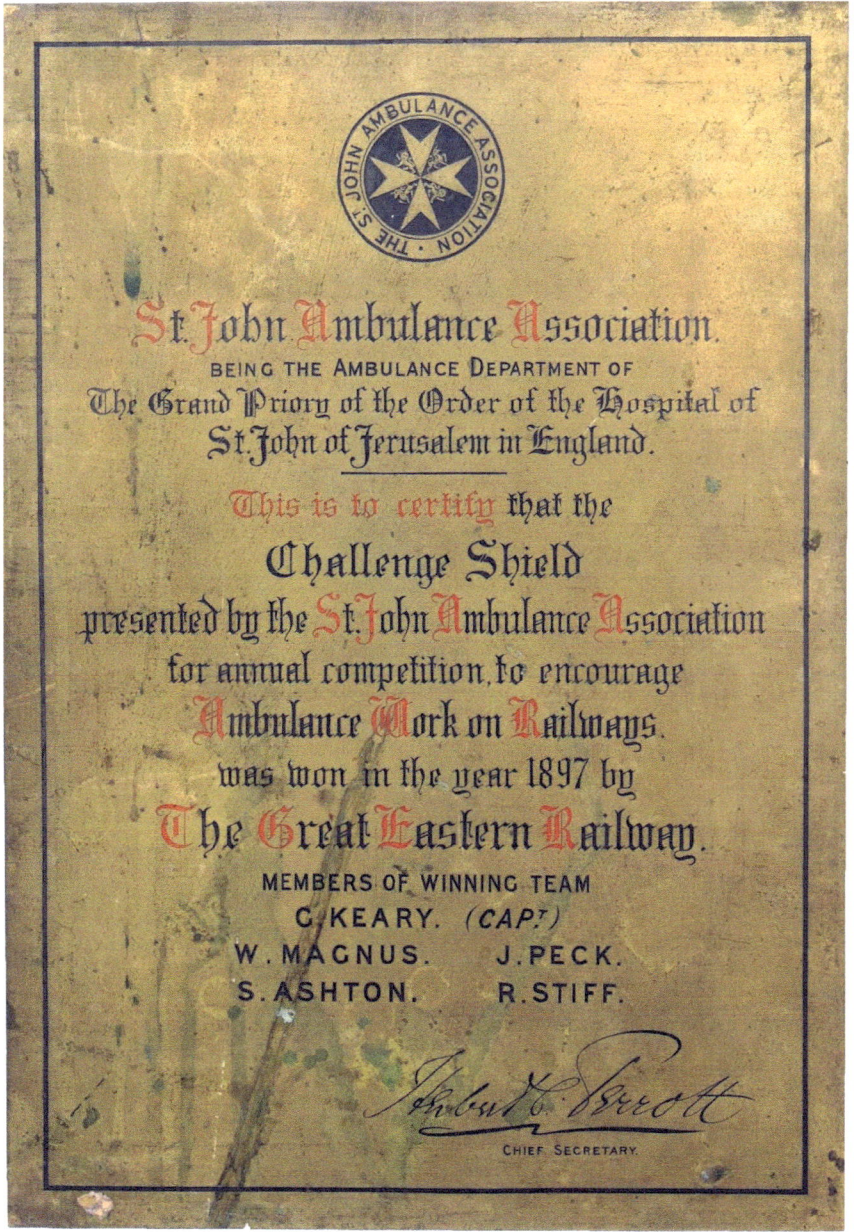

The Plaque presented to winning team in the first Railway Challenge Shield Competition in 1897

Presented retrospectively in 1903 (Photo Courtesy of Alan J Sharkey) 7

---

7 The Plaques were presented retrospectively on the 12 May 1903 for this and previous years of the Competition. The Great Eastern Railway hold four Plaques (The Liverpool Street Team two plaques for 1897 and 1898, with The March Team also holding two plaques for 1903 and 1904). Alan J Sharkey. The Great Eastern Railway Movement ISBN 978-1-905729-53-1 and the Facebook First Aid History Page accessed 12 May 2022.

1898 Liverpool Street - Second National Finals Win

The Liverpool-street team again won the competition's preliminary round and went on to successfully defend their national title, which was formally recognised later in the year by Board of the Great Eastern Railway.

A report in the *Railway News* dated 09 April 1898 detailed the competition –

> Great Eastern Railway Ambulance Corps. – Lord Claud Hamilton on Tuesday night presented the prizes to the successful competitors in the annual displays of the Great Eastern Railway Ambulance Corps, which took place at the Town Hall, Stratford. The corps now contains thirty divisions, four having been added during the year. During 1897 299 men presented themselves for examination, and of this number 263 satisfied the examiners. Twenty teams entered for this year's competitions, and as no division sent more than one team the competition was more representative than was the case in 1897. The sectional competitions were held at Colchester, Stratford, Lowestoft, and Cambridge, and as a result of these, Liverpool Street, Bethnal Green, Stratford, Brentwood, Cambridge, and Lowestoft divisions were left for the final competition for the challenge cup presented by the Great Eastern railway company. These competitions occupied the whole of Tuesday afternoon, the judges being Dr Heaton C. Howard and Dr T. Taylor, hon. surgeons of the Metropolitan Corps, and Brigade Chief Superintendent W. J. Church Brasier, of the St John's Ambulance Corps. The Liverpool Street were adjudged the winners of the challenge cup with 225 marks out of a possible 300, and will, by virtue of the win, represent the Great Eastern railway company in the inter-railway competition for the challenge shield. The Brentwood division was second with 206 marks, the Stratford division third with 183, the Bethnal Green division fourth with 177, the Cambridge with 174; and the Lowestoft division gained 150 marks. The winning team gave a short demonstration of ambulance work, and were heartily congratulated by Lord Claud Hamilton, who mentioned that, besides winning the challenge shield presented by the St John's Ambulance Corps in commemoration of the Queen's Jubilee, the Liverpool Street division were the winners of the company's challenge in 1897.

In another report on 09 April 1898 the *West Ham and South Essex Mail* report the additional information that -

> In the individual competition, two men tied, R. Stiff and S. Bates, and therefore an extra prize was awarded.

The report continued –

> A concert and the distribution of the prizes to the successful competitors took place at the Town Hall in the evening. The Mayor (Alderman Ivey) and Lord Claud Hamilton occupied the chair during the evening. And the Field-Fisher Quartet entertained a large company. With their musical programme.

The Liverpool Street team followed the local and company round of the competitions with their second appearance on the national stage.

The newspaper the *Morning Post*, followed the Ambulance movement with regular reports appearing in its columns, so the National Finals were always worthy of an informative report. In publication dated 13 May 1898 the following appeared

> Ambulance Competitions. Competitions organised by the St John Ambulance Association for Ambulance Corps of different Railway Companies and the St John Ambulance Brigade took

place yesterday at the Portman Rooms[8], Baker Street. Four teams representing divisions of the St John Ambulance Brigade in different parts of the country, and teams representing the five following railways companies (Selected from the sixteen entered), viz., the Great Eastern, Great Northern, Great Western, North-Eastern, and Liverpool Overhead, took part in the respective competitions, at the close of which Viscountess Knutsford distributed the Prizes to the successful teams.

In the railway competition the silver challenge shield presented by the St John Ambulance Association (to be held for one year) and the first prize were awarded to the Great Eastern Railway Ambulance Corps, which holds the shield now for a second year, the second prize falling to the Great Northern, the third to North-Eastern, the fourth to the Great Western, and the fifth prize to the Liverpool Overhead Railway.

In the St John Ambulance Brigade competition, the silver challenge shield given by Mr T. R. Dewar (to be held for one year) the first prize was secured by No. 2 District (Southern and Western), represented by Wellingborough Corps; the silver challenge cup given by Dr A. S. Eccles (to be held for one year) going to No. 1 District (Metropolitan Corps), represented by the East Ham Division; the third prize to No. 4 District (North Western), represented by the Preston Corps; and fourth prize to No. 2 District (Southern and Western) represented by the Westgate-on-Sea Division. Cordial votes of thanks to Viscount and Viscountess Knutsford closed the proceedings.

A report in *Bury Free Press - Bury St Edmunds*, a day later, on 14 May 1898 gave full details of the results and included the marks. It read –

Victory of G.E.R. Ambulance Men. On Thursday the Railway Challenge shield in connection with the St John's Ambulance Association was competed for at the Portman Rooms, Baker Street, London. Five teams were selected for the final and eventually the Great Eastern men again proved victorious with 337 marks; the Great Northern being placed second with 310; the Great Northern third, 267; the Great Western fourth, 249; and Liverpool Overhead fifth with 241.

On 7 December 1898 the newspaper called the *Eastern* reported :-

G.E.R. Ambulance Corps. – On Tuesday the chairman of the Great Eastern Railway, Lord Claud Hamilton, presented Messrs. G. Keary, R Stiff, W. Magnus, J. Peck and S. Ashton, composing the Liverpool Street team of the Great Eastern Railway Ambulance Corps, with an illuminated address in commemoration of the team having for the first two years of its institution won, in open competition with other railways, the Challenge Shield presented by the St John Ambulance Association.

The chart show shows the results of both the Railway and St John Ambulance Brigade Competitions from their inception of their 1897 Jubilee competitions going forward to 1914 from which point they were disrupted by the events of World War I.

---

8 The Portman Rooms became one of the best-known London venues for dances, concerts, charity bazaars, political, religious and social meetings of all sorts, including many events promoting women's suffrage. By, 1913, the main ballroom was declared structurally unsafe. Repairs were carried out, and in 1916 the Portman Rooms were requisitioned as a military hospital and Royal Army Medical Corps barracks. The Portman Rooms re-opened to the public in 1919 as the grand ballrooms and function rooms which they remained until World War 2. Ref https://blogs.ucl.ac.uk/survey-of-london/tag/portman-rooms accessed on 31 January 2022.

What should be highlighted is that William Magnus was part of the 1897 and 1898 Great Eastern Railway team which won the Railway Challenge Shield, at the same time as A.A.Atkins, another Great Eastern Employee, was part of the East Ham team so prominent in the 1897 to 1901 St John Ambulance Brigade, Dewar Challenge Shield Finals. Winners twice and runners up twice, for a time the City and East London had two of the best, if not the best, competition teams in the country.

Annals of the Ambulance Department by N. Corbet Fletcher, Second Edition 1947

Another name on the Railway Challenge Shield should be noted, that of the Great Eastern Railway, March. The March team won the Railway Challenge Shield competition in 1903, 1904 and 1907. This team included William Goodley[9], who promoted competition work at every turn of his St John life. William who had joined the Great Eastern Railway at Norwich in 1894 obtaining his First Aid Certificate in 1895, he moved to March in 1899. During his war service, on 25 March 1917 he was mentioned in despatches. After promotion to Captain he was awarded the Military Cross in 1918.[10] On returning home he transferred to East Ham Division on 22 June 1921 as a Supernumerary Divisional Superintendent, this was just at the time William Magnus was moving to his new position at Norwich, the two had worked together in the First Aid Competitions arena.

Goodley was not however destined to take a role at Ilford, but on 30 September, 1922 he was given charge, as Divisional Superintendent, of No. 72 Barking Division. His Brigade Service was outside the railway, but he took on the appointment of President of Liverpool Street Ambulance Division in 1930. He was appointed Assistant Commissioner and in 1933 Commissioner of London (Prince of Wales's) District. After long and distinguished service having seen London District through the 1939 -1945 War period William Goodley OBE. MC died in January 1947.

---

9 Alan J. Sharkey, The Ambulance Men of March ISBN 978-1-905729-40-1
10 RAMC Journal February 1919.

The St John Ambulance Brigade Ilford

Liverpool Street and East Ham 1899

On 29 April 1899, *The Essex County Standard* reported on another success for William Magnus and the Railway Team.

> G.E.R. Ambulance Competition – Presentation of Prizes by Lord Claud Hamilton. The Great Eastern Railway Ambulance Competition has resulted in placing Liverpool Street first (for the third time in succession), with 265 marks; Stratford second, with 214 Mark; and Brentwood third, with 193 marks. The competing teams in the final were: -
> Liverpool Street: Messrs. W. Magnus, J. Peck, R. Stiff, G Keary, and S. Ashton
> Brentwood: Messrs. W. Bishop, J. Oakley, G. Hales, A. J. Baker, and T. Lucas.
> Stratford: Messrs E. Leverett, T. Mees, H Aldred, S. Bates and J Burrows.
> The subjects for the competition were viva voce, individual bandaging, artificial respiration, and stretcher drill. The prizes were: First Challenge cup, given by the directors of the Great Eastern Railway, and five electro-plate tea services; second, five cases of carvers; third five electro-plated cruet stands.
>
> The prizes were presented by Lord Claud Hamilton at a crowded meeting in Leyton Town Hall. Ipswich and Cambridge won fourth and fifth prizes, and the individual prize for the highest number of marks gained was won by Mr Keary, of the Liverpool Street team.

The Diss Express 12 May 1899 recorded that the Liverpool Street team of the Great Eastern Railway did not retain the Challenge Shield in 1899. It reported -

> Railway Ambulance Competition. The inter-railway competition for the challenge shield presented by the St John's Ambulance Association, to encourage first aid on the railways, took place on Wednesday in London. Five teams completed in the final, and the result of the competition was announced to be as under; -1, London and North Western; Great Northern; 3, Great Eastern; 4 North London; 5 Cheshire Line Committee. The prizes were presented by the Duchess of Buckingham, assisted by Earl Egerton, of Tatton. – Lord Knutsford congratulated the London and North-Western team on their success in having beaten the Great Eastern Team, which had previously won the shield for two years in succession.

Whilst this was happening the team from No 15 East Ham Division under the leadership of Superintendent Edwin Hodgson won the Dewar Shield both in 1899 and they won it again in 1901 this time under Superintendent A. A. Atkins. There was no Competition in 1900 because of the South Africa War. As mentioned before both men play a part in William Magnus's story going forward.

The *West Ham and South Essex Mail* reported on 24 February 1900 that an

> Ambulance Concert was given at Stratford Town Hall on Monday evening in aid of the funds of Leyton and Leytonstone division of the St John Ambulance. The hall was crowded. Among those present were the honorary surgeon, Dr A. Todd-White; hon. superintendent Mr W. T. Brooks; superintendent, Mr J. J. Olley; first officer, Mr A. F. Paddon; Second Officer, Mr W. R. Magnus; staff-sergeant, Mr T Mees; sergeant Mr C. J. Fitch; and the Hon Sec., Mr H. Marston. This division numbers some 40 members, with five officers and three superintendent officers. The program was enthusiastically received.

The article continued with full details of the program. Magnus had been promoted from Supernumerary Officer to Second Officer on 28 October 1899.

1901

The 1901 Census was conducted on 31 March. It shows that William Magnus was living in Leyton Parish of West Ham District. His occupation was shown as a Railway Clerk. The area was located near the Stratford GER Depot. The entry shows the family Robert, William's father, who was a Widower, and Williams grandparents the time of the Census.

1901 Census

On 10 August 1901 *Eastern Counties Times* carried a report of a duty on Wanstead Flats carried out principally by No 4 Leyton and Leytonstone Division. Magnus is shown as being the second officer of the Division and was on duty that day. It gives a feel of the day's events.

> "First Aid" on Wanstead Flats. As usual, much practical assistance was afforded by members of the St John Ambulance Brigade on Wanstead Flats on Bank Holiday. The following officers and members turned out for public duty: Dr A. Todd-White, hon. surgeon; Supt. John. J. Olley; first officer, Mr A. F. Paddon; second officer W. Magnus; supernumerary office C. J. Fitch. Bugler, A. Burland; Privates, W. G. Hancock, A. Reynolds, G. Bray, A. J. Shrimplin, E. J. Mason, E. Wallis, A. J. Allison, J. Whittingham, J. T. Olley, H. F Olley, C. A. Bolton, W. Fox, and J. Hawkins; nursing sisters, Mrs Beeton, Miss Botterill[11]. And Mrs Grinner (Children's Home Division). Assistance was given during the day by Mr Belcham, Mrs Robins and Mr Harris. The commissariat was superintended by Mrs A. Burland, Miss M. Leeley, and Miss A. Marrison. Supt L. McKenzie kindly had a space fenced off, and the police gave their usual valued assistance. Cases treated during the day; Concussion 1,Contusions 3; wounds (incised) 3; wounds (lacerated) 1; gun-shot 2; diarrhoea 1, faints 2, epilepsy, 1; exhaustion 1; total 13. One case was taken to West Ham Hospital of gun-shot wound in the leg and was detained.

Another report on 7 September 1901, the *Eastern Counties Times* showed details of Leyton and Leytonstone Divisions social activities.

> Leyton and the St John Ambulance Association.
>
> The annual outing of the Leyton and Leytonstone division of the St John's Ambulance Association took place on Saturday at Hainault Retreat, Lambourne, three three-horse brakes being chartered to convey the excursionist thither. The party comprised Supt. J. J. Olley and Mrs Olley, 1st Officer A. F Paddon and Mrs Paddon, 2nd Officer W. Magnus and lady, 1st class supry. Officer T. Mees and Mrs Mees, Nursing Sister, 2nd class supry. officer C. J. Fitch and lady, 2nd class supry. officer H. Marston and Mr Marston, Bugler A. Burland and Mrs Burland, store-keeper B. Green and Mrs Green and many members and their wives and honorary members to total number of sixty-seven. After a pleasant drive the party partook of a substantial tea which was provided in an excellent manner by Mr Groves the proprietor.

---

11 Miss Botterill's membership number was No. 8, she was the first Superintendent of No 17 Leyton and Leytonstone Nursing Division.

The St John Ambulance Brigade Ilford

After tea, Supt J. J. Olley made a short speech upon the position of Leyton and Leytonstone division and conduct and smartness of its members. He referred also to the honorary members who numbered 20 to date, and to the support so kindly given by them, after which eight ladies and gentlemen asked to have their names put on the list of honorary members and paid a year's subscription, for which the Superintendents returned thanks on behalf of the members. The Superintendent also referred to seven members[12] who had volunteered for duty in South Africa, five of whom had returned, three being present, viz., Mr H. Dixon[13], Mr P. G. H. Fitch[14], and Mr W. H. Clements[15], who were received with great cheering.
Mr E. Reynolds of Ilford, responded on behalf of the honorary members, and Mr S Bate on behalf of the member of the Division.

First officer Mr A. F. Paddon spoke of the many kindnesses shown to the division by Mrs Olley in providing accommodation at Acorn Villa for the meetings of the division.
The rest of the evening was spent very pleasantly, songs and recitations being given by member and honorary members. The homeward journey was started at 8 p.m. and the part safely arrived at Leytonstone at 10 p.m.

---

12 This does not tally with the Grand Priors South Africa Report Page 26 Appendix III which shows from a strength of 35 Leyton and Leytonstone Division had only two volunteers accepted. This could mean the remaining five may have served in other capacities or with another corps possibly Great Eastern Railway.

13 R. H. Dixon Regimental No 129 - No 355 Served with St John Ambulance in South Africa Second Boar War Awarded Queens South Africa Medal. Information accessed on Ancestry.co.uk website 21 January, 2022.

14 P. G. H. Fitch Regimental No 1784 - No 1568 Served with St John Ambulance in South Africa Second Boar War at No.3 General Hospital – Awarded Queens South Africa Medal with Clasps Cape Colony and Orange Free State. Information accessed on Ancestry.co.uk website 21 January, 2022.

15 W. H. Clements Regimental No 1785 – No 1553 Served with St John Ambulance in South Africa Second Boar War at No.3 General Hospital – Awarded Queens South Africa Medal with Clasps Cape Colony and Orange Free State. Information accessed on Ancestry.co.uk website 21 January, 2022.

The St John Ambulance Brigade Ilford

Chapter Three – Approach to St John Ambulance

The initial approaches were made to the St John Ambulance Brigade in East Ham regarding the provision and extension of the organisation in Ilford. On 19 October 1901, *The Essex Guardian* reported on the subject.

> Mr Cameron Corbett's Gift to Ilford.
>
> (Special for the "Guardian")
>
> It will be remembered that, some weeks ago, Councillor Burleigh introduced the subject of the need of procuring an ambulance litter or carriage for Ilford. He found that the Urban District Council could not purchase the same, and with characteristic persistency he contemplated starting a subscription list with a view of obtaining what was necessary to an enterprising, up-to-date community. Word reached Mr Boyd (Agent for Mr Cameron Corbett, M.P), and that gentleman was not slow in communicating the fact to the popular M.P., and Mr Corbett expressed his readiness to present the town of Ilford with the best horse ambulance carriage money could buy. The councillors naturally hailed the idea and the magnificent offer, and a week ago Councillor Burleigh said, at the Town Hall, Mr Boyd had decided to get an expert's opinion on the matter of the purchase of suitable vehicle. The matter was left in the hands of the Councillor, Mr Boyd, and the expert, we now learn that the expert whose valuable service were secured was Superintendent E. Hodgson of the East Ham Division of the St John's Ambulance. Mr Hodgson is well known at Ilford, having resided for some years at Brandon Terrace, Ilford Hill and now fills the post of headmaster under the East Ham School Board. He is in charge of the team, which for two years won the Dewar Shield (presented by J. Dewar, Esq), open to all England, and of course, are the holder of it now. Superintendent Hodgson has been actively engaged in training hundreds of men in ambulance work for South Africa, over 1,500 having passed through his hands[16]. His experience with ambulance work is wide and varied. And his services have been rewarded, for he was awarded by Her late Majesty Queen Victoria, the Honorary Brotherhood of the Order of St John's of Jerusalem, and was publicly presented to him by Lord Knutsford at Westminster Town Hall.
>
> This was the last declaration granted by her Majesty in connection with Ambulance Work before her death, and is, therefore, much appreciated and valued by Mr Hodgson. By the St John's Ambulance Association, the East Ham corps is acknowledged to be one of the best in England.
>
> On Saturday last, the expert – who, by the way, is the holder of many other medals in connection with his ambulance work – accompanied Mr Boyd and Councillor Burleigh to the St John's Ambulance Association to inspect their most improved ambulance carriage. And as a result of their deliberations we understand that plans and specifications are to be prepared for the building of a carriage for Ilford, and the specifications considered by the carriage expert again.
>
> The cost, it is estimated, will be about £150, and the carriage will take about four months to build. It will be fitted with a locker, and with the necessary appliances for dealing at once with injuries. It will not be confined to cases of accident, and people of Ilford will be glad to learn that there will be in the town in a short time means of conveying serious cases from the home to the hospital, and vice versa, if necessity arises, but no infectious cases will be taken.
>
> As to location of the carriage, we understand that the General-Purpose Committee are considering the matter, but it is highly desirable that it should be placed as near to the fire

---

[16] Edwin Hodgson (Divisional Superintendent No15 East Ham Division) did receive a mention in the Grand Priors Report on the South African War, it covered his work at St John's Gate in the drill yard. Edwin had also been appointed an Honorary Serving Brother of The Order of St John, in one of the last lists signed and approved by the Sovereign Head of the Order, H.M. Queen Victoria, before her death.

> station as possible, so that someone may be on hand at all times. And a position is a central one.
>
> We would suggest, when the gift is formally accepted, that an ambulance display be given in the park for what we feel sure Supt. Hodgson and others would gladly take a leading part at such an exhibition.
>
> We feel sure we are but voicing the opinion of the people generally when we thank Mr Boyd for his kind interest he has taken in the movement, and congratulate him upon the success which attended his initiation of so noble a work. A need of praise is also due to Councillor Burleigh and the expert, for the no small part thy played also in the matter.

Superintendent Edwin Hodgson had resigned from No 15 East Ham Division, St John Ambulance, in late 1901 when he and his family moved to Kent and he had taken a new teaching position. Hodgson's place was taken by his deputy, First Officer A. A. Atkins, who was promoted to Divisional Superintendent of East Ham Division. Atkins, an employee of the Great Eastern Railway and a member of the GER Ambulance Corps, Bethnal Green Division.

1902

On 14 February 1902 *The Recorder* noted the arrival of the Ambulance Carriage. An article on the Ilford Urban Council proceedings reported

> Councillor Burleigh, in eulogistic terms, moved that a vote of thanks be passed to Mr Cameron Corbett, M.P. for his handsome gift of an ambulance carriage to the town (hear hear). In passing, Councillor Burleigh said they owed a great deal to Mr Boyd for the care and attention he had given to the matter (hear, hear). The ambulance carriage was duly delivered in Ilford on February 1st, and it had been placed in the charge of Mr Emery. – Councillor Aitcheson seconded the motion, and it was unanimously agreed to. – Councillor Burleigh[17] then moved the Surveyor be formally instructed to take charge of the ambulance carriage, and be responsible for it. And further that the Surveyor draw up conditions under which the carriage might be used the object of the giver was that it should not be used for infectious case (hear, hear). This was seconded by Councillor Bodger, and agreed to.

On 12 April 1902 the *Essex Newsman* newspaper reported

> G.E.R. Ambulance Corps. The annual ambulance competitions among the Great Eastern Railway station staffs for the challenge cup, presented by the Directors, took place on Thursday evening at the Leyton Town Hall. Twenty-one teams entered, and after severe tests the Liverpool-street station contingent were declared the winners. Colchester came second, Stratford third, and March fourth.
>
> The individual prize was carried off by Mr W. Magnus (Liverpool Street). Miss Ida Hamilton presented the prizes to the successful competitors. Lord Claud Hamilton, Chairman of the Company, said there were now 32 Divisions of the corps throughout the line.

---

17 4 May 1917 *The Essex Chronicle* reported that John Lawrence Burleigh, was reported "killed in action" he was the son of Councillor and Mrs Burleigh.

The St John Ambulance Brigade Ilford

Great Eastern Railway, London, Liverpool Street. c1900. Photographer Unknown. Authors Collection

William's was seeing Miss Maud Shelly (sometimes spelt Selly), born in 1878, who lived at 27 Carnarvon Road, West Ham. Maud's occupation was described as a Mantle[18] Makers Assistant in the 1901 Census. Her mother's name was Jane Shelly (née Griggs), whilst her father, named Edwin, was a Carpenter and Joiner by trade.

William Magnus married Maud Beatrice Shelly on 24 May 1902 at St Paul's Church[19], Maryland, Stratford.

---

18 The name refers to its original heat source in gas lights which illuminated the streets in the late 19th century. *Mantle* refers to the way it hangs like a cloak above the flame.

19 St Paul's Church, Stratford, is at the south-east corner of the junction between Maryland Road and Waddington Road. It started about 1850 in a City Missionary Sunday school, and an iron hall was put up in 1859. That was replaced by a permanent church in 1864. In 1945 the building was destroyed by a German V1 rocket. The present building was consecrated in 1953. A bell was added to the tower in 1954. Accessed 1 November 2021 https://www.historyfiles.co.uk/ChurchesBritain/London/East_Newham14.htm

Chapter Four – The Beginning of St John in Ilford 1903 - 1910

17 July 1903 - *Leominster News*
Divisional Superintendent A. A. Atkins of No15 East Ham Ambulance Division had known William Magnus for some time and there is little doubt that discussion took place about forming an Ilford Section of East Ham Division. As William now lived in Ilford he had become the officer of choice to run the section. So, he moved from being Second Officer with No 4 Leyton and Leytonstone Ambulance Division, joining No 15 East Ham Ambulance Division as First Officer and being officer in charge of the embryonic Ilford Section. William served in this capacity from the 22 July 1903 until 31 December 1905.

29 August 1903 edition of *Ilford Guardian* published a letter from H. C. Bull the Hon, Secretary to the Section.

> Dear Sirs, - Will you be good enough to inform the public through the valuable medium of your paper, than an Ilford Section of the East Ham Division of the St John Ambulance Brigade gas now been formed under the command of Superintendent Atkins, whose first officer Mr W. R. Magnus, has been placed in charge in charge of the new section.
>
> It may interest your readers to know that the Ilford Men's Meeting is directly responsible for this new formation, inasmuch as its recruits were nearly all members of the first aid classes organized by that body towards the latter end of last year.
> Any person who holds a first aid certificate issued by the St John Ambulance Association, and physically suitable is eligible to join the St John Ambulance Brigade.
>
> In order to become thoroughly efficient however, the section requires funds for the provision of adequate first aid equipment. Subscriptions for this purpose will therefore be welcome by the treasurer, Dr E. King Houchin, of Cranbrook Road, Ilford, or by the undersigned, from whom further particulars may be obtained.-
>
> Yours truly
> H. C. Bull
> Hon Secretary to Section
> 24th August 1903

The Barking, East Ham and Ilford Advertiser announced on 5 September 1903. –

> Ambulance Brigade – An Ilford Section of the East Ham Division has been formed under the command of Supt Atkins, whose First Officer Mr W. R. Magnus, has been placed in charge of the new section. The Ilford Men's Meeting is directly responsible for the new formation. Mr H. C. Bull has been appointed hon. secretary, and Dr E. King Houchin treasurer.

Originally Ilford Section was part of East Ham Division and was later registered, in its own right as No 46 Ilford Division. Dr Edmund King Houchin, also joined No 15 East Ham Division on 22 June 1903 and then went to Ilford Division on its formation, and at the same time William Magnus was promoted to Divisional Superintendent of new Ilford Division.

At the 50th anniversary dinner, some years later the then Divisional Superintendent Mr Dean[20] alluded to the early days of the Division. it was he said

---

20 Transcript of Speech given at the Golden Jubilee Dinner by Mr Dean. Accesed at the Redbridge Museum and Heritage Centre

amusing to note among the old minutes a reference to the financial balance in 1903, a sum of 1/1 (one shilling and one penny) in hand being recorded illustrating a meticulous attention to detail even in those days. Also, a note of dismay at being informed by the "School Board" of a charge of 17/6 (17 Shilling and 6 pence) for a room later to be altered favourably by its successor the "Education Committee" to 5/- (Five Shillings).

1904

The Recorder on 29 July, 1904 carried a full article under the headline

> St John Ambulance Brigade. Ilford Section.
>
> On Monday last, at Christchurch Schools, Ilford, as interesting presentation was made to Sergt. C. J. Fitch, of the Leyton and Leytonstone division. As is doubtless already known in Ilford, section of the East Ham division was formed in June last year, from among the numerous holders of certificates obtained through the St John Ambulance Classes, held under the auspices of the I.M.M [Ilford Men's Meeting][21]. In inaugurating the section, the first officer, Mr W. R. Magnus, was ably assisted by his friend Sergt. Fitch, who undertook the instruction of the necessary military and stretcher drill, and also successfully coached the candidates for promotion. As evidence of the work accomplished under his tuition, it may be mentioned that on the occasion of the visit of the Brigade Sergt-Major to conduct the examination for promotion, the latter stated that he was surprised to find such a very high state of efficiency attained in so short a time.
> In recognition of Sergt. Fitch's services to the section it was unanimously resolved by the members to present him with a testimonial. This took the form of a silver cigarette case and match box, both with the recipient's monogram, and the former also bearing a suitable inscription.
> At the conclusion of the usual fort-nightly drill the hon. surgeon to the section (Dr E. King. Houchin) presented the testimonial to Sergt. Fitch, and in an excellent speech expressed the sense of indebtedness which the whole of the section felt for the services rendered by him, and asked his acceptance of the testimonial in recognition of the same, and as a token of the esteem in which he is held by the whole of the members (Applause.)
> Sergt. Fitch, in thanking the members for the gift, stated that it came upon him as a complete surprise, and that whatever he had done for the section had been done firstly as a friend of the first office, Mr W. R. Magnus, with whom he had been associated in ambulance work for over 15 years; secondly, as an ambulance enthusiast desirous of seeing the work progress for the good to be achieved through its instrumentality. He very much appreciated the kindly thought which had prompted the gift, which would always bring back to him remembrances of very pleasant times, He would also always be only too happy to render any assistance on a future occasion should it be necessary. (Applause.)
>
> The proceedings were brought to a close, with a vote of thanks to the hon. surgeon for making the presentation.

A happy occasion was the birth of William and Maud's daughter, Lena Elsie Magnus, who was born 26 September 1904

---

21 Norman Grunby in his Potted History of Ilford privately published in 1997 noted "Mrs Sarah Ingleby (1823-1906) was a resident at "Valentines" for over 60 years She was the Ilford representative on the Romford Board of Guardians. During her occupancy "Valentines" and its grounds were frequently made available for various functions organised by the Ilford Men's Meeting.

The section started to receive valuable donations, one such donation came via Dr King Houchin and was noted in *The Recorder* on 2 December 1904, as follows –

> Ilford St. John Ambulance.
> Presentation of an Ashford Litter.
>
> Through the instrumentality of their hon. surgeon, Dr E. King Houchin, the Ilford section St. John Ambulance Brigade has had presented to it, by an anonymous donor, one of the latest standard pattern Ashford litters with rubber tyres, supplied by the St. John Ambulance Association, together with a first-aid box, containing all necessary appliances for the efficient rendering of first aid. The litter has been stationed at the shop of Mr A. W. Rowe, a member of the section, at 25 York-road, and is available at any time for use in case of accident or sudden illness in the district.

East Ham Echo edition 27 November 1904 reported –

> St John Ambulance Brigade
> Annual Parade at Little Ilford.
>
> The East Ham divisions of the St. John Ambulance Brigade held its annual parade on Sunday morning, St. Michael's Church at Little Ilford being visited. Besides the local contingent, several members attended from the Ilford, Leyton, Leytonstone, Walthamstow, Beckton, North London, Toynbee Hall, Deptford and Rotherhithe branches, as well as a number of nursing sisters, under the charge of Mrs Randall, and the Ilford Volunteer Band (Bandmaster Kingsnorth), Superintendent A. A. Atkins commanded the East Ham Division, and among the surgeon's present were Drs. F J McKettrick, P. K. Wallis, and E. King Houchin (Ilford).
>
> The service was conducted by the rector (Rev.P.M. Bryne.), whose discourse from the text, "Sir, I have no man, when the water is troubled, to put me into the pool"- was of a thoroughly appropriate and interesting nature. In the course of his remarks the preacher said: I have had the privilege for some years now of referring on these occasions to some aspect or other of the works of the St John Ambulance Brigade. This morning we are pleased to welcome you to our church again, and I venture to submit to you on this occasion a few thoughts before us in text. Your brigade, as it seems to me, is a noble answer to that cry of suffering humanity. Your object, I take it, is to follow in the steps of Him "who went about doing good." You try to catch His spirit of particle practical and loving Sympathy, and to watch and imitate His method of dealing with individuals struck down in the battle of life. This being so, it is well, indeed it is essential, that you should take up the work in a religious' spirit. Hence the value and importance of such a service as this. You come here to-day to lay before God the work of the past twelve months, asking him to accept what you have tried to do, and to pardon what has been done amiss. You come to thank Him for all His goodness and to seek His blessing on the coming year. Is it not so!
> There has been talk of late about having a fixed Sunday every year, to be known as Ambulance Sunday throughout London, much as Hospital Sunday is observed, when the subject of first aid and ambulance work might be brought to the notice of the people generally, and wider interest aroused in the movement. There is a good deal to be said in favour of that idea – though I must confess we are getting rather over done with special Sundays. But, in any case, we at least in these parts do something in that direction by having a St John Ambulance Church Parade, we appreciate and enjoy our gathering together here, and there is a special fitness in appointing this particular Sunday for the purpose. This is, as you know, the last Sunday of the Christian year. Today we wind up the series of Sundays after Trinity, and then, Sunday, we begin the Churches' year again, with the Advent season. It is usual for us, on this last Sunday in the Christian year, to look back and gather up the

fragments of teaching and of blessings which we have received, and then, as we look forward to the future, we ask God, in the collect for to-day, to "stir us up to greater efforts in His service." So, with yourselves and your brigade work, I rejoice to know that, since we met last year, your work has grown and prospered, and that now you have an Ilford section attached to your division at East Ham. May you go on and prosper, with the hand of God still strong upon you to bless you in all you undertake. This coming year may bring perhaps important changes in the organization and development of your operations. There has been some discussions lately, so I understand, about handing work over much, if not all, of your work to the local and municipal authorities in London and elsewhere. Well, this is not the time or place to enter into the question as a whole, but personally I may be allowed to state that I for one should deplore any decided steps in that direction, or any action that would tend to take this work out of your hands. I don't want to see our hospitals and kindred societies put upon the rates – do you? I prefer to see works of charity depending upon voluntary effort and self-sacrifice. It is better for you that it should be so, and better for all concerned, though the strain thus put on voluntary effort may increasingly severe, we must be prepared for that. But by this way. "Lengthen your cords and strengthen you stakes" by all means. Grapple with the growing needs of London and other places. Devise new methods for meeting new demands that are being made upon you, but don't allow the reproach of the text to be brought against you, as if you had failed to do your part, or as if any large number of sufferers were bound to be left neglected. I verily believe that your order has a splendid future before it, as we all know, it has a splendid record in the past. Let that record be ever present to your mind as a constant inspiration to spur you on to fresh enthusiasm, and then we need not fear about the future. There are some people nowadays who have no respect for age, either in person or in institutions. The mere fact of their being old is to some a sufficient ground for wanting to remove them. Such people little know the wondrous vitality which belongs to an ancient order such as yours, and that man is blind and dull indeed who cannot see and value at their true and proper worth the cheerful readiness to be of use, the loyal obedience to irksome discipline, the willing surrender of precious time which have always marked your work. But here I must stop to-day. I have kept you already, I fear, too long. Take away with you, if you will, the picture which St. John has given us in the text. Keep before you the thought of suffering humanity, crying out for a brother's help. Remember it is Christ, our incarnate Lord, who is the central figure in the picture, and who is, still the Good Physician of men's souls and bodies, and bearing all this in mind, give yourselves no rest until the means of recovery and healthfulness are put within reach of us all. Well may we, on a day like this, thank God with all our hearts for the increasing opportunities and means that are now afforded for the relief of distress and pain. Who can doubt that this progress in the relief of human pain is one of the glories of our day and generation. The healing water are being marvelously moved, but still, as of old, there is need of the personal agents – men and women like ourselves -to be God's instruments for man's relief. Claim you share, dear friends, in this glorious enterprise, and do it as unto Him. The "Work of the world" (a poet has truly said) – "The work of the world is done by few. God asks that a part may be done by you.

The band accompanied all the hymns, and at the conclusion of the service played the National Anthem. Mr F.E. Wilson presided at the organ.

The Recorder dated 30 December, 1904 reported on a Fatal Accident at Ilford Station, the article continued

> About nine o'clock on the night of the 22nd [December 1904], during the dense fog that prevailed, an elderly gentleman named Black, who lived at No 11, Horace-road, Forest Gate, was the victim of a fatal accident at Ilford Railway Station. While walking along one of the platforms he stepped over the edge and fell across the rails. Happily, no train was approaching, and he was rescued as soon as possible, but the fall fractured his thigh.

Mr Arthur Rowe, of York-road, who is a member of St John Ambulance Association, and some of his comrades, being called by Mr W. Pallant, station-master, were quickly on the scene, with the new ambulance, which was recently given anonymously, and now used for the first time. It was necessary, however, after the sufferer had been brought out of the station, to transfer him, under the direction of Dr Jobson, to a horse ambulance, on which he was removed to the cottage hospital in Shrewsbury-road, Forest Gate.

The sufferer was afterwards removed to West Ham Hospital, where he succumbed to his injuries on Tuesday morning."

The East London Advertiser dated 10 June 1905 carried the following news item –

Dr King Houchin and First Aid.
Under the auspices of the I.M.M., many agencies have been established, and including in the number is a local section of the St. John Ambulance Brigade. On Sunday the members attended the meeting at the Congregational Church, High Road, Ilford, in uniform and a very brave show they made. The officer in command were Superintendent A. A. Atkins and First Officer Magnus, while hon surgeon's Dr McKettrick and Dr E. King Houchin were also present, the latter being accommodated in the pulpit, the latter being chairman for the afternoon. After appropriate musical selections by band and choir, and the hearty singing by all present of the National Anthem, Scripture lesson from the 5th Chapter of St Luke's was read by the First-officer Magnus and prayer was offered by the Rev. C. H. Vine.

In his capacity as Chairman, Dr E King Houchin made a capital speech congratulating the I.M.M. on the work of the organization generally, and the initiation of ambulance work in the town in particular. He first alluded to the great honour and privilege he felt conferred upon him in being "called to the front," to preside over such a magnificent assembly and thanked on behalf of the "Knights" of St. John for the invitation to attend that meeting. He claimed that they were really doing good work along the lines of the I.M.M. motto- "For God and Humanity." The members of the Brigade had taken the trouble to equip themselves to render first aid to the injured, to be master of such peculiar and often difficult situations as arose through accidents in our crowded streets. The birthplace of the Ilford section was Ilford's Men's Meeting, and he trusted that the parent had no reason to feel ashamed of the child. Dr Houchin concluded with a reference to the fact that while the members of the Ambulance Brigade endeavoured to render aid to the injured and repair the body, ministers, such as Mr Vine, were doing greater work ministering to the soul and preparing it for the life to come.

By 1905 campaigning for a hospital in Ilford had also gained momentum and public events were held to support a hospital. The photograph below shows one such event in July 1905 held in Seven Kings Ward. The Division and its members became keen supporters of the hospital movement in Ilford.

1905 Campaign Supporting the Ilford Emergency Hospital Scheme - Photographer unknow

1905 Drowning in Wanstead Park.

The Recorder carried a story in which William Magnus featured. The report appeared on 4 August, 1905. The headline read -

Bather – Drowned in Wanstead Park.

Many of the pleasure seekers in Wanstead Park on Sunday were shocked by a sad tragedy that occurred near the East London Waterworks. Three brothers, who could swim a little were bathing in the Roding, and one of them, named Harry Harding, suddenly sank in deep water. His companions were unable to help him, but called for assistance. One of the park-keepers rowed a boat to the spot, and after the river had been dragged for best part of an hour the body was brought to the surface. It was conveyed to Wanstead Mortuary to await an inquest. It may be added that First Officer Magnus of the Ilford, St John Ambulance Corps, was present, and for 25 minutes he did his utmost to promote artificial respiration, but without success.
An inquest was held at the Public Office, Wanstead, yesterday (Thursday) morning, when the verdict of "Accidentally drowned" was returned. Deceased was 17 years of age, and a native of West Ham.

The Annual report of No 15 (East Ham) Ambulance Division for the year ending 1905, records Ilford Division's formation and notes William Magnus's promotion to Divisional Superintendent and the Surgeon included Dr E. K Houchin, the full report reads as follows –

No. 15 (East Ham) Division [formed 5.4.95 [1895]
Head-quarters: Public Offices, Wakefield Street, East Ham.
Honorary Surgeons.

F. J. McKettrick, M.B   E. K. Houchin   S. A. Stride, L.S.A

Superintendent.   1st Officer.
A. A. Atkins, 41 First Avenue   W. R. Magnus
Manor Park, Essex

Honorary Secretary.   Inspector of Stores.
Corpl. F. G. Cosburn, 129 Carlyle Road   Pte. J. Brickell.
Honorary Treasurer.
Pte. T. Hurden.
Officers 5. Sergeant 1. Corporals 4. Privates 45 Total effective 55.

Increase since last report 11. Drills held 70, Average attendance 14. Cases attended on public duty 60. Cases attended not on public duty 82. Annual Inspection 27th May. Total on parade 41. Absent with leave 9. Absent without leave 5. Annual re-examination, 27th January. Members passed 40. Did not appear 12. Medallions 31, Service Badges 15. Nursing Certificates 25. Regulation uniform worn. Material: 2 litters, 6 Stretchers, 2 haversacks, box of first aid materials, 2 large hampers, 2 marquees, 2 bell tents, oil stove, cups, saucers etc., blankets, waterproof sheets, etc. Division supported by members subscriptions, donations, etc.

The work of this Division for the past year has, on the whole, been satisfactory, but attendance at public duty leaves much to be desired. The Bank Holiday duties were well attended, and the whole of the work efficiently performed. The attendance of two member of the Cyclist Division upon these occasions was of great assistance. The Beckton Division also joined us, which materially lessened the work of the Division. We beg to thank these Divisions for assistance so freely given. The Ilford Section has been formed into a separate Division, to date from October 1st, 1905. This will reduce our strength by 1 Hon. Surgeon, 1 First Officer, 1 Sergeant. 2 Corporals and 22 Privates. We wish the new Division (No. 46) every success, and congratulate First Officer Magnus upon his promotion to Superintendent.

The East Ham Borough Council have again extended their patronage to this Division, and have very materially assisted us. The annual Church Parade of the Division was held on Sunday. October 23rd, 1904, and was attended by a total of 150 of all ranks. The following Divisions were represented: - Nos, 3,4,7,10, 29, 33, 40 and Nos 4 and 8 Nursing. The most important local duty performed was on the occasion of the visit of T.R.H the Prince and Princess of Wales to East Ham on Saturday, March 18th, 1905, when 69 members of all ranks were on duty, eight stations being formed on a route of 2 ¾ miles. The number of cases treated was 14.

1906 – Ilford Division First Church Parade

On 20 July 1906 *The Essex Chronicle* carried a piece on the Ilford Summer flower show held at Valentines Park. It reported that the Ilford Section of the St John Ambulance Brigade attended under Hon-Surgeon Dr E. King Houchin and First Officer, W. R. Magnus.

Church Parades were, and still are, an important part of St John life. The following report dated 12 October 1906 and published in the *Eastern Counties' Times* reflects this. It covers the first church parade of the Ilford Ambulance of the St John Ambulance Brigade. It read –

> Ambulance Parade at Ilford – Rev. C. H. Vine on the mystery of Pain. – The first church parade of the Ilford Division of the St John Ambulance Association took place on Sunday, when over 100 members of the Ilford, North London, Leytonstone, East Ham and Beckton Divisions gathered in York-road for a march to High-road Congregational Church. The officers in charge of the Ilford contingent were Dr King Houchin and Supt. Magnus. Other medical men present included Drs. McKettrick and Stride. Supts. Olley, Kimber, Atkins and Perry. 1st Officers J. Olley., 2nd Officer and Mrs Harrop Superintendent of East Ham Nursing Division also attended. The procession to the church was headed by the Essex Volunteer Band, playing appropriate music.
> The church was crowed to excess, special seats being reserved for the visitors. The Rev. C. H. Vine conducted the service, assisted by the Rev. J. Mayo. The fine choir, under the leadership of Mr W. J. Walls, rendered the musical service in a highly-finished and devotional manner, the anthem "The Lord is exalted" being particularly good.
> Mr Vine preached a thoughtful sermon on the subject of pain.

1907

An update on the work of Ilford Section, now a Division, appeared in the newspapers, the *Eastern Counties' Times*, dated 21 June 1907, carried the following the article being headed-

> Ambulance Work in Ilford. And a word about the carnival – Presentation of Certificates
>
> The article continued "A meeting of the members of the No. 46 (Ilford) Division of the St John Ambulance Brigade was held at Christchurch-road Schools on Monday evening, after the usual fortnightly drill, to distribute the certificates gained by the students of the class whose course of lessons was recently completed. The attendance included Supt. Woollard[22] and several other members of the Ilford Fire Brigade, Mr W. J. Alderson, Mr Harry Harries, and other members of the teaching profession and others who have also passed through the class, besides Dr E. King Houchin, District [Divisional] Supt. W. R. Magnus, Matthews Sergt. Bull, and a number of Brigadiers in uniform.

---

[22] Later Superintendent Woollard took charge of the Clarnico Fire and Ambulance Brigades, one of the largest Private Brigades in London. It also has its own St John Ambulance Brigade Division

Dr E. King Houchin, whose entrance was the signal for a round of applause presided; and District [Divisional] Supt. Magnus opened proceedings by describing the aims and objects of the Ambulance Brigade, which was formed in 1887. He also mentioned that 2,000 members went to South Africa during the war, to assist in the work of the hospital. The brigade regulation required that every member should attend at least twelve drills in twelve months. But the minimum of twelve drills per annum was too small, because it was insufficient in many cases to keep the members in touch with ambulance work. In this Ilford division they held a drill once a fortnight, making 26 drills a year, and if any of the members of the late class should join the brigade, he hoped they would endeavour to attend as many drills as they possibly could. (Hear, hear.)

Dr King Houchin then presented the certificates gained by the students who had successfully passed the examination of Dr A. C. Tunstall, M.D., as under:-

Mr J. G. Barnes, 100, Claremont-road, Forest Gate; Mr H. Harries, 22 Grosvenor-road, Ilford; Mr H. Bayliss, 47 Courtland-avenue, Ilford; Lieut B. Collier, 106 Cranbrook-road: Mr I. R. Bonallack, 41, Woodgrange-road, Forest Gate; Mr E. D. Wright, "The Nook," Cranbrook road; Mr P. J. Raymond, Station-approach, Ilford; Mr F. W. Metcalf, 36 Lawrence-road, Bow; Mr W. J. Alderson, 3, Gordon Road, Ilford: Mr H. W. Apling, 188 Thorold-road. Ilford; Supt. J. Woollard, Ilford Fire Station; Mr J. Regan, Ilford Fire Station; Mr W. Morris, Ilford Fire Station; Mr C. Ferguson, 62, Woodlands-road, Ilford; Mr K. R. McKenzie, 81, Park-road, West Ham; Mr G. L. Joyce, Beehive; Mr S. Holyfield, 43, Warwick-road, Stratford; Mr H. Wallis, 38, Berkeley-road, Manor Park; Mr W. R. L Aldridge, 42, Queen's gardens, Ilford.

Supt. Magnus commented upon the gratifying circumstance that several firemen had obtained certificates, and he pointed out how the firemen and Ambulance men were sometimes called upon to work together in case of fire resulting in injury to individuals.

Dr King Houchin then presented medals[23] to two firemen to wear on their uniforms, to show that they are members of the Ambulance. Supt. Woollard [Ilford Fire Brigade], who is already in possession of a similar medal, expressed the thanks of the Fire Brigade for the very great kindness shown to them by Dr King Houchin and the other officers and members of the Ambulance Brigade, in assisting them to get through their course, and enabling them to obtain their certificates. (Hear, hear.)

Sergt. Bull Approaching Wedding.

Supt. Magnus said there was still another presentation to make. Sometime ago an ambulance class was started in connection with the Ilford Men's Meeting, and as a result of that class, an Ilford section of the East Ham Brigade was formed. For two or three years that section was fostered by East Ham division, until they found it necessary to blossom forth, and the Ilford Section became Ilford Division. (Applause.)

He proceeded to speak in appreciative terms of the work of Sergt. Bull, who had been with them throughout the hardest part of their work, from the time when they were a class of the I.M.M. This would probably be the last occasion on which he would be with them before he entered into the bonds of matrimony –(cries of "shame!" Laughter) – and the members of the Brigade desired to show their sympathy with him. (Laughter and applause.) He asked Dr Houchin to present Sergt. Bull with a very small token of their esteem and respect, (Cheers.) Dr Houchin then, in a few graceful sentences, presented Sergt. Bull with a very handsome barometer.

---

[23] These were probably the St John Ambulance Association Medallions.

Sergt. Bull, who was taken by surprise, was heartily cheered as he stepped forward to reply. He said he felt very much like the man who was called upon to make a speech, and who didn't know what to say, but some of them knew what he ought to say, and those who did know had better tell the others. (Laughter.) Sergt. Bull passed on to say that he appreciated their gift very much. It was a very handsome piece of furniture, and he should value it for the rest of his days. He saw that it pointed to "Fair" at present.

A Voice: "Stormy." later on. (Loud laughter.)

Sergt. Bull, continuing, said he hoped that so far as the prospects of the division were concerned, the indicators would always remain "fair'; and he hoped he himself should share the same kind of weather in his future life. (Cheers.) He thanked then one and all giving him such a beautiful present in the memory of the most rapid voyage he should ever take – a voyage from the Cape of Good Hope to the United States in less than half-an-hour. (Laughter and cheers.)

Dr Houchin congratulated the students upon having obtained their certificates. He was sure they would not have received them if they had not satisfied the examiner. Dr Tunstall was one of their best men as regarded knowledge of first-aid. He had written a great deal about it, as well as having taught and examined, so that he was thoroughly aware of what was essential in a first-aid man. But he wanted them to bear in mind that they ought not rest contented where they were. They must not be satisfied with having acquired their first-aid certificate. They must remember that admitted a certain amount of knowledge on their part to render first-aid to the injured or the seriously and sudden sick, and it land them in positions of responsibility. From his own experience of surgery, he could tell that the first thing to be done in cases of accident was usually the most important thing; and that often after first aid had been rendered -especially when it had been rendered efficiently. As he knew it would be by them on any occasion to which they might be called – they would find that they had done all that a surgeon could probable have done if he had been there in the first instance. He was pleased for another reason to have presented them with these certificates. It was a compliment to himself as their instructor, and he was sufficiently conceited to acknowledge that compliment. It showed that they had not been mere dummies. They had kept their ears open; their intelligent minds had responded to what had been said; and they had absorbed sufficient to pass a very creditable examination. He now wanted as many of them as were not in the Brigade to join the Brigade, for the simple reason that it would give them opportunities of exercising the knowledge, which they had acquired. (Hear, hear.) It not only did that – it frequently gave them a very pleasurable outing, which was enjoyable itself, and also cleared their consciences, in giving them confidence in their ability to render first-aid in case of necessity, if called upon (Hear. hear.)

He passed on to express pleasure at the serving members of the Ilford Fire Brigade among their number. It was very important that the members of the fire brigade should be thoroughly up in first-aid duties, because in cases of fire it was important to not only rescue persons form buildings, but occasionally they might be called upon to render first-aid to those who were suffering from burns or other injuries. This often meant a great deal to the sufferer, lessening the risk of blood poisoning that might very easily occur if burns were allowed to be exposed for some considerable time. He was very pleased, also, that members of the first brigade had distinguished themselves so far as to receive medallions. (Hear, hear.) He was also glad to see to find that there were School Teachers who had received Certificates. (Hear. hear.) It was very important indeed that school teachers who had guardianship of numbers of children assembled in large masses, should keep thoroughly cool heads, and remain self-possessed in times of special difficulty and danger, so as, for example, to get the children into line and safely out of a burning building, away from danger, and also be able to give first-aid, to those who were either caught in the flames or were injured in any other way.(Hear. hear)

Speaking of Sergt. Bull. Dr Houchin congratulated him upon the step which he was taking, and said they were very sorry to lose him as secretary of the division. (Hear, hear.) During the whole time he had been with them, he had been a considerable stimulus to the men who had attended classes. (Hear, hear.) Turning to some members of the class who were unable for one reason or another to join the Brigade, Dr Houchin said he trusted they would keep in touch with the work of the brigade at all events. The brigade would be glad to see them at the fortnightly drills, or at any post at which they might happen to be on duty, so that they might have the opportunity of assisting in the work of rendering first-aid, and of keeping their knowledge up to the mark. (Hear, hear.)

Supt. Magnus expressed the cordial thanks of the Brigade and class to Dr Houchin for his presence and address. Dr Houchin was a very busy man, but they were always pleased to see him whenever he could spare half-an-hour.(Cheers.) He proceeded to say that in dealing with accidents they often had to make the best of a bad job, and make shift with such appliances as they could procure on the spot. He advocated a splint watchfulness on the part of the men, so that they might be alert to the opportunities of service; and by exercising their minds as to how this or any difficulty could be overcome, they would be ready to cope with accidents when they occurred. He had known people who had obtained certificates and medallions, but two years later were not qualified to render first-aid, because they had forgotten much of what they had learnt. It was necessary that first-aiders should constantly keep in touch with the work of the Brigade, whether they joined the Brigade or not. (Hear, hear.)

The vote of thanks to Dr Houchin was carried with acclamation; and Dr Houchin replied stating he was a most enthusiastic first-aider; and reminded members of the Brigade that they would very soon have the opportunity of working for a local affair, and that was The Hospital Carnival on Saturday, July 13th. (Hear. hear.) He had received an application from Mr Fyson, the Carnival hon. secretary, for the Brigade to render similar service to that which it undertook last year; and they hoped whenever possible to see, with them, those who had taken up this ambulance work.

Their only means of finances were by their annual concert, for which he would be pleased to supply tickets for sale or window bills. The expenses of the upkeep of the Brigade amounted to between £50 and £60 a year, including the purchase of drugs and other necessary equipment. They possessed a tent; and were one of the best qualified ambulance corps in the Metropolitan Ambulance Corps were not known by their numbers – not by quantity, but by their quality. The headquarters of the Ilford Division were at 5, York Road, where Mr Rowe was almost always on duty, night and day, to undertake first-aid. They had complete equipment there. Again, at the Town Hall there was a first-aid equipment box. Mr Drane, the hall keeper, had a box, and in case of accident it was nearly always available. The whole of the members of the Brigade also had outfits, which he hoped was hanging on a nail in their hall, so as to be ready for immediate use. Supt. Woollard, of the Fire Brigade, also had a box. So that throughout Ilford, first-aid outfits were readily obtainable.

Turning to the question of the Hospital movement in Ilford, the speaker said he wished it every success. The Establishment of a hospital in Ilford would materially assist the Ambulance Brigade in their work. He considered it a compliment that Mr Fyson had come to their meeting, and he begged to assure him that the Brigade would be willing and pleased to take up their stations along the line of procession and in the Park of Carnival Day. (Applause.) He also acknowledged the services rendered to the Brigade by their local Press, and moved a vote of thanks to Mr Fyson for his presence and assistance.

Mr Alderson rose, but Dr Houchin claimed the privilege of seconding this motion, at the same time testifying to the services rendered to the Brigade by the press. He trusted the day was not far distant when it would be absolutely necessary for a permanent first-aid station to be established in each populous district, and that would be in telephonic communication with centres in the streets, so that when person required the aid of the ambulance men they might be rung up, as in the case of the fire alarms.(Hear, hear.) The vote of thanks was heartily carried.

The Essex Guardian of June 22, 1907 also report the above proceedings and noted that Sergt Matthews had taken over Sergt Bull's role as the Divisions Secretary, after the latter's five years in the role.

Ilford Division in Valentines Park Ilford c1907 Photograph Author's Collection Photographer Unknown

No. 46 (ILFORD) DIVISION. [Formed 1.10.05.]

HEAD-QUARTERS : CHRISTCHURCH ROAD COUNCIL SCHOOL, ILFORD.

Hon. Surgeon and Treasurer.
E. King Houchin, L.R.C.P.

Superintendent.
W. R. Magnus,
51, Stanhope Gardens, Cranbrook Park, Ilford.

Honorary Secretary.
Corpl. M. G. Matthews,
13, Bathurst Road, Ilford.

Inspector of Stores.
Pte. A. W. Rowe.

Officers 2. Sergeants 2. Corporal 1. Privates 16. Total effective 21. Decrease since last report 3. Drills held 24. Average attendance 14. Cases attended on public duty 51. Cases attended not on public duty 199. Annual inspection, 22.6.07. Total on parade 15. Absent with leave 6. Annual re-examination, 21.1.07. Members passed 17. Did not appear 6. Medallions 15. Service badges 8. Nursing certificates 15. Regulation uniform worn. Material: Ashford litter with first aid box, 4 stretchers, large first aid hamper, 3 havresacs, 2 marquees, 2 folding bedsteads, blankets, waterproof sheets, water bottles, etc.

Public duty has been performed locally on many occasions and also when ordered by Head-quarters. On Whit Monday, the first Bank Holiday duty was undertaken at Hainault Forest, recently acquired and thrown open to the public by the London County Council, and already the necessity for an ambulance station has been proved, as from the first we have been able to report cases, although not of a serious character. The annual concert was held in the Ilford Town Hall on October 18th, 1906, and the Divisional funds were considerably benefitted thereby. The Hon. Surgeon delivered a course of lectures on first aid early in the year, and the strength of the Division was increased by four as a result. During the year first aid boxes, of original design, have been obtained and issued to each member of the Division.

The 1907 Year Book of St John Ambulance – Ilford Annual Report © Museum of the Order of St John

The St John Ambulance Brigade Ilford

1908 - Dr King Houchin – Hon. Life Member of the Association

William Magnus's father Robert James Magnus passed away at 51 Stanhope-gardens Ilford Essex on 20 April 1908. Probate was granted in London on 2 May to William Robert Magnus railway clerk, the estate valued at just over £200- 2s.

One of the key events for Ilford Division in 1908 was recorded in *East London Advertiser* edition dated 13 June 1908. Its headline "Presentation to Dr R. King Houchin". It continued

> An interesting presentation was made last week to Dr E. King Houchin, who is well-known to East London people. Dr Houchin has been the instructor to the Ilford St John Ambulance Association, and at the distribution of awards he addressed the recipients of the certificates.
>
> He spoke of his pleasure at being present, and to find so many there. They had to congratulate themselves on their membership of and upon the fact that they include members of the police force and the fire brigade. Not only were they doing good for themselves but also rendering a good public service (hear, hear).
>
> After speaking of their growth from small beginnings, he said they were being more and more recognised by public bodies, and they were proving that they existed not merely to wear uniform but to render real service. He hoped the Division would not be content with standing still, but would continue in the way they had begun.
>
> Referring to his hope that they would have one or two permanent stations in Ilford, where men should be always on duty, he said there were a certain number of individuals who owned places, such as gateways or rooms in Ilford, which might, if approached, let then have rent free. Of course, the majority of students which they had now were men who could not give their time to be always on public duty, but there was a certain number of individuals who had nothing whatever to do, and who might be pressed to take up the work from a philanthropic and humanitarian standpoint. He trusted that this ideal of his would be realised before the lapse of many years (loud cheers).
>
> He then expressed a hope that the members of the Brigade might always work well and in harmony with the police, giving their aid willingly and with good heart. Dr Houchin concluded with a few word of advice to his men. He counselled them never to be officious in public but to be perfectly decided as to what they were going to do, and in what they did do. Never stoop, he said, to the indignant position of arguing what might be the matter or what to do in public. If a case was a doubtful one, it was better to treat as a serious one than as a trivial matter. If it happened not to be serious then they would not be blamed for taking extra precautions, while if it was serious and they treated it as trivial case they would lay themselves open to condemnation and "show up" the Brigade.
>
> During the evening Dr Houchin was the recipient of a nicely-framed manuscript which read as follows: -

> Presented to Dr E. King Houchin. L.R.C.P., L.R.C.L.
> Sir,
> I have the honour to inform you that at a meeting of the Central Executive Committee, held at St John's gate on Thursday (19th inst.), it was unanimously resolved to add your name to the list of Honorary Life Members of the St John Ambulance Association, in recognition of your able and valuable services as gratuitous lecturer to our classes at Ilford, for which the committee desires to tender its grateful thanks.
> I am, Sir,
> Your obedient servant,
> (Signed) Herbert C Perrott

> This presentation was made by Mrs Magnus on behalf of the Ilford Division. Superintendent Magnus saying a few words in eulogy of Dr Houchin's services.
>
> When the cheers and singing "For he's a jolly good fellow" had subsided a little, Dr Houchin briefly thanked them, and reiterated as an offer to again give his services in lecturing, as hitherto.
>
> Towards the close of the evening, Mr Magnus made an offer of a challenge cup in memory of his late father, to be competed for in a [First Aid] competition.

The Essex Guardian reported on Ilford Division Church Parade on 8 July 1908 -

> Ilford Ambulance Brigade. On Sunday last the members of the Ilford Division, St John Ambulance Brigade under Dr King Houchin and Superintendent Magnus, attended Church Parade at St Paul's Cathedral. About 800 officers and men and 120 Nursing Sisters attended the Parade and the great Cathedral was filled to the utmost, many of the congregation having to stand in the doorways. The service was a fully choral and the Bishop of Mexico preached a most impressive sermon.
>
> On Saturday next the Division will attend the annual inspection, which this year will be held in Hyde Park. It is expected that a member of the Royal Family will be present and make the inspection.
>
> It is interesting to note that this is the 21st Birthday of the St John Ambulance Brigade, which now boasts of a record of long and useful service throughout the world in time of peace and in time of war.
>
> On case of accident or sudden illness the Division will be on duty in the streets on the occasion of the Ilford Hospital Carnival.

William Robert Magnus, a Railway Official, is recorded as having joined the England, United Grand Lodge of England Freemason's. The Membership Registers of 1751-1921 show he was initiated on 12 November, 1908 into Lodge No 879 Southwark Lodge, and then later into Sincerity Lodge of Freemasons 943 Norwich (the latter Sincerity Lodge Number is unconfirmed)

On 22 October, 1909 the *Eastern Counties News* reported on the -

> St John Ambulance Concert at Ilford. The Ilford Town Hall presented a gratifying appearance on Thursday evening, the occasion of the sixth annual concert in aid of funds of Ilford Division (No. 46) of the St John Ambulance Brigade. The building was crowded from end to end by a thoroughly representative audience. The company present included Deputy Commissioner Col. Lees Hall, Assistant-Commissioner W. H. Morgan, of headquarters' staff; Honorary Surgeons Dr Carvell and Dr McKettrick.[24] Also, the officers of Ilford Division, including Dr King Houchin and Supt. Magnus; and other divisions represented were Beckton, Leytonstone, and St Marks.

On 4 December, 1909 the *Barking, East Ham and Ilford Advertiser* carried a short report which read :-

---

[24] Dr McKettrick was Divisional Surgeon of No. 15 East Ham Ambulance Division and one of the founders of East Ham Cottage Hospital. He was also an International Curling Champion.

> Ambulance Brigade – At the annual meeting of the Ilford division on Monday the balance sheet presented showed £13 in hand. – Supt. Magnus, on behalf of the members, presented Sergt. M. G. Matthews and Corpl. A. W Rowe with a medical text book each.

The Essex Times 16 October 1910 reported on -

> Ilford Emergency Hospital – Foundation Stone Laid by the Lord Mayor.
>
> The foundation stone of the Ilford Emergency Hospital was laid by the Lord Mayor of London (Sir John Knill, Bart.) with much ceremony on Friday afternoon. The Lord Mayor and Lady Mayoress, accompanied by Sheriffs (Mr Alderman and Sheriff Roll and Mr Ralph Slasenger) and Mrs Roll, arrived by road in State, at Roding Bridge, where they were met by officer of the hospital. The imposing procession passed between lines of spectators to Ilford Town Hall, where the Chairman of the Urban Council (Mr H. M. Thornton, J.P.) and members received his Lordship and the Sheriffs in the Council Chamber. By permission of Col. J. E. Windus, the band of the 4th Battalion Essex Regiment played a selection on the steps of the Town Hall.

The Lord Mayor was presented with an Illuminated Address before proceeding later to the site of the proposed Hospital on arrival –

> The Lord Mayor was presented with a silver trowel by the Architect (Mr R. Banks-Martin)[25], the stone was lowered into place by the Builder (Mr H. J. Carter), and was set by the Lord Mayor, who declared it well and truly laid.
>
> The inscription on the stone is: "Ilford Emergency Hospital (Incorporated). This stone was laid by the Right Honourable Sir John Knill, Bart., Lord Mayor of London, on the 15th day of April 1910."
>
> Prayer was offered by the Rev. H. W. E. Molony, Vicar of Ilford.
>
> Mr J. W. Godfrey proposed, and Mr Thomas Hughes seconded, a vote of thanks to the Lord Mayor, which his Lordship acknowledged.
>
> A vote of thanks to the Sheriffs was proposed by Mr J. T. Dormer, seconded by Sir John H. Bethell, M.P., and acknowledged by Mr Alderman and Sheriff Roll.
>
> The Ilford Division of the St. John Ambulance Brigade, under the Hon. Surgeon (Dr E. King Houchin) and Supt. Magnus was in attendance.
>
> To start the hospital free of debt a further £2,500 will probably be required, and every effort is to be made to raise the amount before the end of 1910.

---

[25] Robert Banks-Martin 1869–1930. He designed the East Ham War Memorial unveiled in 1921 He was Mayor of East Ham, 1914-1918. He also visited troops from East Ham on the Western Front during WWI.

Chapter Five – 1911 The Coronation Year & 1912 Royal Review

On 25 January 1911 "Recognition of Cadet Units. – The following additional unit has been reported as recognised by Territorial Force Associations – Essex. – Ilford Church Cadets. This was confirmed in June Orders (Order No 161) of 1911 as published by the *Army and Navy News* dated 10 June 1911. Some years later, in 1917, William Magnus was to play a part in the Essex Regiment Cadet organisation.

The 1911 Census was taken on 2 April. Both William Magnus, a Railway Clerk, his wife Maud Beatrice and their daughter Lena Elsie Magnus, who was born 26 September 1904 are listed. It also shows William's mother-in-law, Jane, aged 77, living at the family home at 51 Stanhope Gardens in Ilford. What is sad about the return is that they had two children but only Lena survived.

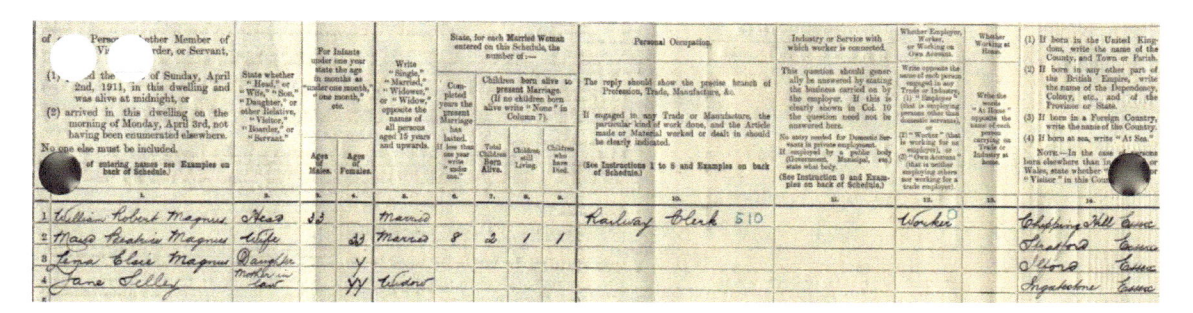

No 15 Ilford Nursing Division was formally registered on the 1 May 1911, under Superintendent Mrs Maud Beatrice Magnus.

1911 - The Coronation of King George V and Queen Mary

The Recorder of 2 June,1911 reported:

> The Ilford division St John Ambulance Brigade, under Supt Magnus, attended the annual company inspection at Manor Park on Thursday last, together with East Ham and Walthamstow Divisions. Colonel Lees Hall, the deputy commissioner, was the inspecting officer, and he complimented the members on their smart turn out and efficient drill.
>
> On Tuesday, the division attended the ceremony of institution and induction of the new Rector of St John's at Clerkenwell, the church of the order. The living is in the gift of the order, and the Lord Bishop of Stepney officiated. The ceremony was historic, and the Knights of Grace and the Knights of Justice, included many members of the nobility, were present in their robes. It is over three hundred years since such scenes were enacted.
>
> On Sunday next the members attended church parade at St John's. On Whit Monday a detachment of men and nurses will be on duty at the great local fete at the Gordon Club Grounds, and a further detachment will attend as usual at Hainault Forest.
>
> A cordial invitation has been extended to members of the Ilford division to attend the investiture of the Prince of Wales at Carnarvon Castle on July 13th next, and arrangements have been made for the division to be represented on this historic Royal occasion.

The Recorder on 23 June 1911 carried the following report following the Coronation on 22 June 1911.

> Ambulance Mems. This is an exceedingly busy week for the members of the Ilford Division, St John Ambulance Brigade, On Monday, Tuesday and Wednesday they were on duty at Earls Court Exhibition; on Thursday and Friday – accompanied by the sisters of the Ilford Nursing Division under Lady Superintendent Mrs Magnus, they leave Ilford soon after daybreak and proceed to their stations on the line of route, whereat they were posted for duty at 5 a.m. An advanced party will remain in London over night to prepare and transport the equipment to allocated stations.

The Recorder on 30 June 1911 carried a detailed article of the Ilford Divisions attendance at the Coronation of King George V and Queen Mary.

> The Ambulance Brigade and the coronation". The story continued "Aided by alarm clocks and other subterfuges the members of the Ilford Division St John Ambulance Brigade, together with the ladies of their Nursing Division, looked as fresh as paint when they paraded at 3.30 a.m. on Coronation Day at Ilford Station, to start their journey to New Admiralty Arch, the station allotted to them for the day. Some of the members who done duty at Earls Court Exhibition until 11 p.m. on Wednesday, remained at Liverpool-street all night to be in readiness to convey the stretchers and equipment to Charing Cross, where they were met by the main body at 4.20 a.m. A side street next to the Admiralty was assigned by the police as a base, and on arrival preparations were at once made to meet any emergency in the way of accident or illness. Early though it was the pavements were already filled with enthusiastic though tired sightseers with five hours still to wait until the first of the processions was due. At 6 o'clock, Corporal Rymer, the head of the Divisional Commissariat announced breakfast. The nurses had made ample provision for the day in the way of foodstuffs, and it was quaint to see Dr King Houchin, Superintendent Magnus, Lady Superintendent Magnus, the nurses and men taking their very early morning meal standing in the street. The Ilford Division had the ambulance care of two large stands of guests of the Admiralty on the Whitehall side of the arch and men were posted thereat. Others were told off at regulation distances along the line of route. Everything done with military precision, and when Lord Knutsford and other high headquarters officials paid their visit, all was in readiness. Luckily for the public the day was cool and cases of heat exhaustion were thereby lessened, but in the course of the duty it transpired that some patients had travelled long distances by train, reached London early on Wednesday evening, and had taken up positions on the pavement as early as 7 and 8 p.m. They had stood through-out the night. The members were kept busy throughout the day, and at 3.30 p.m., after the troops moved off, Colonel Trimble, C.M.G.,[26] the ambulance officer in charge of the route section, gave authority for the division to return home and seek rest to be in readiness for the early duty of the next day. The arrangements made were in every sense complete. Water cups made of paper were carried by each man on duty and used in cases of distress. Oxo in flasks was also provided, and be it said, the readiness and willingness of the nurses and men to do anything and everything required of them made a strenuous duty a real pleasure.

---

26 Dr Charles Trimble was born in 1856 in Co Louth, and he moved to Bamber Bridge as GP by 1881. He was active in the 5th Lancs RGA Volunteer corps from the late 1870s. After the South African War, he was awarded the C.M.G. for his outstanding work, as Senior Deputy Commissioner of St John Ambulance Brigade (No. 4 District). He was also a JP. On 22 July 1915, (aged 59) Dr Trimble embarked for France as Major and established the St John Ambulance Hospital at Etaples, and became its Officer Commanding and was later promoted to Lt Col. The hospital was bombed twice in May 1918 and so badly damaged it had to be dismantled and then in October moved to Trouville until February 1919. He was awarded the Order of St John Life Saving Medal in Gold for his actions during the bombing of hospital at Etaples, also in 1918 he was made a Companion of the Order of the Bath. After the War, he became an Alderman on the County Council, and finally retired to Penwortham. He served St John Ambulance for over 55 years. In 1942 he was made Bailiff Grand Cross of the Order of St John of Jerusalem. He died on 10 October 1944.

A touch of the world-wide scope of the ambulance work was afforded by the presence of members of the Over-seas Brigades – Africa, Transvaal, Australia, New Zealand, India – who had journeyed to England to work side by side with members of the old country. Nurses from other parts of England were billeted by their sisters in the work here in London, and special provision was made for the accommodation of the men who came to London to play their part. The varying brogues as they greeted each other was most interesting, and the air was laden, with a sense of true brotherliness in making the acquaintance of men and women who, all over the world, devote a large share of their time to voluntarily aiding the sick and suffering.

After the long duty on Coronation Day, the nurses had perforce to prepare the commissariat for the next day. This meant but a short rest, for 4.30 a.m. Friday morning saw them at the station again with the men, ready to entrain for Ludgate Circus for another spell of duty on the route of the royal progress. A position outside Messrs. Thos. Cook and sons' office was assigned, and everything went as if by clockwork. Duty ceased at 3 o'clock on Friday afternoon, and both men and nurses expressed themselves grateful that they had been permitted to take their place and share in the voluntary work of rendering first aid where necessary on the occasion of the Coronation festivities of the Sovereign Head of the Order of St John.

There was, however, one regret, Sergeant Row, on whose shoulders as inspector of stores to the division fell the labour of preparing all the ambulance equipment was, owing to sudden illness prevented from accompanying his comrades.

First Officer Matthews, hon. secretary of the Ilford Division, assumed the duties attendant on the honour recently conferred on him, for the first time on Coronation Day, and was the recipient on many congratulations.

Dr King Houchin, Superintendent Magnus and Lady Superintendent Magnus are to be congratulated on the efficiency of their divisions and the arrangements made in conjunction with headquarter, for carrying out their share of the important duty.

Magnus awarded Order Service Medal and lunch with H.R.H. the Duke of Connaught

The Recorder in its edition of 7 July 1911 reported that -

> On the 5th July Superintendent Magnus was presented with his medal for long and efficient service by H.R.H. the Duke of Connaught, the superintendent had the honour of lunching with His Royal Highness.
>
> Sergeant Matthews, the hon. secretary of the Ilford Division, has been promoted to the rank of First Officer.

This was alluded to in the previous coronation report.

St Paul's Cathedral

The Recorder dated 7 July 1911, reported under the headline "*Ambulance Men*". It covered the visit of the King and Queen to St Paul's Cathedral. It read as follows

> The Ilford Division, St John Ambulance spent a useful day in the City on Thursday last, on the occasion of the visit of H.M. the King and Queen to St Paul's Cathedral and the Guildhall. This was the last of the Coronation duties. Dr King Houchin and First Officer Matthews were in charge of the men, and Lady Superintendent, Mrs Magnus, Lady Maud Wilbraham, and

Mrs Law controlled the nurses. For the first part of the day the division was posted at the Old General Post Office, St Martins-Le-Grand, and members were kept busy until the king reached the Guildhall. They then removed their station to a spot near Sadler's Wells Theatre, in Rosebery-avenue, where the press of sightseers was so great that ambulance station had to be based in the theatre grounds. Here they also found plenty to do.

The members and their nurses will be on duty in the streets on Saturday next on the occasion of the Hospital Carnival. The usual encampment will be fixed in Valentines Park.

Investiture of H.R.H. the Prince of Wales at Carnarvon

The Recorder Friday 7 July

Arrangements have now been completed for attending the investiture of H.R.H. the Prince of Wales at Carnarvon[27]. The Ilford Division headed by Superintendent Magnus and Inspector Rowe[28], will be well represented on that historic occasion.

The Daily News on 12 July 1911 reported

Detachments of the St John Ambulance Corps will be in attendance during the Investiture of the Prince of Wales at Carnarvon, and as usual, will carry ample supplies of Oxo for dealing with cases of exhaustion.

Miss Olive Houchin

The Recorder published on 28 July 1911 carried a short report which read

At the prize distribution of the Royal Academy of Music, held at Queen's Hall. Miss Olive Houchin, daughter of Dr King Houchin, Cranbrook-road, Ilford, was awarded the silver medal for pianoforte playing.

The Death and Funeral of Mr Cuthbert Wright

22 September 1911 - *Eastern Counties' Times - London, London, England,* reported the funeral of Mr Cuthbert Wright as follows

Amid many manifestations of sincere sympathy and profound respect, the remains of Mr Cuthbert Wright, of Britannia-road, Ilford were laid to rest in the family grave in the Ilford County Cemetery on the 14th inst. Deceased was very well-known and highly respected representative of young manhood of our town, having been secretary of the Ilford Cycling Club and a member of the Ilford Division of the St John Ambulance Brigade. The coffin was borne on the shoulders of four of his comrades in the Ambulance Corps, who were in uniform, supported by Dr King Houchin, Superintendent Magnus, and several members of the Division, together with the ladies of the Ilford Nursing Division. On the centre of the coffin rested the deceased's ambulance cap and belt, surrounded by most beautiful floral tributes from his relatives and many friends. The mourners included the parents, sister and other relatives and a largely representative section of the Ilford Cycling Club. After the service in the Cemetery the coffin was again raised on the shoulder of his ambulance comrades and borne to the grave. The ambulance officers stood at the salute as their men slowly lowered the coffin to it last resting-place. The floral tributes afforded opportunity for many touching references, and included, amongst others, a cross, inscribed "At rest," from the parents;

---

27 The investiture of David, Prince of Wales, later Edward VIII, took place on 13 July, 1911.

28 This refers to Inspector Rowe being the Divisions Inspector of Stores

wreaths from his sister and Miss Florence Parish; harp, with eight strings, one of them broken, from his seven oldest chums; a cycle wheel, with a broken spoke, from Ilford Cycling Club; and from the Ambulance Brigade an eight-pointed star, the badge of the Order of St John of Jerusalem. The funeral arrangements were conducted by Mr Hawes, of Ilford-lane.

Fundraising

The annual fundraising concert was the subject of an article in *The Recorder*, published on September 29, 1911, it read-

> St John Ambulance Brigade – Next Thursday's Fine Concert. Considerable interest is being manifested in the annual concert in aid of the Ilford Division of St John Ambulance Brigade, which takes place at the Town Hall next Thursday evening. The proceeds are as usual to be exclusively devoted to the voluntary work of rendering first-aid to the injured, in which the Ilford Division has for years past distinguished itself on many occasions, both public and private. The cause should, therefore, make a wide appeal to the public, quite apart from the fact that, from an artistic point of view, the concert is the most ambitious ever attempted by the society., and is certain to eclipse all previous efforts. The patrons include Sir John Bethell, MP., and Lady Bethell; Councillor W. P. Griggs. J.P., E.C.C [Essex County Council], and Mrs Griggs; other members of the Ilford Urban District Council; and the Mayor and Mayoress of East Ham; the headquarter-officers, and other notabilities.

On 13 October, 1911 *The Recorder* continued its coverage of the event in carrying a further report on the concert -

> Ambulance Concert at Ilford. The Town Hall was well filled on Thursday, on the occasion of the eighth annual concert in aid of the funds of No. 1 District, Prince of Wales Corps, Ilford Division, of the St John Ambulance Association. The officers of the Division were present, viz., Dr King Houchin (hon. surgeon), Supt. W. R. Magnus, First Officer M. G. Matthews (hon. secretary), inspector of stores, A. W. Rowe, and a number of members who acted as stewards. The sisters of the Ilford Nursing Division kindly undertook the sale of programmes, and in their professional costumes they gave a characteristic colour to the proceedings.
>
> A full and very excellent programme was provided. Each moiety was opened by Mr Russell Bonner, who also acted as the sympathetic accompanist throughout, by finely played pianoforte selections from Chopin, which charmed the audience and were an added tribute to Mr Bonner's known musical culture. The lady vocalists were Miss Evelyn Clifford, Miss Edith Kirkwood and Miss Mary Palgrave-Turner. The last named being the star of the trio.

Lord Mayors Show 1911.

Later in the year the regular duty, providing cover, for the Lord Mayors show was reported in *The Recorder* dated 17 November, 1911

> Ambulance Mems. – Ilford division under Dr King Houchin and First Officer Matthews and the nurses under Lady Superintendent Mrs Magnus, were on duty in the City on Thursday, on the occasion of the Lord Mayor's Show and rendered useful service. The work of the winter session of the local branch of the St John Ambulance Association has opened under the most encouraging circumstances. The ladies' first-aid class numbers 60 students and the male home nursing class is equally well attended. Doctors King Houchin and Noel Maudsley, assisted by Superintendent and Lady Superintendent Magnus, First Officer Matthews and the members of the Ilford

Ambulance and Nursing Divisions are directing affairs and much good work contemplated.

The final news report for 1911 was published by *The Recorder* on 1 December, 1911. It read:-

Ambulance Mems. The eighth annual general meeting of the Ilford Division St John Ambulance Brigade was held on Thursday at Christchurch Schools, Ilford, under the presidency of Dr King Houchin, supported by Supt. Magnus, First Officer Matthews, Sergt Rowe, and the non-commissioned officers; Mr John Gardener (representing the honorary members), and other members of the division. The balance sheet and statement of accounts were submitted, showing a balance in hand. The educational work is now being carried out by the St John Ambulance Association as distinct from the Brigade. The branch is under the control of the local officers, with Sir John Bethell as president, and is doing splendid work by teaching home nursing, first aid to the injured and military sanitation. Classes are held twice weekly, and the students evince the greatest enthusiasm. A St John Ambulance company[29] has recently been formed from the division to combine with troops in the event of war and the work is in every way developing in its great usefulness.

Ilford New Hospital Opens 1912

News of Ilford's New Hospital featured in the news in early 1912. *The Barking East Ham and Ilford Advertiser* date 27 January 1912 reported -

Ilford's New Emergency Hospital. Interesting gatherings have been held this week in connection with the opening of the new Ilford Emergency Hospital, which is arranged to take place to-day (Saturday).

The hospital; has been erected in Newbury Park, between Barkingside and Seven Kings, at a cost of about £10,000. The hospital movement in Ilford was inaugurated by the members of the Ilford Medical Society some eight years ago. Later they were joined by a number of prominent laymen, and the first Hospital Committee was formed. The work was carried on with great success till 1907, when a Board of thirty governors took on the work and the question of suitable hospital buildings came up for consideration. The result is seen today in the construction of the administrative section, the dimensions of which are ample for the work of a, 100 bed, hospital. When the need arises for an increase the number of beds, now limited to 20 – no further expenditure for building will be incurred beyond that of extending the ward. The foundation stone of the building was laid on April 15, 1910. The scheme has been made possible by the success of which has attended the Ilford carnivals, from which source the greater part, of the funds have come.

During the week the workers and friends in seven wards have been given the opportunity of inspecting the building, and on each evening social gatherings and concerts have been held. On Monday between 500 and 600 were present from the Cranbrook and North Hainault Wards; on Tuesday there was a similar gathering from Loxford and St Clementswood Wards. Wednesday was set apart for the Park Ward, and Thursday for South Hainault and Seven Kings.

The Hospital will be declared open to-day (Saturday) by Mr Ben Bailey, J.P., Chairman of the Board of Governors, and will be open for the admission of patients on Tuesday, January 30th.

---

[29] This may be a reference to the formation of a Voluntary Aid Detachment.

1912 Magnus appointed a Serving Brother of the Order

By 1912 William Magnus's work within the St John Ambulance Association within London and the Great Eastern Railway Corps was recognised by the Order of St John. Magnus was awarded and invested as a Serving Brother of the Order of St John on 27 February 1912.

The Recorder dated 7 June 1912 reported -

> Ambulance Mems [Members]
>
> The members of the Ilford Division St John Ambulance Brigade are experiencing a busy time. A fortnight ago they journeyed to Manor Park to meet their comrades from East Ham and Walthamstow for the purposes of the annual inspection. Now they form part of the Essex Bearer Company, this annual function is shared by the headquarters staff from St John's Gate and the War Office authorities.
>
> Assistant Commissioner Winney represented St John's, and Colonel Cree, R.A.M.C., represented the War Office. Various evolutions and first-aid expositions were indulged in, and at the close the inspecting officers warmly congratulated the men on their smart turn out and highly efficient drill. Supt. Magnus and First Officer Matthews were in charge of the Ilford Division. Colonel and Lady Gwendoline Colvin honoured the function with their presence.
>
> On Whit Monday the division split up into two detachments for public duty. One journeyed to Hainault Forest and the other to the fete at Gordon Ground. In both instances the members were able to render useful service. On Saturday last attendance was given at the High School sports.
>
> Next Saturday week, the members parade at the Guildhall for the presentation of Coronation Medals. The following Saturday they journey to Windsor to take their place in a grand review of upwards of 70,000 ambulance men and nurses gather together from all parts of the habitable globe, trained and equipped for service of rendering first-aid to the sick and injured. His Majesty the King, sovereign head of the Order of St John, is to hold the review and the great event is looked forward to with intense enthusiasm. The annual divisional concert is fixed for October 3rd, and several prominent artistes are already secured for the occasion.

The 1912 Royal Review – Windsor

The Recorder 28 June 1912 -

> Ambulance Review.
> Great Spectacle at Windsor.
> Ilford Takes Part.
>
> Last Saturday was a memorable day at Windsor. The Royal borough has many times been temporarily the hub of all great movements, and on Saturday its streets echoed with the foot-tread of those whose interests lie in the great work carried on throughout the length and breadth of the globe by the St. John Ambulance Brigade. The movement dates back from the days when knights of old gave their lives for the Holy Sepulchre. The members of to-day labour tirelessly without hope or desire for reward for those who are stricken down in the thousands and one dangers which modern life entails.

Saturday will live long in the memory of those favoured ones who visited the great canvas town which had sprung up in Windsor Great Park. The camp was pitched on the right of the road on entering Queen Anne's gate, and here some 13,000 men and women fraternized and refreshed under the able hands of Lyon's and Co., prior to parading on the review ground for inspection.

The Ilford Division under the command of Dr King Houchin and Supt. Magnus, and accompanied by the ladies of the nursing division, under Lady Supt. Magnus, left Ilford at nine o'clock to catch one of the many special trains due to leave Paddington for Windsor at about ten o'clock. At Paddington, with many hundreds of other members, the Ilford contingent entrained, and were straightway conveyed to Windsor station.

The Royal borough had been the rendezvous of some far-distant divisions since Friday night, and was very much astir with martial music made by several bands of the ambulance district. It was indeed a noble sight. No less than 40 special trains were arranged for the day, and just after mid-day the whole of the 11,000 men and 2,000 women had arrived on parade ground, and were there under the command of Sir James Clark. Bart., C.B., the Chief Commissioner of the Brigade. The day was perfect, the sun shone with all its June splendour, and through the heat was great it was tempered with a delightful breeze. The review was held on the usual ground to the left of Queen Anne's Gate, and here huge stands were erected for privileged spectators. These began to fill up long before the hour of the coming of His Majesty.

The King, in honouring the Brigade of which he is sovereign head, once again evinced his great interest in every phase of the life of his subjects who labour in the public service, and he has paid a Royal compliment to a great work which goes on around us ceaselessly and unostentatiously day by day. Though essentially a peace organisation, the brigade proved itself of service when the nation was at war in South Africa, and at present provided a reserve for the work of mercy in the army and navy amounting to 8,000 members.

The Ilford Division, with many others, wore the Coronation medal awarded by His Majesty for the first time, with conscious pride. The sight of marching columns of nursing sisters in their cool grey frocks was as pretty as any seen in the streets of Windsor for some time.

Punctually at 3.30. the King, accompanied by Col. Sir Fredk. Ponsonby and Sir Derek Keppel, rode to the review ground on his black charger, Delhi. There was an escort of Life Guards

The Queen, the Prince of Wales (who had only arrived at Windsor two hours previously), and the Princess Mary followed in an open landau drawn by four beautiful greys. There were five long lines of ambulance officers and men stretching from Queen Anne's Mead almost to Shaw Lane deer pen, and facing them in two huge grand stands stood the 3,000 nurses. The representatives of the Brigade overseas were posted in the centre of No. 1 District Prince of Wales corps, of which Ilford is part, immediately opposite the saluting base.

The King was received by a special reception committee of the Order of St. John and the band of the Grenadier Guards played the National Anthem. Journeying in front of the nurses, the Royal procession passed up and down the long lines of ambulance men, and the King was able to see the practical side of the work, as occasionally the heat overcame a member, and first aid had perforce to be rendered. The inspection occupied nearly an hour, and there followed a shipwreck life-saving display and an example of mine rescue work by brigade members from various collieries. Thousands of people in the great park admired the remarkably smart movements of the men.

After His Majesty had received the Royal salute, at a signal given by the Chief Commissioner the 13,000 men and women, waving their caps and handkerchiefs, gave a salvo of hurrahs for their sovereign head, which stirred the hearts of everyone, and the cheering was continued until the Royal procession had moved off the parade ground. Thus, ended the most enjoyable day in the annals of the St. John Ambulance Brigade.

The Ilford Division, spick and span, in spite of the long and exciting day, reached Ilford station shortly after 10 p.m., where they formed up with their nursing sisters in the centre and March through Cranbrook-road to Dr Houchin's, where the esteemed surgeon took leave of his comrades, and in a characteristic little speech emphasised the fact that the Ilford members had that day reached a zenith, and told how the high and proud position which they had attained must be individually safeguarded and the good work continued. Hurrahs for the doctor preceded the dismissal by Supt. Magnus, after which the members dispersed.

Next Sunday the Division will attend the annual church parade at the church of the order. St. John's. Clerkenwell, and it is hoped that the weather will be fine, as in that event the service will be a drum head one in the open air.

Last Monday Supt. Magnus attended a general assembly of the order of the hospital of St. John, to which he has recently been admitted as hon. serving brother.

The following member attended the Royal review: - Hon. Surgeon Dr E. King Houchin, Supt W. R. Magnus, 1st B.M.C. Officer. M. G. Matthews, Sergt A. W. Rowe, Corporals Rymer, Welch and Aldridge. Privates Butcher, Long, L.G. Mitchell, Dodd, McKenzie, Apling, Ives, Drayson, Chevalier, Shenton. Smith, Newman, Pitcher, H. E. Souster, S.R. Souster, Jackson, Lady Supt. Mrs Magnus, Nursing Sisters Law, Welch, Rymer, Hope, Macey, Alder, Clements, Stenning and Miss White.

12 July 1912 in a follow up to the Windsor Review *The Recorder* reported –

Ambulance Mems.
The Ilford Division St John Ambulance Brigade will be on duty in the streets next Saturday, and will be accompanied by members of the Australian contingent of the St John Ambulance Brigade, who came over for the recent Royal Review at Windsor. The Canadian contingent sailed for Toronto on the 10th, or they too would have joined in the carnival duty.

24 July 1912 The *Daily Mirror* carried a message in the "*Charities Section*". It read

Unique Scheme for the Blind. A Lending Library of Braille Music. Funds are urgently needed, and should be sent to the Secretary, Miss Laura Strickland, 98 Clova-road, Forest Gate, E., a blind lady who has originated the scheme or to the Hon, Treasurer, Dr E. King Houchin, 65 Cranbrook-road, Ilford. President -The Lord Bishop of Barking.

The Recorder dated 8 November 1912 carried an article which showed the tensions rising in Europe and it reported on the Balkan War. Although St John did not officially take part in the conflict, the British Red Cross did and some members of St John volunteered, this is one such case.

Former Ilford Fireman in Balkans. Assisting the wounded Greeks. Mr W. Morteal, a former member of the Ilford Fire Brigade, left England on October 27th with a detachment of the English Red Cross Society to assist in the rendering first-aid to the wounded with the Greek Army in Turkey. Mr Morteal received his instruction in first-aid work under Dr King-Houchin and members of the Ilford division of the St John Ambulance Association, and passing all examinations, received a medallion this year.

Another concert by Olive Houchin

Miss Olive Houchin.[30] Another concert by Olivia, was reported in *The Recorder* on 8 May 1914 The report noted "*Miss Olive Houchin at the Town Hall*". It continued

> This was the second pianoforte recital given by this truly gifted young local artiste took place on Thursday evening last at the above hall.
> There was a good attendance of music lovers, who listened with marked attention to the various items rendered.

The article continued and a gave full listing of the programme.

---

[30] The marriage of Olivia D Houchin (1892 – 2002) took place at St Giles church, London in the second quarter of 1917. Olive Dorothy, youngest daughter of Dr and Mrs E. King Houchin, of Ilford, Essex. She married Sergeant, later Colonel Rupert Bland Crouch. OBE, ED. CD. 1896 – 1958. They lived in Ontario, Canada. They did have issue.

Chapter Six - 1914 and The Start of WWI

The First World War found William working in a key positions both on the Railway and in the voluntary sector with St John Ambulance and various Voluntary Aid Detachments.

Great Eastern Railway

On the Railway, after gaining considerable experience, in the Superintendent's Office at Liverpool Street, in connection with traffic working matters, he was eventually appointed to control of the Superintendent's Train Delay Section, known internally as the "Punctuality Department", heading a large team, with a Deputy and Assistant (who devotes his time looking after Goods Trains), and a dozen Travelling Inspectors.

Taking about his role we hear the voice of Magnus. He was asked -

> It seems to me" said I [GER. Magazine Reporter], glancing through the sheet after sheet of neat returns, "that the main portion – the bulk – of the trains invariably arrive to time?" Oh yes replied Mr Magnus "but we are not content with major portions; we want an absolutely clean sheet' without spot or blemish'; when we obtain that we intend to have it framed.

In April 1914 The April District Officer Dinner took place, it was one of the final social occasions before WWI interrupted the life of the Country. Both Mr and Mrs Magnus were present.

The Deputy Commissioner Col Less-Hall took the chair at the 13th annual dinner of the Officers of the Corps which was held at the Holborn Restaurant on 22nd April. The gathering this year was not so large as it had been previously, but never the less a very congenial company sat down to dinner, and amongst those present were:-

Deputy Commissioner	Lees Hall
Assistant Commissioner	Winny
Assistant Commissioner	Vilven
District Superintendent	Pointin
District Secretary	Hallat
District Treasurer	Lines
Corps Secretary	Hayman
Hon Surgeons	Major Maitland Coffin & Dr. H S Blok
Lady District Secretary	Miss Hunt
Lady Inspector of Stores	Mrs. Allen Paull
Lady Superintendents	Mrs Calvin Lines, Miss Twist, Miss Hankey, Miss Law, Mrs. Harrop, Mrs. Magnus;
Nursing Officers	Miss Edith Bourke, Mrs. Brooks, Mrs Stanley Smith
Superintendents.	Allan Paull W D Liddell, H Langley-Jones, G T Cooper, W R Magnus, A W Saunders, Page, J T Olley, N Burton, C Statham Ambulance Officer. A E Evans, A J Allison, F O W Bemberger, R W Stone, H S Blok, H E Hawkin
Deputy Commissioner	Mr. W H Morgan, Mrs. Morgan, Mr. Smit, Mr. Darvil and Superintendent Wells (Metropolitan Police)

Toast were given by Lees Hall, W H Morgan and Superintendent Wells.

The St John Ambulance Brigade Ilford

A wedding for Ilford Members

A wedding took place in June 1914 of two people with close connections with the Ilford Division. *The Recorder* dated 26 June 1914 carried the following report:-

> Miss Edith Macey and Mr Frederick Rymer.
>
> The wedding of Miss Macey and Mr Rymer, as mentioned in our report of the Barkingside Church Fete, took place on Saturday at the Parish Church. The bride, Miss Edith Macey, is the only daughter of Mr and Mrs F . Macey of "Roadfield," Barkingside, and the Bridegroom, Mr Fred Ouiter Rymer, the eldest son of Mr and Mrs F. J. Rymer, of Belmont-road, Ilford. Both have been closely connected with the Ilford Division of the St. John Ambulance for a considerable time.
>
> The bride was attired in a costume of silver-grey silk and a white hat with a white ostrich feather. The bridegroom wore the well-known uniform of the St. John Ambulance. Miss Macey was attended by the Misses Annie and Dollie Rymer (sisters of the bridegroom, and Mr Long, of Raleigh, acted as best man. The Vicar of Barkingside officiated. Mr A. E. Macey, uncle of the bride, and a composer of some reputation, and also connected with the musical directorship of the D'Oyly Carte plays, presided at the organ.
>
> A reception was held after the ceremony at the residence of the bride's parents, and here it is interesting to note that the happy pair were piloted in a carriage from the church by a number of members of the St. John Ambulance, the escapade causing no little amusement in the neighbourhood. The catering by Mr Ingram was satisfactory in every detail. Mr Coe supplied the motors. The honeymoon is being spent on the Isle of Wight.

The Following report appeared in the *First Aid Journal* July 1914. It covered the Annual Inspection of London District in Hyde Park on the 4 July 1914, only a month before war was declared on the 4 August 1914. The report read –

> Annual Inspection.
>
> The whole of the corps comprising 1,517 men and 342 nursing sisters was inspected in Hyde Park, on July 4th, by Colonel Tyrell, Commissioner of the Brigade. Amongst those present were Colonel Cantile, Mr. W. H. Morgan, Assistant Commissioner Vilven and Winny. The corps assembled at 3.30 p.m at Wellington Barracks in charge of District Supt. Pontin, and marched to Hyde Park, where the parade was taken charge of by the Deputy Commissioner, Colonel Lees Hall. The various Division were made up into companies in charge of the following officer: -
>
> | | |
> |---|---|
> | No. 1 Company, | Supt Liddell; |
> | No. 2 Company, | Supt Olley; |
> | No. 3 Company, | Supt Jones; |
> | No. 4 Company, | Supt Hudson; |
> | No. 5 Company, | Supt. Cooper; |
> | No. 6 Company, | Ambulance Office Godden; |
> | No. 7 Company, | Supt Atkin; |
> | No. 8 Company, | Supt Orchard; |
> | No. 9 Company, | Supt Healey; |
> | No.10 Company, | Supt Stratham; |
> | No.12 Company, | Supt Journet; |
> | No.13 Company, | Supt Magnus; |

No.14 Company,   Supt Saunders;
No.15 Company,   Supt Wallis.

On entering the park parade ground the corps advanced in quarter-column to take up its position on the inspection ground, were Colonel Tyrell inspected the line. The march-past was in battalions in column of companies, each battalion being headed by its band. At the conclusion of the inspection medals for long-service were presented by Surgeon-General May, C.B., Director General of Medical Services for the Royal Navy. Trophies were also presented to the winners. The Osborne Challenge Shield for improvised work was won by Leyton and Leytonstone (No. 4 Division); the Sleath-Gent Challenge Cup for the best man in the district by Lance- Corporal Milburn; the Efficiency Cup for drill by the South Metropolitan Gas Company Division; the Masset Mainwaring Cup for First Aid by the Hampstead Division; and the Nursing Bowl for the best women in the district by Miss Nellie Jennings, Balham and Streatham Nursing Division. The efficiency of the Brigade was commented on favourably by the Inspecting Officer and others.

London District Inspection July 1914 – *First Aid Journal* July 1914 © Museum of the Order of St John

War was declared by Great Britain, on Germany, on 4 August 1914. A month later on the 11 September 1914 *The Recorder* reported

> Under the heading of "Red Cross Hospital for Ilford," Mr W. R. Magnus makes and appeal to the people of Ilford and the district, which I am sure will not go unheeded. "There is now," he says "the prospect of a Red Cross Hospital being formed in Ilford in connection with our Emergency Hospital, to receive upwards of 150 sick or wounded soldiers," he proceeds to ask for promises of beds, bedding, and other equipment, to be collected only on condition of the hospital being required by the War Office

> Ten days' notice will be given to the governors if and when the hospital is utilised, and everything would have to be got ready within that time. Hence the necessity of making every possible preparation beforehand, so that the mobilisation of staff and equipment can be effected in good order and with a little delay as possible

> The nursing staff will be provided by the Ilford Ambulance and Nursing Divisions of the St. John Ambulance Brigade, and they will work under the direction of and in conjunction with the permanent nursing staff at the hospital. Other arrangements are in progress, and Drs. Jobson and Watts have kindly offered to act as resident house surgeons.

Lighting Restrictions were introduced on 11 September 1914, but not until raids started were they more strictly enforced. The Regulation made under the Defence of the Realm Act meant it was left to local authorities to implement. Later in the war, warnings were reinforced, on 21

May 1915 *The Recorder* headline read '*The Zeppelin Raids. Grave Warning to Ilford Residents*'.

The Recorder date 9 October 1914 reported on Ilford Division as follows:-

> Roll of Honour
> ST. JOHN AMBULANCE BRIGADE No. 46 (ILFORD) DIVISION.
>
> The undermentioned members of the Ilford Division volunteered for the Military Home Hospital Reserve, subsequently enlisted in the Royal Army Medical Corps, and are now serving as follows:-
>
> At Military Hospital, Caterham:-
>
> Sergt. A. W. Rowe, ward master and steward in charge of staff; Pte. G. A. S. Ives, assistant to colonel for medical examinations of recruits and vaccination; Pte. S. A. Souster, assistant cook and assistant to linen store keeper; Pte. L. Rogers.
>
> At Queen Alexandra's Military Hospital, Millbank: - Corpl. J. F. Q Rymer, Pte. E. Long, Pte. W. L. Burton, Pte. C. L. Dodd. Pte. A. E. Jacklin, Pte W. S. Chevalier, Pte. A. H. W. Jenkins.
>
> The majority of the above have been inoculated against enteric fever.

The Recorder 6 November 1914 carried the following photograph and a brief write up about Frederick Stephen Oliver[31] born in East Ham (1888- 1954) Private 37954 RAMC awarded War Medal and Victory Medal

> This picture is from a photo of some of the "Kitchener Boys" in camp at Aldershot, and includes more Ilfordians. They belong to F Company, Royal Army Medical Corps. On the left of the picture is F. S. Oliver, late of Ilford Fire Brigade, who holds the St. John Ambulance medallion, having received training under Supt. Magnus and Dr King Houchin, of Ilford. He has enlisted for the duration of the war, and hopes to return to Ilford Fire Brigade after he visits Berlin.

The Kitchener Boys at Aldershot - Photographer unknown

---

[31] In the 1939 Register he is shown as a factory fireman living in Ealing, with his wife Amelia Ann Maile whom he married on 14 September 1919 in St Mary the Virgin, Greater Ilford.

The St John Ambulance Brigade Ilford

Belgian Refugees

The local newspaper recorded that on 10th November 1914, the first group of Belgian refugees of "nine gentleman, eight ladies and four children…of a class similar to Ilford people" arrived at the Mansion.

Valentines Mansion

Valentines Mansion was home to 270 refugees over the course of the war. Most stayed for a short time before finding accommodation elsewhere. A child was even born in the house on 28 November 1914 – she was named Maria Valentine Franck.

Ilford Postal Refugees Committee and the Belgians Outside Valentines Mansion, Ilford in January 1915. 32

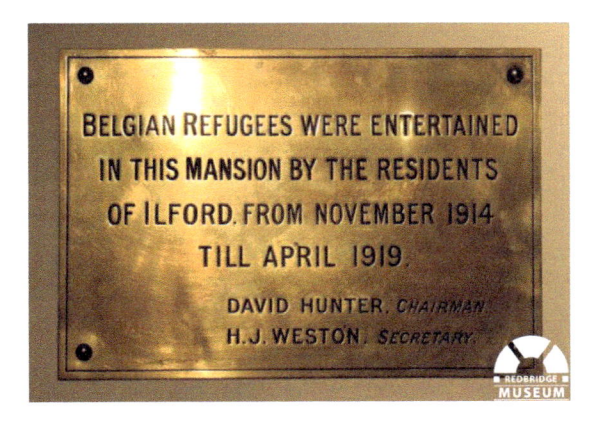

A brass memorial plaque at Valentines Mansion commemorating the Belgian refugees housed there during WWI

Photograph's *Redbridge Museum and Heritage Centre.* 33

---

32 The Valentines Mansion housed 80 fleeing Belgians at a time, by the end of WWI it had accommodated over 250 people.

33 Web page accessed on 14 January 2022. https://redbridgefirstworldwar.org.uk/memorials/belgian-refugees-memorial-plaque.

Chapter Seven - The Ilford New Year's Day Train Crash 1915

New Year's Day Train Crash and The Medical Response.

The Globe dated 1 January 1915 reporting Ilford Train Crash in a Special Edition

The Globe 1 January 1915 gave further details of the response as follows -

> Rescue Work.
>
> The work of rescue was immediately commenced, but great difficulty was experienced in reaching those under the overturned carriages, some of whom were still alive. The noise of the collision brought local doctors and ambulance men to the scene in a remarkably short space of time, and a large force of railwaymen, police, medical men, Territorials who had been guarding the line, and firemen were speedily engaged in extracting the injured.
>
> Third Train's Escapes. The two trains which met with disaster were not the only ones involved, another local train which started from Ilford being struck by falling carriages. One account says that the driver pulled up within yards of the wreckage. There were thus three trains passing through the station at the same time.

The Westminster Gazette 1 January, 1915 recorded one account from Dr Collier, who had been a St John Ambulance Brigade Surgeon of some note having trained the No 15 East Ham Ambulance Division National Champions Competition team some years earlier.

> Dr Collier's Account
>
> Dr Collier, of Grosmont House, Manor Park, who was called to scene of the accident shortly after the occurrence, said the scene when he arrived was "simply too awful for words" "From what I could gather," he told the press representative " a Clacton express train ran through an ordinary train. After passing through the ordinary train the engine of the Clacton train pitched over the embankment, overturning several of the carriages following. Most of those who have lost their lives were apparently killed by the force of the impact of the large engine and the ordinary train. Several bodies were found under the bogey of the engine.
>
> The scene was indescribable, and the bodies which were recovered were unrecognisable. Those who showed any sign of life were immediately attended to on the railway line, other cases not so serious were speedily transferred to the station, where the platforms quickly presented a spectacle reminding one of a hospital surgery. Every doctor in the district was called upon at once, and they did a large amount of work by the side of the wrecked trains. Breakdown gangs were quickly on the spot and started at once to extricate the unfortunate persons who were pinned beneath the wreckage, and the fire brigade also assisted.

The Standard published on 2 January, 1915 reported

> The railway officials acted with splendid promptitude. Medical men in the neighbourhood were summoned, and very quickly Dr Houghton, Dr Jobson, Dr Collier, Dr Cox, and Dr Fraser arrived. Ambulances were brought, and a large force of police took charge of the station. As they were rescued the injured were taken to the Ilford Emergency Hospital, the West Ham Hospital, and the London Hospital. The bodies of the dead were carried to the local mortuary, but it was not till after five o'clock that the last body, that of Mr H. W. Bird – was recovered.
>
> When the express locomotive leapt into the coal-yard it fell on a milk van and horse belonging to Messrs Abbott Brothers. The Carmen Mr W. Saville, narrowly escaped with his life, and he had to be removed to the hospital. The horse was living and in agony. It was shot by a Territorial who was guarding the line.
>
> The tender of the locomotive struck the fence, the driver and fireman only just managed to "jump clear" in time. They were dazed, but not seriously hurt. Happily, there was no outbreak of fire. The local fire brigade "turned out" but the men were needed only to assist in ambulance work[34]

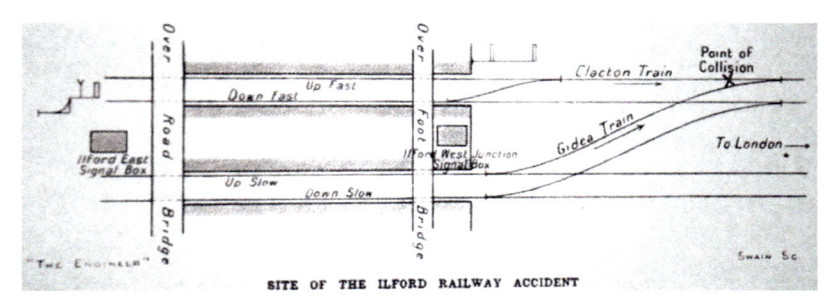

Ilford Station sketch plan showing signals. The Engineer 8 January 1915.

On 08 January, 1915 the *Loughborough Newspaper* recorded the opening of the inquest on the ten victims.

> The names of the victims were:
> | | |
> |---|---|
> | Alexander White, | Seven Kings |
> | August Lambert, | Goodmayes |
> | Frank Simmons, | Hornchurch |
> | J. Delfgow, | Seven Kings |
> | F. H. Daniels | of Messrs Waring and Gillow, Oxford-street |
> | Miss Bertha Christie, | Seven Kings |
> | H. W. Bird, | Seven Kings |
> | George Maylam, | Traffic Manager's Office G.E.R., Goodmayes |
> | C. Richardson | Engineer's Office, G.E.R., Romford |
> | F. G. Allen, | Seven Kings |
>
> Directors' Sympathy Speaking with much emotion, Mr Thornton expressed sympathy on behalf of the managers and directors of the Great Eastern Railway with those bereaved, and also with the injured.
>
> The inquest was adjourned for a fortnight.

---

[34] The firemen of the Ilford Fire Brigade were trained by and held "First Aid to the Injured" Certificates of the St John Ambulance Association.

Ben Bailey, Chairman of the Governors of Ilford Emergency Hospital wrote the following letter which was printed in *The Recorder* on 8 January 1915. He wrote -

> My notes would be incomplete were I not to record how splendidly the matron (Miss Green) at the Ilford Emergency Hospital and her staff met the extra-ordinary pressure. Fortunately, there were three doctors at the hospital performing an operation at about nine o'clock – Dr Watts, Sen., Dr Watts jun., and Dr William. – on receipt of a telephone message from me to the matron, they remained to receive the cases as they arrived. Later, when the last injured person had been dealt with at the scene of the disaster. I visited the hospital and found Drs Coleman and Houghton in attendance, in addition to the three already named, and almost all the injured had been thoroughly overhauled, fresh dressing applied and each made comfortable as medical skills could make them. The doctors named, as well as many others, including Dr Carrol and his partner, Dr Jobson, Dr King Houchin and Dr Steen, did noble and praiseworthy work in the highest form.
>
> Mr Hare, the secretary of the hospital on hearing of the accident, went direct to the hospital and did excellent work there. As did Mr James Mein, the late secretary of the House Committee.
>
> Our carnival and other workers - have in-deed, all interested in our hospital- have now some very tangible proof of the necessity for and usefulness of the institution, and the work we have been able to do on this occasion is a fine reward for all the years of toil and the self-denial exercised by so many in raising of this monument for the relief of suffering humanity. I am sure the public at large will be glad to hear that matron has just informed me (Wednesday Evening) that all of our cases are making satisfactory progress.
> In conclusion, I would like to add that I have received thanks of the directors and the management of the Great Eastern Railway for the assistance rendered by all connected with the Ilford Emergency Hospital.
>
> Yours faithfully,
> Ben Bailey
> Chairman of Governors, Ilford Emergency Hospital
> 5 Cranbrook-road, Ilford
> 6th January, 1915

The role of St John Ambulance in the Ilford Train Accident.

The Recorder published the following letter from the Divisional Secretary of the St John Ambulance Ilford Division on 15 January 1915. It read as follows -

> The Work of the Ambulance Brigade
> To the Editor of the "Recorder".
> Dear Sir, - You will doubtless be glad of some first-hand information concerning some of the details of succour rendered to the injured in the recent lamentable railway accident.
>
> Two officers of this division (No 46 (Ilford) Division, the St John Ambulance Brigade), each carrying pocket first aid outfits and restoratives , were standing on the platform at the time of the accident was occurring, and were therefore first amongst those to reach the scene. The incident is one we have on more than one occasion imagined for the practical instruction. Of our members, and to that extent the means to be adopted were already planned and were set in motion without a moment's delay.

There were a multitude of eager and willing helpers ready to act messengers, and they were despatched for doctors, first aid requisites from an ambulance station adjoining the railway, police, ambulance men, and nurses, fire brigade (the member of which, thanks to the foresight of the Ilford Council, have all been trained in ambulance work by the officers of this division). This done, attention was next directed to cases needing the arrest of serious haemorrhage and shock, and helpers were cautioned as to the harm which might accrue from the unnecessary movement of the injured who were clear of the wreckage, until effective first aid had been rendered. Officers of territorial units were extremely prompt in mustering the soldiers present to act in many useful capacities, and a posse of special constables was soon got together to supplement the regular police who were present under Inspector Hamilton.

The manner in which onlookers who were not able to render and useful service heeded the request of the police and military to withdraw from the scene so as not to impede the services of the railway, medical and ambulance officials was beyond praise.

Railway Disaster at Ilford 1 January 1915 Photo by Barrett

There was no panic, at least at the scene of the disaster, and speaking as one with a long experience and training in emergencies of this kind, I am of the opinion that intelligent coolness displayed throughout was worthy of the best traditions of our race. The pluck of the injured was marvellous, and the manner in which the surgeons worked begot the admiration of us all.

Dr Fraser was the first to arrive, and he was quickly followed by Dr Houghton, Dr Whiting, Dr Coleman, Dr Carroll, Dr Houchin, our divisional surgeon, and many others. On their arrival the cases needing first attention were indicated, and within a short time patients were ready for transportation to hospital.

Simultaneously with surgical attention, squads of lay helpers collected shutters and other material for improvising stretchers and biers, splints, etc., under the direction of railway officials and ambulance officers, one by one, as the patients were prepared by surgeons, the removal to hospital or home was undertaken.

Residents of houses in York-road kindly provided coffee, tea, brandy, rugs and other comforts, which were especially useful.
As soon as possible, those who had received fatal injuries were suitably covered and borne reverently from the scene.

From an inspection made immediately after the accident occurred, we formed the opinion that in each case death was instantaneous.

One poor fellow pinned under the overturned coach was found still breathing, though terribly injured, and the work of rescue was nobly undertaken by a squad under the direction of Mr F. Wilmott, with several doctors in attendance. At great personal risk Mr Wilmott laboured assiduously under the coach until his labours were rewarded by the extrication of the poor fellow alive. To mention Mr Wilmott is but to name one of the many lay helpers who rendered signal service.

There were over a dozen doctors present, and everything possible was promptly done to save or prolong life, to prevent further injury, to secure speedy removal to hospital, and to alleviate shock and suffering. From the onset the manner in which the several units, professional and lay, trained and untrained, worked together systematically and courageously reminded one of an ordinary drill.

It is against our principles to seek anything in the nature of an advertisement, but seeing that the residents of Ilford and the neighbourhood provide us with funds as a means of training men and women in first aid work and providing requisites for use in such emergencies, it will be of interesting for them to know that the Ilford Division played its part. Many of our members are away on active service, but Dr King Houchin, Superintendent Magnus, Ambulance Officers Matthews and Allinson (Leytonstone), Mr Apling, Mr Hurdon, Lady Superintendent Magnus, Nursing Sisters the Misses White and several students of the recent first aid classes, including police and firemen, were on the spot engaged in the work of rescue and succour, a work to which they devote a large portion of their lives.-

Yours faithfully
Morrison G Matthews
Hon. Secretary".

One other item appeared in the *Essex County Chronicle* on 15 January 1915

Ilford
Bravery. - P.C Arthur Youngs, of the G.E.R Police has been awarded the certificate of honour of the St John Ambulance Association for praiseworthy attempt to save the life of a man injured by a train.

The Inquest on the Ilford Train Crash

Nine inquests were held in Ilford by the Ilford Coroner and one at the London Hospital by the East London Coroner. The Ilford Coroner's jury verdict was recorded as Accidental Death which found that the

Collision was caused by an error of judgement on the part of the driver of the Clacton express in misreading one signal for another near the scene of the accident, thus working on a false presumption, he being ignorant of any error all the time.[35]

---

[35] Framlingham Weekly News *30 January 1915*

The verdict given by Jury to the East London Coroner on the tenth victim, Mr Frederick Allen, was "Accidental Death" and attributed the accident to the driver of the Clacton Express omitting to notice that a distant signal was at danger.[36]

Railway Disaster at Ilford 1 January 1915 Photo No2 by Barrett

Great Eastern Railway Magazine[37], carried two letters from H. W. THORNTON, the General Manager of the GER which read as follows -

> Dear Sir,
> On behalf of the Great Eastern Railway Company I shall be glad if you will allow me the courtesy of your columns to express my deepest sympathy with the relatives of the passengers who met with their death in the accident at Ilford yesterday, and with all the passengers who were injured. At the same time, I should like to convey my sincere thanks to all who rendered assistance after the accident. I am communicating personally with some, but there were numerous instances of unobtrusive work by many whose names I cannot ascertain and I can only thank them collectively through the press. I should also like to place on record my appreciation of the services of the territorials, the police, the local firemen, the boy scouts, the nursing sisters and the ambulance men, the local doctors and the staff at Ilford, West Ham and London Hospitals. Further, I feel it is proper to say how well pleased I was with the admirable manner in which our railwaymen worked in clearing the line and reorganizing the traffic.
>
> Yours faithfully,
> H. W. THORNTON, General Manager.

The second letter read

> On behalf of the Great Eastern Railway Company, I write to ask you to accept my most grateful thanks for the prompt and generous assistance which you so kindly afforded on the occasion of the accident at Ilford Station on 1st January, 1915.
>
> I can assure you that much suffering was alleviated by the quick and cheerful response that was made to the calls for help, and I appreciate what was done more than I can express.

---

36 *Birmingham Mail 27 January 1915*

37 *Great Eastern Railway Magazine 37 Volume 1915 1 58*

Yours faithfully,
H. W. THORNTON, General Manager.

The accident investigation was conducted by the Board of Trade and the final report was written by Lieut. Col P. G. von. Donop. It was published on 16 February 1915. In the report primary cause of the accident is given as driver error and excessive speed. The Secondary cause was the lack of an AWS (Automatic Warning System). The result was a Signal passed at danger, causing a sidelong collision. 10 fatalities, 502 injured.

Chapter Eight – WWI Gathering Momentum

St John Ambulance and the Voluntary Aid Detachment (VAD).

In *The Recorder* dated 11 September 1914 the following report appeared. It read, under the heading of "Red Cross Hospital for Ilford." Mr W. R Magnus makes an appeal to people of Ilford and the district, which I am sure will not be allowed to go unheeded. "There is now" he says-

> the prospect of a Red Cross Hospital being formed in Ilford in connection with our Emergency Hospital, to receive upwards of 150 sick and wounded soldiers," and he proceeds to ask for the promise of beds, bedding, and other equipment, to be collected only on condition of the hospital being required by the War Office.

William Magnus was appointed Commandant of Oakwood V.A.D. Hospital, also known as Oakwood Military Hospital, based at 203 High Road, Chigwell, Essex. It opened in March 1915 and its first patients were 6 servicemen suffering from frostbite. The Hospital had 20 beds (later increased to 27) and was affiliated to Colchester Military Hospital. It was mainly used as a Military Convalescent facility.

It was run by the Essex 82 Voluntary Aid Detachment (although William was with Essex 27 Voluntary Aid Detachment). Trained Nurses were posted by the Joint War Committee and two local General Practitioners provided medical care. The hospital closed in February 1919.[38]

Oakwood V.A.D Hospital, Chigwell

The Hospital Board and the key role of William Magnus was reported in *The Recorder* dated 2 April 1915. The article read -

> The principal business before the Board had reference to the arrangements for accommodating the twenty wounded soldiers who are to be sent to the hospital soon after Easter, to which subject I referred last week. There will be others to follow later, and it is regarded as certain that in the course of a few months at latest Newbury Park School, adjacent to the hospital will have to be requisitioned to serve as an adjunct to the hospital for use of the wounded. Mr W. R Magnus, divisional superintendent of the St John Ambulance Brigade, is working with the governors and the medical staff in this matter, and is rendering valuable assistance.

---

[38] Lost Hospitals of London Internet access 12 January 2022 https://ezitis.myzen.co.uk/oakwoodmilitary.html

Air Raid Scheme Implemented on 1st February 1915[39] with the concurrence and the approval of the Police, No. I District of the Brigade this day brought in the Ambulance Air-Raid Scheme for rendering prompt assistance during attacks from the air.

The various London Police Stations were selected as the rendezvous where members of the local Divisions automatically reported for duty on receipt of the air raid warning, and where ambulance stores were deposited.

In addition, a contingent of members was on duty each night at District Headquarters as mobile squads for rapid transport by motor cars when required. Experience proved the wisdom and serviceability of this Air-Raid Service, which remained in continuous operation up to Armistice Day, 1918, although no hostile raid occurred in London after 19th May of that year.

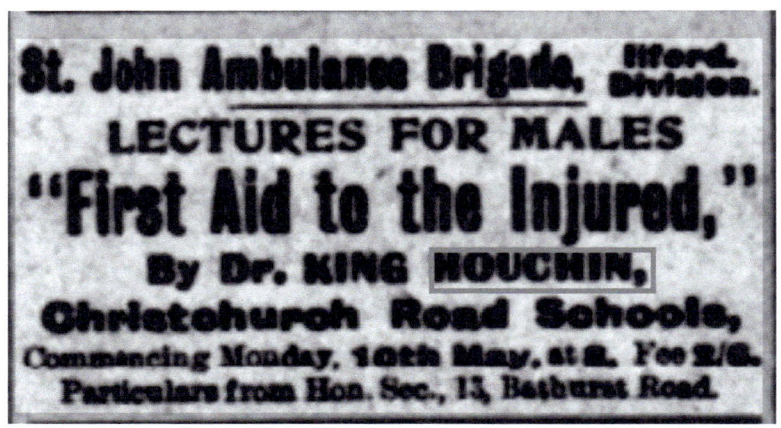

30 April 1915 First Aid Class Advertisement

The following report shows the organisational skills of William Magnus in dealing with the arrival of the first war casualties in Ilford. This is an edited account of *The Recorder's* article dated 7 May 1915. The headlines read.

> Arrival of Wounded Soldiers. Busy-Midnight Scene at the Ilford Emergency Hospital. Interesting and Pathetic Scenes at Newbury Park. Twenty Wounded, including some Canadians.

The St John Ambulance transferred wounded from Newbury Park to the Ilford Emergency Hospital. The paper stated –

> The scene at Newbury Park Stations and the Emergency Hospital will long be remembered by the small party comprising the Governors, the medical men, and the men and nurses of St John Ambulance Corps which awaited the arrival of their stricken countrymen. The transference from the train to hospital was expeditiously and carefully carried through by the ambulance corps, and the wounded who only left Boulogne at four o'clock in the afternoon were made comfortable in hospital bed by one o'clock on Tuesday.

---

[39] Fletcher, N.C. The St John Ambulance Association: Annals of the Ambulance Department. (Hertford: Stephen Austin & Sons, Ltd. 1949)

The Old Newbury Park Station.

A telegram was received from Dover by the Matron at about six o'clock that 20 cases would arrive that night, and Mr Hare. Hon. Secretary to the hospital, at once advised everyone concerned, and at 10 o'clock all was in readiness at Newbury Park station.

There were in attendance about 12 men of the St John Ambulance Association under the command of Mr W. R. Magnus, with Dr King Houchin, their Divisional Surgeon, and some of their men. Beguiled the time by practising the stretcher and other drills. Outside the station were some ten vehicles, consisting of ambulance motors and various kinds of vans, which had kindly sent for the purpose, in addition there had emerged a little crowd of about 40 of the public. The Red Cross train arrived at 11.45pm.

The members of the Ilford branch of the St John Ambulance Brigade who assisted included: Dr E. King Houchin. Divisional Superintendent W.R. Magnus, Ambulance Officer M. G. Matthews, Corpl Aldridge, Privates Mitchell, Apling, Drayson, Souster, Pitcher, Burton, Dunster, King, Claxton, Pratt and Jackson.

Transport arrangements were in the hands of the Ilford Division St John Ambulance Brigade.

Motor wagons supplied from St John's Gate Two public ambulance cars lent by the Ilford Urban District Council and Romford Union. Laundry vans by the Ilford Steam Sanitary Laundry Company. Motor by F. Coe.

Ilford Emergency Hospital – VAD Nurses and Patients Photographer Unknown

In Ilford, the *Sheffield Telegraph* dated 13 May 1915 reported under the headline

"Remember the Lusitania"
In Rowan Road, Ilford, twelve shops were attacked, in six cases the premises were absolutely sacked. For three hours the work of destruction went on. Ever kind of article of furniture was thrown from upstairs windows, and in one house a piano was completely smashed to atoms. Dozens of people were to be seen laden with valuable property. The temper of the crowd was extremely ugly, and the police were absolutely powerless.

The Recorder of 14 May 1915 headlines were much the same "The Anti-German Crusade – Wild scenes at Manor Park –

Four shops and a private house looted and wrecked – Mob kept out of Ilford."

Extraordinary scenes were witnessed at Manor Park late on Wednesday night, when a crowd of at least 5,000 persons attacked German owned and other shop and private dwelling house. A strong body of police under Sub-Divisional Inspector Hamilton, reinforced by 300 special constables, made strenuous and sustained, but only partially successful attempt to cope with the disorder, which raged long after midnight, and it was two o'clock on Thursday morning before the crowds were wholly dispersed. Five person were arrested.
The shops that were wrecked and looted included a butcher's, one baker's, a barber's and a little general shop. One of these establishments is carried on by a naturalised Englishman another by a British-born subject, but the unreasoning crowd made no distinction. While police were guarding one shop, the wreckers penetrated it from the rear, the interior was speedily ransacked and in ruins. In all cases the windows were smashed, as well as the furniture. While goods were stolen wholesale, and the premises presented scenes of as of devastation by fire. In the case of the private house, everything was in the place was stolen except a piano, which was too cumbersome to move. The owner is also said to have been struck and injured.
Having wreaked their vengeance upon the supposed enemy aliens west of the Roding, the mob commenced a march upon Ilford, but Inspector Hamilton skilfully marshalled his forces and with the individual assistance of the "specials" he forced a barrier that effectively dammed the dangerous tide at Roding Bridge.
In East Ham other scenes took place and in all 40 arrest were made.

The Recorder of 21 May 1915 the headline was again "Anti-German Crusade" It gave more details of the previous week's events –

On Thursday night stones were thrown at the Cauliflower Hotel, High Road [Ilford], and smashed some of the windows. The same night, while Inspector Hamilton was directing the operations of the police at Manor Park, an attempt was made to pull him from his horse. Also, a stone was hurled at him which cut his head, but happily no seriously. The special constables again rendered valuable service at Ilford Broadway in dispersing the crowds during the exodus of the Hippodrome audiences and other places of amusement.

In Southend the St John Ambulance Brigade, then part of London (Prince of Wales's) District, were also assisting the police and army with rioting there, which was near the Kursaal. *The Evening Standard* on 13 May 1915 reported –

Over 200 special constables were on duty. The St. John Ambulance Brigade and the 34th Voluntary Aid Detachment were out with stretcher, but there were no casualties.

The following report appeared in the *Chelmsford Chronicle* on 17 May 1915. It shows the progress made in Essex and units recognised and registered by the War Office for service. Mrs W. R. Magnus is recorded as one of the Commandants for Ilford.

> British Red Cross Society
> Progress in Essex
>
> Since the beginning of the year several new men's and women's detachments have been raised by the Essex Branch of the British Red Cross Society and the St John Ambulance Association, and they have been recognised and registered by the War Office for service as may be required. These include the following:-
>
> One men's and one women's detachment at Saffron Walden, of which Dr and Mrs J. P. Atkinson are Commandants. Two women's detachments in Romford, of which Miss Bardsley and Mrs Walter Frost are commandants. A women's detachment at West Ham and another at Ilford, of which Mrs Eva Scott and Mrs W. R. Magnus are Commandants, in addition to a men's detachment at Westcliff-on-Sea, with Mr Alwin Flide as Commandant. These bring up the total number of detachments formed by these societies in the County of Essex to 78, with a total membership of 2,473. Other detachments are in the course of formation.

The Recorder dated 28 May 1915 reported on the death of a serviceman at the Ilford Emergency Hospital.

> Death of a wounded soldier in Ilford Hospital. We regret to report that Private [H] Thomas Crosby[40], one of the wounded soldiers in Ilford Emergency Hospital Died yesterday (Thursday) morning from his injuries. He had suffered from a gunshot wound in the thigh, and his injuries were such as to cause grave anxiety from the first. His wife has been with him during the past fortnight and was present at the end. The body will be removed to Stockton-on-Tees for burial.
> Another case of severe injuries to the head is regarded as very serious. All the other soldiers are progressing favourably, and some are now nearly convalescent.

The Recorder on 18 June 1915 continued the above story when one of the twenty men, Private J. J. Studd [41], died in the Emergency Hospital -

> Funeral of Private J. J. Studd. One of the wounded who died in Ilford Hospital.
>
> With full military honours the funeral took place on Saturday afternoon at the City of London Cemetery of Private John James Studd, of the 1st Rifle Brigade. The late Private Studd was

---

40 Commonwealth War Grave Commission Record In Memory Of Private H T Crosby. Service Number: 2539, 5th Bn., Durham Light Infantry who died on 27 May 1915 Age 29 Son of Thomas Crosby; husband of Maud Elizabeth Crosby, of 5, Appleton Rd., Newtown, Stockton-on-Tees. Born at Norton-on-Tees. Remembered with Honour Stockton-on-Tees (Durham Road) Cemetery EI. A. 14.

41 Commonwealth War Grave Commission Record *"In Memory of Rifleman J. J. Studd. Service Number: B/33 1st Bn., Rifle Brigade who died on 06 June 1915 Age 43 Son of William and Ann Studd. Remembered with Honour City of London Cemetery and Crematorium, Manor Park Screen Wall. 203. 80586."*

one of the twenty wounded soldiers admitted to the Ilford Emergency Hospital on May 3rd, and he died in that institution on June 6th.

The deceased, who lived in Bethnal Green, was 43 years of age, was suffering from shrapnel wounds in the head, and from the first his case was regarded as hopeless.

The coffin was carried on a gun carriage, which with a firing party, was supplied by the 13th Service Battalion of the Essex Regiment. The firing party assembled at the deceased house in Bethnal Green, and on route to the cemetery met the band of the 1/4th Battalion Essex Regiment and a detachment under the direction of Capt. H. G. Henderson commanding adjutant of the 3rd line depot, at Katherine-road, Manor Park. The band played funeral music, including the dead march from "Saul."

At the funeral the Ilford Emergency Hospital was represented by the acting commandant, Mr A. Hare, and Mr Magnus, the superintendent of the local ambulance branch of the St John Ambulance Brigade.

Mrs Edith and Mr Frederick Rymer had son during the second quarter of 1915, he was named James F Q Rymer.

The Metropolitan Police issued advice to the public in June 1915, when The Commissioner of Police for the Metropolises, offered official advice to Civilians about what to do in an air raid.

The Recorder 30 July 1915

> A penny collection has been in progress all week in Ilford for the benefit of the St John Ambulance Association and Red Cross Society. The Idea, which has already been carried out with marked success in a number of towns, is that every individual in ever house shall be asked to contribute one penny. As the amount is small, and the whole fund will be for the relief of the wounded, there ought to be no hesitation on anybody's part about falling into line.

The St John Ambulance Brigade Hospital, Étaples

6 September 1915 The St. John Ambulance opened its hospital in Étaples, near Boulogne in France. At the time, Étaples was home to a very large British army base which was notorious for its military training. It was also a stopping point for soldiers making their way to the front.

The hospital played an important role during the First World War. It provided 520 beds for soldiers wounded by the nearby fighting. It was described as 'one of the finest and best-equipped hospitals in France'. [42]

Later in the war, on 19 and 31 May 1918, the hospital was almost destroyed by hostile aircraft. 'The staff exhibited magnificent gallantry in their attempts to protect the patients, of whom 11 were killed and 18 were wounded'. [43]

---

42 Fletcher, N.C. The St John Ambulance Association: Annals of the Ambulance Department. (Hertford: Stephen Austin & Sons, Ltd. 1949), Page No 131

43 Ibid Fletcher, N.C Page 131

The St John Ambulance Brigade Ilford

The provision of hospitals, in war, does not, just happen. They require considerable efforts, especially in the area of fundraising much of which was done on the home front. In the case of the Etaples Hospital most counties supported the effort. An event, in Ilford, was recorded in the *Eastern Counties Times* on 26 March 1915. The article announced -

> St. John Ambulance Brigade Hospital - Hospital for North of France.
>
> Saturday last was a red-letter day for members of the Ilford Ambulance and Nursing Divisions of the St. John Ambulance Brigade, as a result of their day's collection on behalf of the hospital shortly to be sent to the North of France shows.
>
> The total amount collected in the boxes was £48. 6s., and this was made up to £50 by two generous friends, Messrs. Lester and Henderson., who were present at the counting. This amount, together with what had been privately collected, brings the total up to £60. , and there are still some promises of further amounts.
>
> This is a very opportune moment for old students of first aid and home nursing classes to show their appreciation of the gratuitous service rendered by our ambulance friends, by remitting to Mr Magnus their donation in order that at, viz., £100, may become an accomplished fact.
>
> The following divisional members were collectors: Divisional Superintendent Magnus, Lady Superintendent Mrs Magnus, Ambulance Officer Matthews, Nursing Sisters Mrs Law, Miss A. White, Miss E. White, Miss Alder, Miss Rymer, Miss Sten[n]ing, Mrs Waldron, Mrs Wells, Miss Lobb, Miss Lawson, Miss Furness, Mrs Vaughan, Corpl. Aldridge, Privates Pitcher, Claxton, Pratt, Dunster, Jackson, Souster, and King, assisted by Mrs Matthews, Mrs Aldridge, Mrs Souster, Miss Lee, Miss Handley, Miss Stoneman, Miss Matthews, Miss Magnus, Mr Brazier Martin, and Master Freddy White.
>
> It is desired to thank all who helped by their contributions.

Photograph by Brian L Porter of the Ilford Bed Plaque Courtesy of Redbridge Museum and Heritage Centre

The plaque[44] came back from the St John Ambulance Hospital, Étaples[45], France, which was close to the frontline during major battles of WWI. It is not known how the bed plaque came back to Ilford after the war, but was in the care of Divisional Mrs M. B Magnus, for a time, who returned it to the Division in 1961. It was in the care of Superintendent George Everitt, he later handed his collection to Redbridge Museum and Heritage Centre [46].

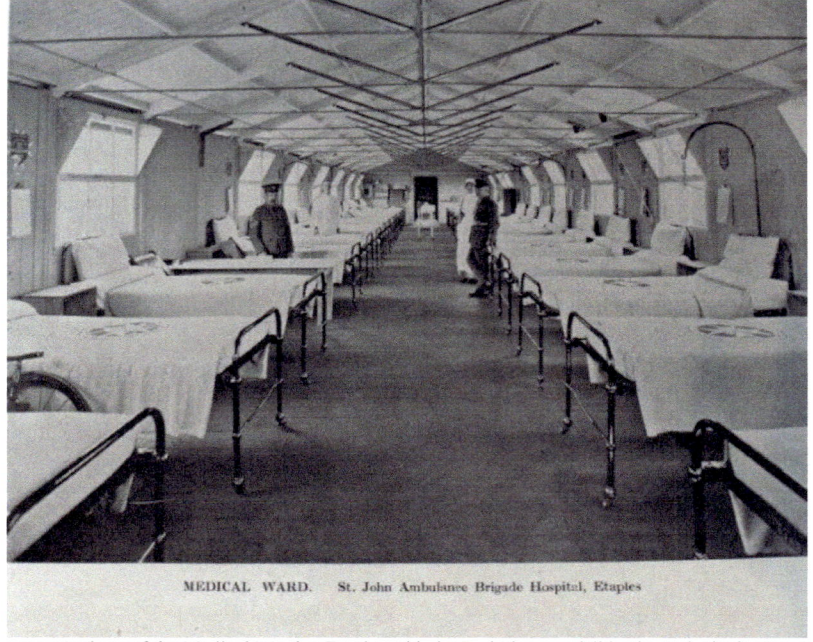

MEDICAL WARD. St. John Ambulance Brigade Hospital, Etaples

A photo of the Medical Ward at Etaples with the Bed Plaques visible above the beds

The Recorder 30 April 1915

Dr King Houchin entry in the 1915 Medical Register read as follows:-
"HOUCHIN, Edmund King, "Ravensworth," 66, Cranbrook-rd. Ilford. Essex (Tel. 614 Ilford) -L.R.C.P. Ed.& L.M., L.R.C.S.Ed.1880: L.S.A.1875; (Lond. Hosp.& Ed.); Mem. Hon. Soc. Middle Temple; Surg. Orph. Working Sch. Haverstock Hill; Proprietor & Originator of the " Aix Treatm.in London "Fell. Hunt. Soc.Lond.; Mem. B.M.A. & Coroners' Soc.; late Surg. H Div. Metrop. Police ; Dep. Coroner East Lond. & Pres. U.K. Police Surg. Assn. Author, "Case of Asphyxia from Foreign Body in Larynx," B.M.J. 1887 ; The Aix-Treatm. of Syphilis in London" (read before Balmeol. & Climat. Soc.) 1901."

---

44 © Redbridge Museum Ref 1996.278.

45 St John Ambulance Brigade Hospital in Étaples was the largest voluntary hospital serving the British Expeditionary Force during the First World War. The hospital had a staff of 241, all from the St John Ambulance Brigade, and was considered by all who knew it to be the best designed and equipped military hospital in France, caring for over 35,000 patients throughout the war.

46 On the 31 May 2018. The Court Circular Issued at Kensington Palace recorded "The Duke of Gloucester, Grand Prior, the Most Venerable Order of the Hospital of St John of Jerusalem, this morning attended a Service at the Priory Church of St John, Clerkenwell, London, EC1, to commemorate the Centenary of the Bombing of the St John Ambulance Brigade Hospital at Étaples and was received by Her Majesty's Lord-Lieutenant of Greater London (Sir Kenneth Olisa).

RMS Lusitania was a British ocean liner launched by the Cunard Line in 1906 and held the Blue Riband appellation for the fastest Atlantic crossing in 1908. It was briefly the world's largest passenger ship. Its sinking by a German U-boat, U20 on 7 May 1915, contributed indirectly to the entry of the United States into WWI.

The Lusitania sinking led to wide spread disturbance across the country and London and the East End were badly affected as the following headlines in the *Stratford Express*, on the 15 May 1915, testify:

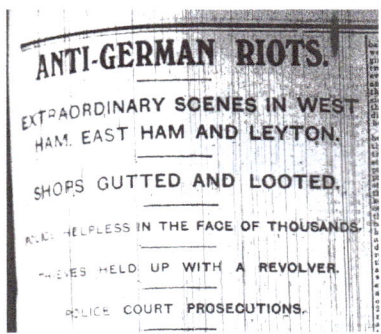

ANTI-GERMAN RIOTS.
EXTRAORDINARY SCENES IN WEST HAM, EAST HAM AND LEYTON.
SHOPS GUTTED AND LOOTED.
POLICE HELPLESS IN THE FACE OF THOUSANDS.
THIEVES HELD UP WITH A REVOLVER.
POLICE COURT PROSECUTIONS.

The situation in between Manor Park and Ilford was serious especially in the evenings

On the night of 31 May /1 June 1915, army airship LZ38 conducted the first air raid on London. The Metropolitan Police reported[47]:

> An aircraft, supposed to be a Zeppelin, the engines of which were distinctly heard, passed over Chigwell Row, Essex, shortly before 11 pm on Monday, 31st ultimo, travelling in a westerly direction. It appears to have reached Dalston shortly after 11 pm, dropped bombs, and returned via Leytonstone - where more bombs were dropped - Wanstead, Barkingside, and Chigwell Row, between which two last points it seems to have left the Division at about 11.30 pm.
>
> 'Police at Wanstead and Barkingside also report having heard an aircraft, which they could not with certainty describe, passing overhead an hour later, i.e. at 12.30 am 1st instant. Whether this last aircraft was hostile or not is unknown.

The following letter was received by No 1 District Headquarters following Air Attacks on East London and Essex.

> "NEW SCOTLAND YARD,
> August, 1915.
> DEAR SIR,
> I am desired to express to you the Commissioner's appreciation of the prompt manner in which members of your Brigade responded to the call on their services on the occasion of the recent hostile Air Raid. It is gratifying to know that the arrangements to make their services effective were successful when this opportunity arose in the locality affected, and where their names were previously noted as willing to co-operate with the Police.
> Yours faithfully,
> (Signed) E. H. PARSONS, Major,
> Chief Constable."

---

[47] *Ilford Historical Society Newsletter, No.121 August 2016*

The Recorder reported on 22 October, 1915 of further wounded soldiers arriving at the *"Ilford Emergency Hospital"*. The article continued -

> Seventeen wounded soldiers arrived on Sunday night, all stretcher cases. They were received at Newbury Park Station by Mr Ben Bailey, Chairman of the Hospital Governors. Dr E. King Houchin and the commandant. The Transport arrangements were carried out by the St John Ambulance Brigade, under the superintendence of Mr M. G. Matthews.
> The commandant would be glad to receive financial assistance towards payment of railway fare to enable the men to be visited by their relatives, who, except in one instance, live in distant parts of the country. The thanks of the governors are again due to the directors and management of the Ilford Steam Sanitary Laundry Co. for the loan of motor and horse vans, and to the drivers for their service. The Governors also wish to express their gratitude to the following for the loan of motor cars for taking the men for drives, viz., Mr Droesse (twice weekly), Mr Kendell, Mr Leonard King, Mr Turner, Mrs Peach, Mrs Mills and Mr Rose.

At least one Ilford resident benefited from the fundraising efforts of the Ilford Division and form the St John Ambulance Brigade Hospital in Étaples, France. *The Recorder* reported on 26 November 1915 the case of one soldier who came into their care.

> Ilford Sportsman at Loos.
> A well-known participator in junior football in Ilford, 2nd-Lieut. J. A. Mason, of 59 De Vere-gardens, on Saturday returned to England from the front, suffering from appendicitis. Lieut. Mason, who was educated at Cranbrook College, joined the 13th City of London Regiment, the London Irish Rifles (Kensington Rifles) on the outbreak of war. In May of this year he was given a commission in the now famous Territorial Regiment, the London Irish Rifles, the 18th City of London. Within a week of completing his officer's course of instruction at Perivale, he was ordered to France and for a time was at Havre, but then was sent up straight away to the trenches at Loos. For the past two months he has been right in the thick of it in the front line, with only a couple of days' break on rare occasions. While in the first line trench a fortnight ago he was suddenly struck down with appendicitis, and for nearly 24 hours had to lie in a small dugout, it being impossible to remove him. However, he eventually arrived at the St John Ambulance Hospital at Etaples, where he remained for over ten days. On Saturday last he was carried on board the hospital ship and arrived at Charing Cross the same night. At present he is being attended by, Sir Frederick Treves, at Prince Henry of Battenberg's Hospital in Hill-street, W. Latest reports announce satisfactory progress, but it has not yet been decided whether an operation will be necessary or not. Lieut. Mason was a member and one of the founders of the Maybrook Football Club. He is also a keen cricketer.

1916

William Magnus's services were in demand by January 1916 and he was delivering Ambulance lectures to 'A' Company of the Essex Women's Voluntary Reserve[48].

The Great Eastern Railway produced new Ambulance Trains at their Stratford Works. These trains were exhibited at Railway Stations across the network. Thousands flocked to see the trains before they entered service. Below is an Ambulance train being displayed at London's Liverpool Street Station in February 1916.

---

48 21 January 1916 Eastern Counties News

Liverpool Street February, 1916. Ambulance Train. Science Museum Group Collection

The unveiling the "Gift" Memorial Tablet at Ilford Emergency Hospital - *The Recorder* March 3, 1916

On Friday 9th June 1916 the following was reported in the *Echo and Mail* -

> St John Ambulance Nurses.
> Lady Maud Wilbraham[49] - Inspects Local Divisions
>
> Some 200 nurses of the East Ham, Ilford, Manor Park, Beckton, West Ham and Barking Nursing Divisions of the St John Ambulance Brigade Paraded at Lathom-road School, on

---

[49] Lady Maud Wilbraham 1861-1922 Daughter of Edward Bootle-Wilbraham, 1st Earl Lathom. The inspection was held in a School named in honour of her father. Awarded an OBE in 1920 for her work as District Superintendent of the St John Ambulance Brigade, London District.

Wednesday evening, when the annual inspection of the units by Lady Maud Wilbraham, chief lady superintendent of the No.1 (London) Prince of Wales District, took place.

Lady Maud was accompanied by Miss Rideout, passed down the assembled lines, paying close attention to equipment of the nurses, and at the close complimented them upon their smart appearance and bearing.

The East Ham division was under the command of Mrs Harrop, senior superintendent, the superintendents in charge of the other units being: Ilford, Mrs Magnus; Manor Park, Mrs Jacobs; Beckton, Mrs Norman Sampey; West Ham, Mrs Scott; and Barking, Miss Smith. Sergt Harrop, of the East Ham Corps, was also in attendance, while a member of the 1st East Ham Troop of British Girl Scouts, under Capt. Northfield, formed a guard of honour.

The following is believed to be the second member of the Ilford Division killed in action. The Commonwealth War Grave Commission details are as follows -

In Memory of Private ROBERT LIVINGSTONE MCKENZIE Service Number: 26594 11th Bn., Essex Regiment who died on 18 August 1916 Age 23 Son of Robert and Catherine McKenzie, of 249, Thorold Rd., Ilford, Essex. Remembered with Honour CATERPILLAR VALLEY CEMETERY, LONGUEVAL IX.E.8.

Once gain McKenzie was a member who had attended the 1912 Royal Review at Windsor. He lived in the same road, Thorold Road as the Apling family, another prominent St John family.

08 September 1916 - *Eastern Counties News* reported-

Thirty-eight wounded at Ilford Hospital.
Another large party of wounded soldiers arrived recently at the Ilford Emergency Hospital. They numbered thirty in all, thirteen being cot cases and fifteen sitting. They were conveyed by train to Newbury Park Station, whence they were removed in vehicles to the hospital by members of the local branch of the St John's Ambulance Brigade, under the direction of Mr Matthews, in the absence of Mr Magnus, who is on holiday. A motor van and three horse vans were kindly lent by the Ilford Sanitary Steam Laundry, Ltd., and a motor was kindly placed at the disposal of the men by the officer in charge of an aerodrome "on the outskirts of London." There are now thirty-eight soldiers in the hospital. The new arrivals are all progressing well. Among the regiments represented are the following – Gloster's, Norfolk's, Argyle and Sutherland Highlanders, R.F.A., R.E., Wilts, Somerset., Machine Gun Corps., London. R. Irish Rifles, Warwick, R. Berks, Oxford and Bucks, Grenadier Guards., Duke of Cornwall, Loyal N. Lancs and Australian Engineers (7 men).

The St John Ambulance Brigade Ilford

Chapter Nine - The Gallantry of William Stephen Chevalier

Train Accident at Gezaincourt, Near Doullens, the Somme, France 24 November 1916

Gallantry Medals Awarded

Lt Col John Handfield Brunskill – Distinguished Service Order
Captain Charles Reginald Hoskyn – Albert Medal First Class.
(Rugby Division, St John Ambulance)
Sergeant 27253 James Orr - Meritorious Service Medal (and Bar).
Acting Corporal 9824 William Stephen Chevalier - Meritorious Service Medal.
(No 46 Ilford Division, St John Ambulance)
Acting Corporal (later Sergeant) 29989 Sidney Heley - Meritorious Service Medal.

This is the story of these brave men, two of whom, Hoskyn and Chevalier, belonged to the St John Ambulance Brigade.

This research started because of a 1931 St John Ambulance Brigade leaflet published by Ilford Division. The leaflet mentions an Ilford member being awarded a "Military Medal". After some considerable work cross checking names, I found the member concerned was first mentioned in *The Recorder* dated 9 October 1914 when it was reported as follows:-

> Roll of Honour
> ST. JOHN AMBULANCE BRIGADE No. 46 (ILFORD) DIVISION.
>
> The undermentioned members of the Ilford Division volunteered for the Military Home Hospital Reserve, subsequently enlisted in the Royal Army Medical Corps, and are now serving.

It goes on to mention

> Pte W. S. Chevalier, who was serving at Queen Alexandra's Military Hospital, Millbank.

William was born on 20 August 1889 in Edmonton, London. The 1911 Census shows he was aged 21 and his family were living a 64 Dudley Road, Ilford. His father, also William, aged 72, was a GPO Pensioner, Elizabeth his mother, aged 51, and Mabel his sister, aged 22, was a Librarian. Elizabeth had 3 children of whom only two were living, Mabel and William.

After an extensive investigation I found the record card for Acting Corporal W. S. Chevalier, No. 9824, who was in 1917 serving with the RAMC as part of the 29th Casualty Clearing Station.

A first-hand account of the train accident is mentioned in the book 'Hired to Kill' by John Morris[50] (Charles John Morris, 1/5th Leicestershire Regiment, later Gurkhas). This excerpt attracted my interest as he was apparently on the train:

> I was offered leave [1/5th Leicestershire War Diary states 24th Nov 16] to go home for a week and left for Calais the same afternoon. While our train was ascending a little incline

---

50 "Hired to Kill" by John Morris. Publisher: Rupert Hart-Davis, London. Publication date: 1960 Page 38

outside Doullens, a goods train in front of us broke its couplings and most of it came rushing down the hill and cannoned into us. The front part of our train was at once derailed and almost immediately caught fire. The carriages were overcrowded and escape was not possible. I was fortunately in one of the rear carriages and suffered only a few bruises. We did not at first know what had happened; but when it became clear that there was some sort of breakdown, we got out and went to investigate. By this time the whole front part of the train was well alight and we could not approach near enough to be of any assistance. The screams of those trapped in the burning wreckage horrified me in a way that sudden trench-death never did. There was something obscene about this drawn-out agony, so unlike the quick death in battle.

William Stephen Chevalier was awarded the "Meritorious Service Medal." This award appeared in the *London Gazette* dated 13 February 1917. The card is marked "For Gallantry in War Area" and it also noted he was "recommended for extra pension".

Meritorious Record Card – Find My Past Internet accessed June 2022

The incident leading to Chevalier's gallantry was a train accident at Gezaincourt[51], the Somme, near to the 29th Casualty Clearing Station commanded by Lt Col Brunskill M.B., B.Ch.

It is likely that he was responsible for all the citations, other than his own, relating to the Gezaincourt accident. He also assisted at the incident and was mentioned in despatches.

The citation on William Chevalier's Medal Index Card reads –

> On the occasion of the train accident at Gezaincourt on November 24th 1916, A/Cpl Chevalier was most conspicuous in his efforts to rescue an injured man from the blazing wreckage. He showed great gallantry, fought the flames without ceasing having his hand severely burnt owing to his efforts to raise up the burning masses of timber in order to free an injured man.

---

[51] Gezaincourt a small village, in the Somme Department of the French region of Picardie. It had a population of 447, in 2006.

> on the occasion of the train accident at Gezaincourt on the 24th November 1916. A/Cpl. Chevalier was most conspicuous in his efforts to rescue an injured man from the blazing wreckage. He showed great gallantry, fought the flames without ceasing having his hand severely burnt owing to his efforts to raise up the burning masses of timber in order to free the injured man.

Reverse of the Meritorious Record Card[52]

The Gezaincourt Train Accident occurred on 24 November 1916 and the War Diary of 29th Casualty Clearing Station at Gezaincourt records the following for that date.

> Serious railway accident occurred about ¼ mile to West of camp, at 4.30 a.m. Trucks from preceding coal train broke away and ran down incline into Boulogne Leave train. Many coaches and trucks were de-railed. Five coaches were set on fire. The Unit turned out and got injured out of train, then brought them to camp. Several of the wounded were burnt to death being pinned down by beams. Major Gordon, 43rd Cameron Highlanders of Canada was Officer-in-charge of the train.
>
> Casualties: 3 officers and 14 other ranks were dead or died almost at once when got out of fire.
> 15 officers and 49 other ranks injured and attended to in this camp and Officers Hospital.
> 2 French civilians injured and brought in here.
>
> Forwarded names of Capt. Hoskyn, Sgt Orr, Cpls. Chevalier and Heley for their gallant conduct.

For these actions Capt. Charles Reginald Hoskyn was awarded the Albert Medal with Sergeant 27253 James Orr, Acting Corporal 9824 William Chevalier and Acting Corporal 29989 Sidney Heley being awarded the Meritorious Service Medal.[53]

War Diary: Matron-in-Chief, British Expeditionary Force, France and Flanders records[54] -

> 28.11.16
> Letter received from Sister in charge, 29 C.C.S., giving a description of the serious railway accident which had happened to a leave train when 18 officers and 51 men were badly injured and 3 officers killed and 7 bodies found in such a charred condition as to be unrecognisable

---

52 Courtesy of Ancestry UK Photo Keith Chevalier posted 7/7/2019 accessed June 2022

53 Internet accessed June 2022 greatwarforum.org/topic/242768-train-crash-at-gezaincourt-24th-november-1916/

54 Crown Copyright: The National Archives, WO95/3988-91

The St John Ambulance Brigade Ilford

owing to the fact that some of the carriages had overturned and caught fire and the men were unable to get out.

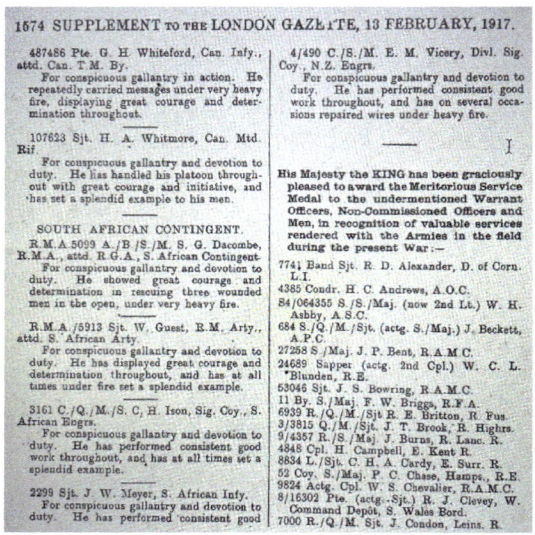

London Gazette 1574 dated 13 February 1917 - William Chevalier

William Chevalier in later Life[55]

Meritorious Service Medal[56]

The newspaper reports of this *London Gazette* announcement seem to have been few. The one found, was published in *The Scotsman* dated 14 February 1917.

Below is the Medal Record for William, which shows he went to France on 28 August 1915. As a result, he was also awarded the Victory, British War Medal and the 1915 Star.

---

55 ibid Ancestry

56 The Meritorious Service Medal was instituted on 19 December 1845 for the British Army, to recognise meritorious service by non-commissioned officers. Recipients were also granted an annuity, the amount of which was based on rank. During 1916-1919, army NCOs could be awarded the medal immediately for meritorious service in the field. They could also be awarded the medal for acts of non-combat gallantry.

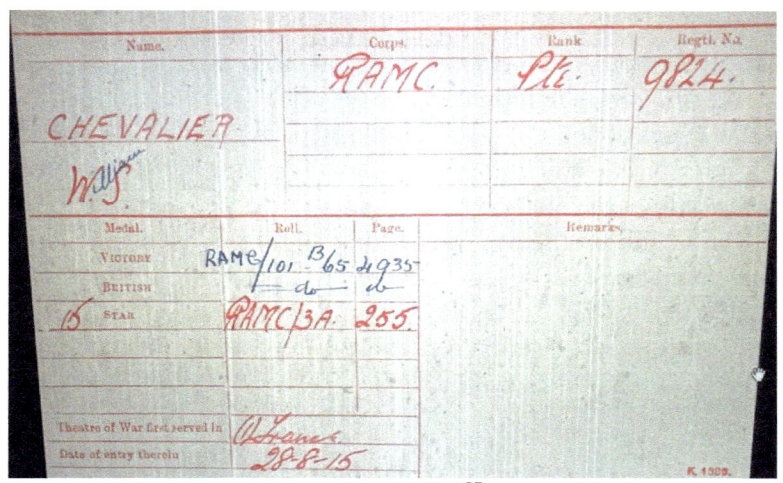

Medal Record Card [57]

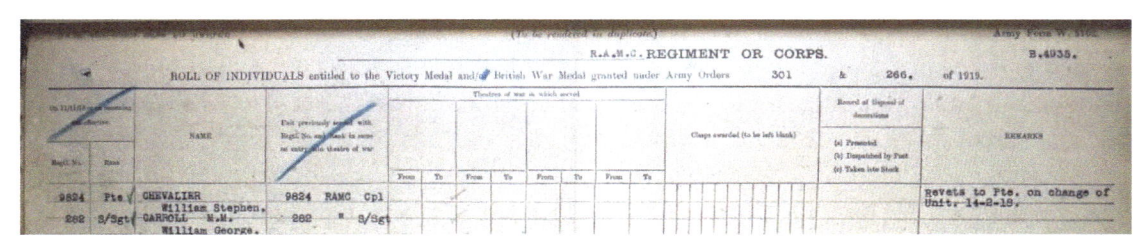

Medal Roll 1919 – Note the remarks "reverts to Pte on change of unit 14-2-1918"

Before the war William worked for the Metropolitan Water Board (MWB), and after the war he returned to his job. He is also remembered on the Metropolitan Water Board Memorial in the Steam Museum, Green Dragon Lane, Brentford. His name is inscribed on its Roll of Honour to Members of the Board, Officers and Employees serving with HM Forces. Under the Officers of the MWB appears the name of "Chevalier, W. S., Cpl"[58].

In 1919 he married Gladys Leila Paine at Great Ilford, St Mary the Virgin, Essex, England. According to the 1921 Census, they lived at 65 Poplar-grove, New Malden after their marriage. They had three children.

Gladys, died at the age of 44 on 30 November 1934. In 1946 he married again, to Dorothy Kathleen Stapley, aged 26. William died at Kingston on Thames on 23 August 1973. Dorothy died in 2006.

William's three children from his marriage to Gladys were William Trayton Chevalier b 4/8/1922 d 5/2/2015, Marcelle Chevalier b 19/12/1931 d 23/5/2014 (Married Victor Herbert Bulmer-Jones 1927 to 2009 with issue) and Jack Kenneth Chevalier 1921 d 9/11/2008 (Married Eileen Patricia Howson with issue).

What of the other four men involved ?

John Handfield Brunskill, John Orr, Sidney Heley, and Charles Reginald Hoskyn.

---

57 Find My Past Internet accessed June 2022

58 http://www.west-middlesex-fhs.org.uk/WMlinks/BrentfordWM.pdf accessed June 2022.

Lt Col. John Handfield Brunskill was a student at Trinity College, Dublin and played for Dublin in cricket at county level, scoring 25 and 58 when Dublin beat the MCC on tour in 1895. He gained a commission in the Medical Services, at the rank of Lieutenant, on 29 November 1900, then went to West Africa 1901-1903, gaining promotion to Captain on 29 November 1903. He was then posted to India from 1905 to 1909. On 29 August 1912, John was promoted to Major, and was serving under this rank when war broke out. He embarked for France on the 9 August 1914, as Deputy Assistant Director for Medical services for the 5th Division. On 26 August 1914, he was in the village of Reumont, which was under heavy shell-fire. Shells smashed into the roofs of houses and onto the roof of the church where the wounded were being treated, and so orders were issued for the field ambulance there to retire with its wounded.

Unfortunately, there were only two ambulance wagons available at the time. These wagons were loaded to capacity, so John, along with two other R.A.M.C. officers remained to care for and transfer to German hands the remaining 60 wounded. He stayed there himself until captured and became a prisoner of war. Because of his devotion to duty at this time, John was mentioned in one of the first of the Commander-in-Chief's despatches. He was repatriated (exchanged) on 29 June 1915, but returned to France the same year. He served under the rank of temporary Lieutenant Colonel from the 23 September 1915, and became the Officer Commanding No 29 Casualty Clearing Station. He remained with this unit until 1917, when he was transferred to Mesopotamia, and served at Dunsterforce, N. Persia and Norperforce. His post as temporary Lieutenant Colonel ceased on 29 October 1917, but he gained full promotion to Lieutenant Colonel on the 28 August 1918

In early 1913, in Kensington, London, he married Elizabeth Mabel[59], the daughter of the late A Robinson, and was a specialist in Bacteriology. John retired on pay on the 27 April 1920 but re-joined the army in 1921 and continued to serve. He was "Mentioned in Despatches" four times, awarded the DSO[60] for the Gezaincourt Trian Crash and an OBE for work in Mesopotamia[61]. He died in Lincoln on 21 July 1940. His wife survived him by nearly 17 years and passed away on 26 March 1957 in Kingston-upon-Thames.

Capt. Charles Reginald Hoskyn RAMC.

On the December 16 1916 Dr Hoskyn was recommended for an Albert Medal to be awarded "For Gallantry in Saving Life on Land".

---

59 The 1939 Register showed that Elizabeth Brunskill served with the ARP and Red Cross

60 Instituted on 6 September 1886 by Queen Victoria in a Royal Warrant published in the London Gazette on 9 November. The first DSOs awarded were dated 25 November 1886. Whilst normally given for service under fire or under conditions equivalent to service in actual combat with the enemy, a number of awards made between 1914 and 1916 were under circumstances not under fire, often to staff officers, causing resentment among front-line officers. After 1 January 1917, commanders in the field were instructed to recommend this award only for those serving under fire.

61 Web site accessed June 2022. http://www.ramc-ww1.com/profile.php?cPath=211_654&profile_id=5663

The Albert Medal First Class

> Capt. C R, Hoskyn, R.A.M.C.—In addition to other plucky acts he crawled under some burning debris at great risk and commenced to amputate the leg of a man who was pinned down. In doing so he loosened the man's body, and he was got out alive.
>
> The Commanding Officer wishes to express his appreciation of the gallantry and initiative displayed by the officers and N.C.O's mentioned in the report.
>
> The Director-General of Medical Services, British Armies in France, also mentions Dr Hoskyn and others in his orders, and adds : " I wish to express to you the greatest admiration which I feel for your splendid conduct under conditions calculated to try the courage of the bravest. You all showed courage, resource, and coolness, and I consider that your behaviour is an honour to yourselves and a credit to your Corps.

The Northampton Daily Echo reported the story on the 20 December 1916 as follows -

> Doctor's Heroism. Operation in Burning Train Wreckage.
>
> Dr. C. R Hoskyn of Rugby, who for the last 18 months has been away on active service as a captain in the R.A.M,C., as we understand, been recommended for the Albert Medal of the First Class[62] – the highest award given for saving life outside the firing line.
>
> The probable bestowal of this coveted honour on Captain Hoskyn is the outcome of a particularly thrilling deed of heroism on his part on the occasion of a serious railway accident at Gezaincourt last month. It appears that six loaded coal trucks broke away from a luggage train and rushed downhill, crashing into a leave train, and overturning the first five coaches,

---

[62] Today this would equate to the award of the George Cross.

which took fire. One of the men was found pinned down by his leg in the wreckage in a sort of cave of fire, the roof comprising piled up and blazing debris.

The man could not be got free, and some of the frenzied spectators were imploring that he should be shot and put out of his of his misery. Captain Hoskyn went to his Commanding Officer and asked leave to amputate, but was at first refused because of the awful danger of the whole lot falling in on him; but he succeeded in getting the necessary permission, and protected as much as possible by bucket of water dashed over him by a line of soldiers, crawled into the wreckage.

The only instrument he had was a sharp dinner knife produced by one of the Tommie's, and with this, and beneath the blazing mass, he commenced to sever the imprisoned limb. Then, by lying out flat and crawling still further under, he managed to loosen the man's body, and together they were both dragged free of the wreckage, only a few moments before the whole blazing mass fell in. The poor fellow who had such a terrible ordeal died in hospital some time later from burns he had received.

Dr Hoskyn was luckily very little burnt, thanks to the Commanding Officer and the men having kept him soaking wet all the time by throwing buckets full of water over him.

The splendid conduct of Captain Hoskyn on this occasion has been specially referred to in the general orders issued to the Fifth Army by the General Commanding. The Director General of Medical Services, British Armies in France, also mentioned Dr Hoskyn and others in his order, and adds: "I wish to express to you the greatest admiration which I feel for your splendid conduct under conditions calculated to try the courage of the bravest. You all showed courage, resource and coolness, and I consider that your behaviour is an honour to yourselves and a credit to your Corps"

Dr Hoskyn is Divisional Surgeon of the Rugby Division of the St John Ambulance Brigade.

Over a year later the announcement came in the *London Gazette*, 30453 Page 143, dated 1 January 1918 and the citation for an Albert Medal awarded to Capt. Charles Hoskyn:

In France on the 24th November, 1916, as a result of a serious railway accident, a man was pinned down by the legs under some heavy girders. The wreckage was on fire, and the flames had already reached the man's ankles. Captain Hoskyn crawled into a cavity in the flaming wreckage, and after releasing one of the man's legs, amputated the other, whereupon the man was drawn out alive, Captain Hoskyn retaining hold of the main artery until a tourniquet could be put on.

The *Kenilworth Advertiser* 12 January 1918 ran a story on the award of the Albert Medal to Dr C R Hoskyn. It read –

Rugby Doctor's Remarkable Surgical Feat.

Soldier's Leg Amputated in Burning Train.

Captain C. R. Hoskyn, Royal Army Medical Corps, who has been awarded the Albert Medal, is a Rugby Doctor, and divisional surgeon of the St John Ambulance Brigade. He recently returned to civilian practice, after spending over two years with the forces.

The rest of the story was a repetition of report in *The Northampton Daily Echo* of the 20 December 1916, which was quoted previously, however the final paragraph concluded –

The man unhappily died in hospital some time later of the burns he had received. Captain Hoskyn was fortunate to escape with minor injuries.

Dr Hoskyn's name also appeared in the St Bartholomew's Hospital Journal, Roll of Honour in April 1918, where his award of the Albert Medal was noted. The May 1918 edition also featured his name, under births -Hoskyn, On March 18th, at 1 Whiteside Road, Rugby, the wife of C.R. Hoskyn MD., B.S. Lond., a daughter.

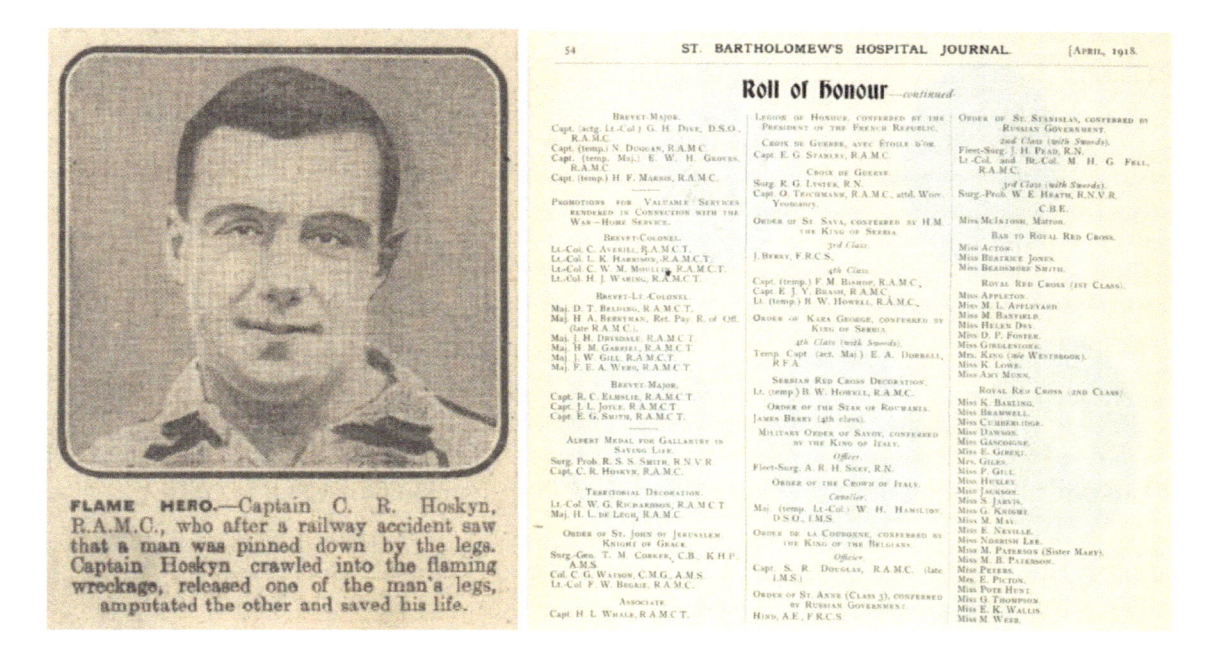

Sunday Pictorial 6 January 1918   *St Bartholomew's Hospital Journal* Copyright Barts Health NHS Trust.

Charles Reginald Hoskyn was born in a part of India that is now Pakistan, and was educated at Bedford Grammar School[63], where he was captain of the school, captain of rugby and captain of rowing. He went on to St Bartholomew's Hospital, where he was also captain of the XV rugby team and played for Middlesex County Cricket team.

He moved to Rugby in 1910 where he started as a general practitioner. The following year, 1911, he was appointed assistant surgeon at St Cross where he continued to work until 1948.

He continued to support the St John Ambulance Brigade in Rugby. I have recorded a few reports of his activities in later years for illustrative purposes.

The Advertiser dated 6 June 1930 reported on the St John Ambulance Brigade Inspection conducted by the Assistant Chief Commissioner Colonel C. A. Moore., CGM. It goes on to mention that "Dr C. R. Hoskyns was to have received a service medal for fifteen years' service but was unfortunately unable to attend to receive it".

The Advertiser dated 11 February 1938 carried the following information in relation to the doctor –

---

[63] From the Commemorative Book compiled by Ted Sparrow in July 2014 titled "Valiant men of Bedfordshire" Pages 26 – 27

Ambulance Division Appointment. – Dr C. R. Hoskyn, A.M., M.D., B.S., has been appointed to succeed Dr G. H Waugh as divisional surgeon to the Rugby Division St John Ambulance Brigade. Dr Hoskyn is also divisional surgeon to the Rugby Cadet Division, where he is very popular as the donor of the "Hoskyn" Cup.

In 1941 it was noted that "The King, George VI, has been graciously pleased to sanction his promotion to the Venerable Order of St John of Jerusalem" – as a Serving Brother, *London Gazette* 27 June 1941 issue 35203 page 3674).

21 October 1941 – *Rugby Advertiser* Announcement of VAD Appointments.

> Mrs. E. D. Miller (Vice President B.R.C.S. Rugby and District), Dr. C. R. Hoskyn (Commandant of Medical and Casualty Services), Mrs. Tyson Davidson (Commandant VAD Warwickshire 68).

20 January 1948 - The *Rugby Advertiser* 20 January 1948 informed its readers that C.R. Hoskyn had been presented with a warrant signifying his appointment as a Corps Surgeon of the St John Ambulance Brigade with effect from 1 January. He was, up to that point, Divisional Surgeon of Rugby Town Division of the Brigade. The presentation took place at the Annual Dinner of the works division of the English Electric Company Ltd.

Dr Hoskyn's has an interest in Welfare activities at Hamilton House at 12 Bilton Road.

Hamilton House was being used as a home for unmarried mothers and their babies. During the war it became a children's home and after the war it reverted to being a home for unmarried mothers and their offspring. It so happened that a member of the hostel committee, Dr D J Jones, Medical Officer of Health for Rugby, was also a member of the Hoskyn Cripples' Fund Committee and when lack of funds forced the home to close and transfer its inhabitants to another town, he arranged for Dr Hoskyn and his team to take over the premises. In autumn 1952, the Hoskyn Centre opened its doors for the first time.

Dr Hoskyn's retirement was widely reported. The following report is taken from *Leicester Evening Mail* 21 February 1953.

> Farewell gifts from Rugby Ambulance
>
> To mark his retirement from the St John Ambulance Brigade active list after 39 years, South Warwickshire Corps Surgeon Dr C. R. Hoskyn was, last night, presented with a wrist-watch and a pipe.
>
> The Presentation took place at dinner in the brigade headquarters in Regent-place. The gift, subscribed to by the members of the corps, the county officers and friends was handed to Dr Hoskyn by Supt L.F Hazell.
>
> The dinner was presided over by the County Commissioner. Dr G. A. Macdonald, who was accompanied by his wife County Nursing Officer Mrs Macdonald. Other visitors included the asst. County Commissioner, Mr J.G. Fowler, of Coventry; County Supt. Miss C.M. Orton, of Staverton; County Supt. A. E. Russell, of Coventry; Ald. Mrs Randall Hosking, County Officer; A. H. Booth, Coventry; Area

Cadet Office F.G. Warwick. Coventry; and Rugby Corps Supt Miss E Sellvester [Selvester].

Mrs Hosking [Hoskyn] was presented with a bouquet by Miss Selvester.
The County Commissioner presented the Rugby Division a certificate from the Chief Commissioner in London, to commemorate the division's 50th anniversary.

The Rugby Advertiser, Friday, February 27th, 1953 also ran a similar report, but it noted a few more details in that Dr Hoskyn had gone on the reserve list. The presentation was made by Corps Superintendent Mr L. F. Hazell who joined the division in 1914, the same year as Dr Hoskyn.

ST. John Ambulance Brigade Annual Brigade Dinner was held at St. John Ambulance Hall on Friday. Left to right: Dr. C. R. Hoskyn, Mrs. Hoskyn, Coun. P. A. Batt, Mrs. Batt. Front row: The Mayoress (Mrs. S. A. Hall), the Mayor (Coun. Mrs. E. F. Monck).

Dr. C. R. Hoskyn

The Rugby Advertiser 6 February 1959

His son was also a doctor who predeceased him, aged 48, in 1960.

He was awarded an OBE in the 1964 Birthday Honours list for his work in the Community and he was also granted the Freedom of Rugby, a year earlier, for his outstanding work as a doctor and humanitarian.

Dr Hoskyn died on 3 March 1965. *Coventry Evening Telegraph* carried the following article following the doctor's death the same day.

Rugby Death of Man who aided Town's Cripples.

Dr Charles Reginald Hoskyn died in the Hospital of St Cross, Rugby early today following a short illness. He was 83.

He was one of the best-known figures in Rugby and became the borough's third honorary freeman in 1962. The following year he was awarded the O.B.E. for his work on welfare of crippled and handicapped people at Hamilton House.

Dr Hoskyn, who lived with his wife at 114, Ashlawn Road, was born in India. He studied medicine at St. Bartholomew's Hospital. He came to Rugby in 1910.

Medal winner - His long association with the Hospital of St Cross began in 1911 when he was appointed assistant surgeon and continued his link until 1948.

During the First World War he served in the Royal Army Medical Corps and was awarded the Albert Medal first class for his bravery in saving the life by amputating the leg of a soldier who was trapped beneath a burning train.

The decoration was awarded where deeds of exceptional gallantry were performed not in the presence of the enemy. The comparable award nowadays is the George Cross.

After the war he resumed his work at the hospital and settled down to devote his time and energy to the welfare of the sick and crippled.

Clinic's driving force - One of his great interest was St John Ambulance Brigade which he served as divisional surgeon and corps surgeon for nearly 40 years.

The care of the handicapped persons was his main interest in the past 43 years and he was the driving force behind the building of the Rugby Orthopaedic clinic and the sun pavilion at the Hospital of St Cross.

In 1949 friends and admirers started the Hoskyn Cripples Fund which is in operation from Hamilton House. This house is equipped as a disabled persons' club and occupation centre.

In his younger days' Dr Hoskyn was a prominent Rugby footballer being captain of St Barts Hospital. He also played in the Middlesex XV.

The funeral will take place at St Andrew's Parish Church, Rugby on Monday at 2pm. A private cremation service will follow at Canley Crematorium.

Citation on John Orr's Medal Index Card.

On the occasion of the train accident at Gezaincourt, 24th November 1916, he fought the flames without ceasing in his efforts to rescue the wounded. He showed great gallantry in endeavouring to raise a blazing mass of wreckage to extricate an injured man who was pinned down by heavy beams of timber across his legs.

John Orr was also awarded a Bar to his Meritorious Service Medal in 1917.

Citation on Sidney Heley's Medal Index Card.

On the occasion of the train accident at Gezaincourt on November 24th 1916, A/Cpl S. Heley showed great gallantry in endeavouring to raise burning wreckage in order to free an injured man. In addition to this plucky act he displayed great resource and initiative in handling the injured who had been removed from the wreckage and were waiting to be removed to the C.C.S. on stretchers.

The St John Ambulance Brigade Ilford

Report of Railway Accident, Gezaincourt on 24/11/1916.[64]

D. of R. No. 1539A -25/11/1916 -- RAMC446/19 (in pencil)

Railway Accident, GEZAINCOURT
At 4-20 hours 24/11/1918

Coal Train No 4016, started from Bethune heavily laden.
It was drawn by two engines – No. 3135, driver Marez – No. 4048 driver Legrand.
Each engine could draw 485 tons – There were 42 trucks with approximate weight of 930 tons.

When mounting gradient from Gezaincourt to Candas a coupling broke and 34 trucks slid dawn hill and crashed into the Boulogne leave train at "kilometre 38,600" ½ mile from Gezaincourt Goods Station.

Of the goods trucks, 24 were smashed and in the leave train 6 carriages, the fourgon [for gone] and engine were overturned – the wind blew the fire from the engine towards the leave train and the carriages caught fire 5 to 10 minutes after the accident.

There were 34 officer and 281 other ranks on the leave train.

The R.T.O.[65] Gezaincourt (Lt. A. H. B. Marshall) reported 24/11/16 as follows:-

*   *   *   *   *   *

An officer immediately came down to warn me. I at once 'phoned to the 29th Casualty Clearing Station. Owing to the marvellous organisation of this C.C.S., doctors and stretcher bearers were on the spot at once. It was chiefly owing to the splendid work of Lt. Col. Brunskill the C.O. that a great many were saved.

As soon as I had wired the C.C.S., I showed some soldiers who had come down, where the fire buckets and water were and I provided handspikes to help get the men buried under debris, I immediately went to the spot.

Everybody was trying to get the men burning under the debris out but were not able to do a great deal owing to the strong wind and the masses of debris. I gave French orders to pull the rest of the train out. They took most of it, but left two unburnt carriages, owing to the fact that the front one was derailed. I told them to bring this engine back and try and pull those two out, after some hesitation (thinking it was impossible) they tried and did it.

Meanwhile the C.C.S. men, the men off the train and my own men did their best to get the burning bodies away. Two cases of heroism are very noticeable. Capt. Hoskyn R.A.M.C., of 29th C.C.S, crawled under the burning debris as great personal risk and began calmly

---

64 Wellcome Collection First World War and Later Material Licence Attribution -Non-Commercial 4.0 International (CC BY-NC 4.0)
Date1916-1920 Reference RAMC/446/17-26 Part of Royal Army Medical Corps Muniments Collection
65 RTO = Rail Transport Officer.

amputating one of the burning men's legs, in trying he helped to loosen the body and the man was got out alive. Capt. Hoskyns behaved with wonderful coolness and pluck the whole time.

The Rev. Capt. Oddie C. F[66]. one of the passengers also did good work running in burning debris and trying to save men. His face was badly cut about and burnt.

The C.C.S. had got all the men they could out, they began seeing to them and for a minute the work was suspended. I then got men on to try and clear the unburnt debris as much as possible so as to localise the fire. While doing this one of the Frenchmen declared there was still a man unburnt right in front of the engine. We managed to clear the ground and found the body. His head was crushed to pieces but the rest of the body was untouched. He had been thrown out of the train too far to be burnt but was crushed by debris.

After this all the men worked at clearing the line, the French giving great assistance, and we extracted burnt bodies. They were beyond recognition. The fire smouldered till about 8 hours, but only burnt fiercely for 2 hours.

These are the numbers of the wounded got from the C.C.S., The names are not got yet.

FRENCH.

The conductor of the leave train.	Burnt to death
One engine driver of leave train.	Slightly Wounded
The garde du frein[67] of the coal train	Slightly Wounded

WOUNDED BRITISH.

Officers   15
Other Ranks   49

KILLED.

3 Officers, 11 Other Ranks (5 of which were so mangled as not to be recognisable – 1 of these was perhaps the "conducteur[68]" of the leave train).

The O.C. of the train was Maj. Gordon, 43rd Cameron Highlanders. He was assisted by Major Boxhall, 61st Divl. Artillery did very fine work in encouraging the men and getting details of the accident. There was one case of great heroism which I did not see. In a carriage immediately next to the burning engine, which itself was on fire, an office assisted Major Gordon in pulling out through the window2 officer 1 slightly 1 severely wounded. These officers had to be lifted through the roof. The officers name is not yet known.

    *   *   *   *   *   *

D.A.D.R.T[69]. (III) (Capt. F. T. Bacon) reported 24/11/16 as follows:-

---

[66] Rev. Philip Francis Oddie, Royal Army Chaplains' Department awarded a Military Cross in the New Years Honours List 1/1/1917
[67] Translates as Brake Guard
[68] Translates as Driver
[69] Deputy Assistant Director of Railway Traffic

*   *   *   *   *   *

I wish also to bring to your notice the very prompt and able assistance which was rendered by Col. Brunskill and the officers and men of the 29th Casualty Clearing Station at GEZAINCOURT, without which the casualties would undoubtedly have been more numerous. Col Brunskill appears to have arrived with his men in a few minutes and took charge of the work or rescue with great efficiency. Col. Brunskill mentioned to me the following names of officers and men who were especially conspicuous in the work of rescue and considerable personal risk: -

Capt. C. R. Hoskyn		R.A.M.C.
No. 27253	Serjt. T. Orr	R.A.M.C
No. 29989	Corpl. S Heley	R.A.M.C
No. 9824	Corpl W.D. Chevalier	R.A.M.C

*   *   *   *   *   *

A. D. R. T. III (Col. W. S. Gray) to D. R., G.H.Q., No. 3/113 25/11/16 as follows:-

It was however mainly due to the energetic measures taken by Colonel Brunskill, after he had received notice of the accident, that many of the injured were saved from the burning debris. Colonel Brunskill wishes to especially mention those of his staff named by Captain Bacon. I have ascertained from officers and men who were present at the time of the accident and immediately after it, that Colonel Brunskill behaved in a most gallant manner. In the instance quoted by Captain Bacon when Captain Hoskyn most gallantly attempted to amputate a man's leg in order to free him from the debris, Colonel Brunskill himself held up a portion of the burning wreckage to make it possible for Captain Hoskyn to carry out this operation, and both these officer run great personal risk before the succeeded in freeing the unfortunate man who was pinned under the wreckage. On an occasion of this description it is difficult to notice all that is done, but all who were present are unanimous in their praise of the work of the two officers I have mentioned, Colonel Brunskill and Capt. Hoskyns.

The whole of the available staff of the 29th Casualty Clearing Station turned out most promptly and assisted in the clearance of wreckage and in the saving of life. Our thanks are due to them for the great assistance they have rendered apart from the gallantry which distinguished the work of some of them.

*   *   *   *   *   *

The St John Ambulance Brigade Ilford

The Commonwealth War Graves Commission information on the Train Accident at Gezaincourt on 24 November 1916. However, the list remains incomplete.

Gezaincourt Connunal Cemetery Extension[70]								
4000103	McINTOSH		J	0	24/11/1916	Private	Army Service Corps	
4000100	BAXTER	HERBERT ARTHUR	H A	0	24/11/1916	Private	Northumberland Fusiliers	8th Bn.
35179	BARKER		H	23	24/11/1916	Driver	Royal Field Artillery	47th Bde. Ammunition Col.
35269	DART	Henry Cullen	H C	0	24/11/1916	Private	Army Service Corps	2nd Mobile Repair Shops
35512	MOSS	JOHN STEPHEN NOEL	J S N	20	24/11/1916	Second Lieutenant	Royal Engineers	57th Field Coy.
35329	GABITES		G	22	24/11/1916	Private	Manchester Regiment	21st Bn.
35183	BARTLE		G	27	24/11/1916	Private	West Yorkshire Regiment (Prince of Wales's Own)	12th Bn.
35424	KERR	LESLIE HENRY FOX	L H F	23	24/11/1916	Lieutenant	Army Service Corps	106th Coy.
35636	SMITH	CHARLES	C	0	24/11/1916	Rifleman	ALIAS	
35631	SKELCHER	JOHN WILLIAM	J W	27	24/11/1916	Corporal	Oxford and Bucks Light Infantry	5th Bn.
35683	TRAILL	SINCLAIR GEORGE	S G	26	24/11/1916	Captain	Cameron Highlanders	1st Bn.
35177	BARBER	WILLIAM THOMAS	W T	0	24/11/1916	Rifleman	Rifle Brigade	7th Bn.
	NEILL		W P		24/11/1916	Second Lieutenant	Royal Scots	
	GABB (believed to be Casualty from 24/11/1916		S F		08/12/1916	Second Lieutenant	Machine Gun Corps	76 Company
Thiepval Memorial. Pier and Face 1A and 8A [71]								
808443	PARSONS	JOSEPH	J	0	24/11/1916	Gunner	Royal Field Artillery	"A" Bty. 46th Bde.

The War Diary of the 29th Casualty Clearing Station. [72]

27 August 1915 Having mobilised at Aldershot, moved to Southampton and sailed on the ship "Manchester Importer". 28 August 1915: landed at Le Harve. 24 September 1915 after a rail journey via Rouen, arrived at Gezaincourt. Remained well over a year. 8 May 1917: moved to Grevillers. 23 March 1918: moved to "Edgehill" (Somme). 25 March 1918: moved by rail to Gezaincourt. 24 September 1918: moved by rail to Wavans but did not open there. 29 September 1918: moved by rail to Delsaux Farm (near Beugny). 19 January 1919: arrived at Calais. 7 February 1919 moved by rail to Bonn in Germany and relieved 1st Canadian CCS. 31 October 1919: war diary ends with 29 CCS still in Bonn. [73]

---

70 The Cemetery extension contains 3 unidentified graves.

71 Gunner Joseph Parsons died on 25 November 1916 (no known grave) according to CWGC he 'Died' on 24 November. Family legend has it that he was killed in a train crash. The only significant train crash, that day was the one at Gezaincourt described in this article..

72 National Archives WO95/415.

Chapter Ten – The War Years 1917 - 1918

In January 1917 the *First Aid Journal* recorded that W Magnus of No 46 Division was awarded a Bar to his Service medal, at the same time as Assistant Commissioner Col. James Cantlie. FRCS.[74]

In January 1917 *The Recorder* carried the following article-

> Ilford's New Emergency Hospital. It read "Interesting gatherings have been held this week in connection with the opening of the new Ilford Emergency Hospital, which is arranged to take place today (Saturday).
>
> The hospital has been erected at Newbury Park, between Barkingside and Seven Kings, at a cost of about £10,000. The hospital movement in Ilford was inaugurated by members of the Ilford Medical Society some eight years ago. Later they were joined by a number of prominent laymen, and the first Hospital Committee was formed. The work was carried on with great success till 1907[75], when a Board of thirty governors took on the work and the questions of suitable hospital buildings came up for consideration. The result is seen today in the construction of the administrative section, the dimensions of which are ample for the work of a, 100 bed, hospital.
>
> When need arises for increasing the number of beds – now limited to 20 – no further expenditure for building will be incurred beyond that of extending the wards. The foundation stone if the building was laid on April 15, 1910. The scheme had been made possible by the success which had attended the Ilford carnivals, from which source the greater part of the funds, have come."
>
> During the week the workers and friends in the seven wards have been given an opportunity of inspecting the buildings, and on each evening social gatherings and concerts have been held. On Monday between 500 and 600 were present from Cranbrook and North Hainault Wards; on Tuesday there was a similar gathering from Loxford and Clementswood Wards. Wednesday was set apart for Park Ward, and Thursday for South Hainault and Seven Kings.
>
> The Hospital will be declared open to-day (Saturday) by Mr Ben Bailey, J.P., chairman of the Board of Governors, and will be open for the admission of patients on Tuesday, January 30th.

A personal account from Julie Pickford (edited)[76]

> My Grandfather William Newman Wright was invalided home in late 1916 and he died in January 1917 in Ilford.

---

74 Sir James Cantlie KBE FRCS KStJ (17 January 1851 – 28 May 1926) was a British physician., he was a pioneer of first aid. The Corbet Fletcher, Annals of the Ambulance Department Second Edition by N. Corbet Fletcher, Second Edition 1947 Page 160. Sir James interest in Ambulance work dated from 1878 when in conjunction with Dr J. Mitchell Bruce, he was asked by Dr Peter Shepherd to revise his notes and assist in production of the first Text-book of the Association.

75 In 1907, the Ilford Emergency Hospital was incorporated under the Companies Act. Internet accessed 2 April 2022 Lost Hospital of London.

76 Internet access Facebook page of "Remembering British women in WW1 – The Home Front and Oversea" 14 May 2019

After investigation I was able to advise that William Newman Wright, born in 1873. He was a Battery Quartermaster Serjeant, No 926545 with the Royal Field Artillery. Awarded Long Service and Good Conduct Medal. He died at the age of 44 in Ilford Emergency Hospital on 2 January 1917[77] He was buried at Great Ilford, St Mary the Virgin on 6 January 1917[78] His wife was Mrs Letitia Wright, 42, Mayfair Avenue, Ilford, Essex. Grave Inscription for William Newman Wright at Ilford Buckingham Road Cemetery is recorded as

Who Dies for England Never Dies

Ilford Emergency Hospital, Essex, 19 June, 1917. Photo accessed on Internet 2 April 2022. - WWI photos. org

1 June 1917 *The* Recorder recorded -
The following is believed to be the first member of the Ilford Division killed in action.

> Rogers. – Killed in action, in France, on May 14th, 1917, Pte. L. F. Rogers, London Regiment, the second and only son of Mr and Mrs Rodgers, of 172 Mortlake-road, Ilford, in his 21st year.

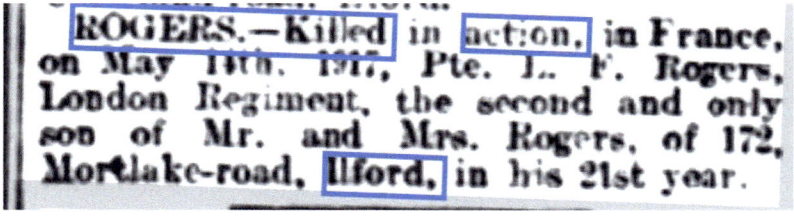

Leon Frederick Rogers

The Commonwealth War Graves Commission recorded his death as follows –

> Private LEON FREDERICK ROGERS Service Number: 281450 2nd/4th Bn., London Regiment (Royal Fusiliers) who died on 15 May 1917 Age 20 Son of Walter John and Edith Rogers, of 172, Mortlake Rd., Ilford, Essex. Remembered with Honour ARRAS MEMORIAL Bay 9.

---

[77] CWGC, Ilford Cemetary Essex No 1 Schedual "A"" Page 1 and 2
[78] Find My Past, Essex Records accessed 20 October 2022

Ilford Air Raid

On the 25th May 1917, what is described as a Great Daylight Raid occurred. There was an incident that happened in the sky above Ilford. The Royal Flying Corps, Captain C. W. E Cole-Hamilton, who with Captain C. H. C Keevil as observer, had gone up in a Bristol Fighter from No. 35 Training Squadron at Northolt, attacked three enemy machines over Ilford. The Gotha's returned his fire, and he only broke off the unequal combat after his gun jammed and Keevil was killed[79].

The Commonwealth War Graves Commission (CWGC) records show that Captain Cecil Horace Case Keevil is remembered with honour and that he is buried in Hampstead Cemetery Ref 0.6.75. He served with Royal Flying Corps (and 18th Bn. West Yorkshire Regiment (Prince of Wales's Own) who died on 13 June 1917 aged 36. He was the son of Richard and Georgina Keevil, of Clitter House Farm, Cricklewood, London.

The Pilot, Captain Con William Eric Cole-Hamilton, did not survive the war and died only a month later. He is remembered with honour in St Albans (Hatfield Road) Cemetery Ref E.A.24. He served Royal Flying Corps (and 2nd Bat Royal Scots) he died on 2 July 1917 aged. 23 He was the son of the late Capt. W. A. T. Cole-Hamilton, Royal Irish Fusiliers and Mrs L. A. Cole-Hamilton.

On 1 June 1917 *The Recorder* carried the short article below, indicating that an effort was underway to raise funds for a Motor Ambulance.

> Ilford Ambulance Fund
>
> Mr W. R. Magnus desires to acknowledge a further sum of £1 from Mr R. Middlemas' ditching party towards the Ilford Ambulance and Nursing Division Motor Ambulance Fund; also £5. 10s from the Goodmayes Choral Society, as a result of their performance of "Judas Maccabeus" – on May 12th

The New Ambulance and Local Concerns.

The Recorder 15 June 1917 carried a report of the Ilford Ambulance Dedication -

> Ilford's Motor Ambulance Dedicated.
> Notable Ceremony in Valentines Park.
> Bishop of Chelmsford's Stirring Address
>
> At the bandstand in Valentines Park on Saturday afternoon, the Lord Bishop of Chelmsford[80] dedicated the motor ambulance that has been purchased by public subscription, under the

---

[79] The German Air Raid in Great Britain 1914-1918 by J.Morris. First Published in 1925 by Sampson Low, Marston & Co. Ltd. – Managing Director Fred J Rymer, who was also a member of Ilford Division.

[80] John Edwin Watts-Ditchfield (17 September 1861 – 14 July 1923) was an eminent 20th century Anglican priest and distinguished author. When diocese of Chelmsford was created in 1914, Watts-Ditchfield was appointed as its first bishop. He began his career with a curacy at St Peter, Highgate (1891-1897) after which he was Vicar of St James the Less, Bethnal Green (1897-1914). He died in post in 1923. There is a statue to him within Chelmsford Cathedral.

auspices of the Ilford Ambulance and Nursing Divisions, for the conveyance of wounded soldiers from the railway station to the Emergency Hospital. The ambulance stood on the west side of the bandstand. It is a handsome vehicle, roomy, and admirably equipped for its purpose. A large crowd of invited guests, including subscribers, gathered within the enclosure, which was ringed by the officers and men of the 3rd Cadet Battalion, Essex Regiment, under the command of Major F. Leighton. The band of the regiment was also in attendance.

Accompanying the Lord Bishop on the stand were the Vicar of Ilford (Rev. A. W. Otterway), the Vicar of All Saints' Goodmayes (Rev. Hector Reindorp), chaplain of the cadets, who acted as chaplain to the Bishop. The Vicar of St. John's Seven Kings (Rev. J. A. Telford), Sir John Bethell, Bart., M.P., Lady Bethell, and Miss Bethell, Sir Peter Grigg, J.P., C.A., and Lady Griggs, Divisional Superintendent and Commandant, W. R. Magnus, and Mrs Magnus (superintendent of the Nursing Division), Ambulance Officer M. G. Matthews, Mrs Law (secretary of the Nursing Division). Major F. Leighton, and a large body of Nurses in uniform. The attendance in the circle below included the chairman of the Urban Council (Councillor F. D. Smith. J.P.) Councillor W. T. Cadness, and J. Lowe.

The service opened with the singing of the hymn commencing "Thou to whom the sick and dying, ever same, nor come in vain." The Bishop and congregation read alternatively the verses of Psalm xli [41] and his lordship then descended the steps to the Ambulance and recited the special prayers for the occasion.

Re-ascending the stairway, and addressing the company, the Bishop said: It is with peculiar pleasure that I am here to-day to take part in the dedication of this Ambulance. Needless to say, that in these days of war, one is apt to look perhaps, simply at the black side of the war. The awfulness, the terribleness seems to over shadow so much, that we scarcely realise that there are any benefits connected to war. And yet I venture to say that there are certain things which we must put on the credit side. The war had drawn out the best that was in the nation. We have only to contrast our nation of two years before the war, and the two years after, to see the extraordinary, the wonderful change that has taken place in the whole character of our national life. It has produced unity where unity seemed to be impossible. In the account of the advance this week, for which we all thank God, we read of men from Ulster and men from the South of Ireland fighting shoulder to shoulder against the common foe – typical of what is seen in all other ranks in life. How marvellously capital and labour have managed to work together! There has been no talk of aristocracy on one side and the labouring man on the other, but every man seems to have gone fourth simply as an Englishman to do his bit, to stand by the side of his fellow, whether he came from the mansion or slum. Then again, it has drawn forth a wonderful sprite of philanthropy, using that term in the highest and best sense. I think it is true to say that during the last three years more money had been freely subscribed, voluntarily given, for the help of other people in some way or other than in the history of our nation before. It is impossible to calculate the millions upon millions that have thus been freely given. And here to-day in Ilford you have another instance of the sprite which has brought forth the presentation of those millions. I am thankful for this local effort. I have always held that no such gift as this can be made without causing those who are giving it to reap, shall I say, as much benefit indirectly, morally and spiritually, as those for whom it was intended. Our lads on the front who come home wounded, do they not deserve the best we can give them? How wonderfully they have fought at the front! We are all proud of our Essex Regiment, equally as we are of our Canadians and Australians; and we must never forget that while we thank God for the wonderful spirit of the Dominions beyond the sea, yet the brunt of the battle has practically fallen upon our English lads – all honour to them (Applause.)

I am glad you gift is associated with nursing, because the one thing the war has proved to the utmost is the extra-ordinary part that women must play in the future development of our country. We speak with pride of our lads earning the V.C. When I think of those heroic nurses who have gone to the front, strong physically and mentally, and have worked and worked until they returned to the homeland shattered and broken in body, without the hope of ever their part in the life of home or nation again. I think those women have as freely given themselves to their nation as the lads who have died in the trenches. (Applause.) All honour to the women of our country, to the mothers and wives who have given their sons and husbands, sent them forth with a "God bless you." And then, after days of agony and suspense, it may be, the fatal telegram – Oh yes, they have given much.

Now we are in the midst of this of this war. Thank God it is going on. Oh, it is not over. I wish I could say to-day use any words that would point to a speedy conclusion of this war; but although we trust and still hope for a speedy conclusion. I think the signs point to a prolonged war, far beyond, it may be, this year. That will mean much to us, but do let us remember that when we drew the sword on August 4th. 1914. We did not draw it willingly, with light heart: we did not draw it with any though of self: we drew it for the certain purpose and it would be worse than folly, it would be a crime of the highest magnitude, to put that sword by until those purposes for which it was drawn have been secured. (Applause.) I am not, I need scarcely say, actuated by any vindictive or blood-thirsty spirit, but I do feel that it is madness to talk of peace until certain conditions have been fulfilled. For instance, I feel that justice demands punishment, not upon the innocent women and children – I am against reprisals of that kind – but what I do feel is that when you have had such deeds of barbarism perpetrated, when you have had Belgium laid low, when you have had the horrors of the sinking of the Lusitania, when you have has all those regulations into which Germany entered at the Hague Tribunal thrown aside, when Germany has gone on like the barbarous nations of bygone days – I say there must be punishment, and, as far as possible, those men who have plunged the world into bloodshed must be punished. (Applause.) I would go so far as to say that capital punishment must be for ever abolished if the men who have thrown the whole world into an agony of heart-breaks are to go unpunished at the end of this war. (Applause.) Then there must be reparations. How can we talk of peace and leave Belgium as she is to-day? There must be reparation, and, as far as money can repair the wrong, money must be paid.

Personally, I rather feel with those seamen who refused to carry men across the seas (alluding to the delegates to the Socialist Congress) unless those men say that the widows and children of those gallant lads of ours who have been sent to the bottom of the North Sea are provided for and the enemy who has done this dastardly thing punished. (Applause.)

Again, I say, how dare we talk of peace unless we have secured the freedom of the weaker nations? It is said there should be no annexation. I do not talk of annexation – I talk of liberation. (Applause.) Are we going to allow Armenia to remain in the hands of the Turk? (Cries of "No.") Are we going to leave German East Africa in German hands? (Loud shouts of "No.") I have been talking during the last week with men who have lived in German East Africa, and they have told me things that I cannot repeat hear in public that have been done under the administration by Germany of that great area in the treatment of the natives. What quarrel with Germany about to-day are her ideals, which we believe to be wrong.

If we in England to-day are not willing that England shall be under the domination of Germany, have we any right to hand over those natives of German East Africa to be under her domination? Therefore, I feel that we must, before we can talk of peace, decide that these smaller nations, these feebler folk, shall be free from that thraldom and domination which we Englishmen would not suffer for a single day. (Applause.)

Then we must secure before peace comes, as far as possible, some mode by which this shall be the last war. I do not want to leave Germany in such a position that our lads of seven and eight and ten years of age will have to encounter another war in 20 or 30 years. – I do not want to leave them a legacy of another German war, worse, if that be possible, than this – I want this war to be the end of war. (Applause.) Therefore, we must see to it that this war fought to such a finish that those great ideals of justice and freedom and mercy shall prevail in the world: and until that day comes, we, God helping us, will be true to the traditions of our fathers. (Applause.)

His lordship proceeded to urge his listeners to keep steady and cool while doing their bit, and to encourage each other to rally round the old flag, and around the King and the Royal Family. It had been a great privilege to be in every part of the British Empire, in every continent, and he said frankly that he did not think our King was getting quite his due. We all remember how it was said that King Edward did a great deal to cement the European Alliance, but why was it that we had got Australia, Canada, India on our side to-day? If any of them had been to either of those dependencies they would know the answer. Our present King had done for out colonies what King Edward did for Europe, having visited every part of our empire and been in touch with ever prominent statesman. An Australian statesman said to him (the speaker) "We don't care whether Asquith, or Balfour, or Lloyd George is Prime Minister – we have got seven prime ministers of our own – but we all rally round the Throne, that is the keystone of the arch." His lordship thanked God that we had a man on the Throne who, he could testify from personal knowledge, was God-fearing, and a man of prayer.

To what kind of England were our boys coming back? Was that lad who had fought for England, who had lived in a slum in the East End, whose wife perhaps, was living in two rooms – was coming back to live in the old ally, to see his wife and children grow up pinched and wan? Or were we going back to make England worthy of the blood that had been shed for her? There would be talk of money, but a nation that spent a thousand millions on war, and had not gone bankrupt, could never again say she had no money for well-thought-out social reforms. But we must build carefully or we might pass into the danger zone of recrimination, where men would seek to set class against class, where men who had suffered wrongs would make their wrongs known, and the voice of the agitator would be heard in the land. When that time came we wanted one centre around which all could resolve.

It was by the Gospel of the Lord Jesus Christ, alone that England and the Empire, and the world could ever be at peace. Into whose hands, in this great time of stress and strain, had we counted the destine of our country and our Empire? It was a very surprising and thought-provoking thing that we had given our destinies, not into the hands of a set of infidels, but practically every man who held any great position to-day was a God-fearing and praying man. He instanced Haig, Robertson, Beattie, the governors and viceroys of our dominions and the Prime Minister himself, who, when he went down to Wales, preached in a little chapel. It was not to the infidel that we turned in this great hour of our nation's trouble, nut to the praying man, to the man who got his strength from his God. After eloquent urging his listeners to put their trust in God at the present crisis, his lordship closed by congratulating Mr Magnus, who had had a great deal to do with the furthering of the work that had brought them together, and all those who had been associated with him. In handing over this splendid ambulance for the work to which they had dedicated it, he trusted it would be the forerunner of much greater effort for our brave lads than had been put forth in the past. (Applause.)

The audience then sang the final hymn, "Thy Kingdom come, O God," and this was followed by the National Anthem, the band effectively leading as before.

The Bishop of Chelmsford, and some other visitors, made an inspection of the ambulance, before leaving the park.

In a separate section of the paper a further, more general, report appeared. The content is reproduced below –

> The dedication of the motor ambulance purchased by public subscription for use of wounded soldiers arriving at the Ilford Emergency Hospital, provided a pleasant afternoon function in Valentines Park last Saturday. The basis of the proceedings was a religious service, but the occasion provided many opportunities for social intercourse and the exchange of greetings by friend of the hospital and the St. John Ambulance Brigade from all parts of the town: furthermore, it furnished the Bishop of Chelmsford with a text upon which to deliver one of breezy and vigorous addresses, which are appreciated in no part of the diocese more than they are at Ilford.
>
> Superintendent W. R. Magnus received honourable mention in his lordship's utterance, and this was only fair and proper, for it is owing to his zeal and energy that this much need ambulance has been added to the equipment of the local division.

The Recorder 15 June 1917 carried a report of an accident which occurred in Ilford Lane and provided a backdrop to public discussions on the use of the new ambulance by St John. The report read -

> Street Accidents.
> Mrs O'Leary, aged 37, living at No. 47 Madras-road, Ilford-lane, while crossing the Broadway on Saturday evening was knocked down by a motor bus and badly injured. She sustained laceration of the scalp and her foot was crushed, the toes being broken. After being attended by Dr Drought, divisional surgeon to the police, the patient was conveyed to the London Hospital.

The editor of *The Recorder* received a letter signed A. Ingram. He decided to publish details and *The Recorder* carried the story in its edition of 22 June 1917 in the "Editorial Gossip" section of the paper.

> Last week, shortly before the "Recorder" went to press, I received a letter signed "A. Ingram," and the address given is "Thorold-road, Ilford," which having regard to the fact that there are four hundred houses in that road, is virtually no address at all. The letter is about the motor ambulance recently purchased by the Ilford Ambulance and Nursing Divisions of the Ilford St John Ambulance Brigade with money provided for that purpose by public subscription. It is not a pleasant letter. The sub-heading of the letter is an interrogatory: "Have the public been tricked?" and the suggestion running through the communication is that the money obtained from the public was secured by false pretences; that is to say, that the subscription was raised "on the understanding that it (the motor ambulance) was for Ilford – that is for the town – not for the St. John Ambulance Brigade."

In another letter in the same edition the following letter appeared -

> Ilford Ambulance and Nursing Divisions Motor Ambulance.
>
> To the Editor of the "Recorder"
>
> Dear Sir, - Owing to numerous enquires with regard to the Ilford Motor Ambulance, I should like to state that the help I and my supporters gave was for a Motor Ambulance for Ilford.
>
> 1. To convey the wounded soldiers from station to hospital
> 2. For Accidents that might occur in Ilford:

and I was assured by Mr Magnus that it would be kept in Ilford for this purpose, otherwise I should not have put my name to it.

On Saturday last, a serious accident occurred, a women being runover by a motor bus and nearly killed: and I am told delay, which might have serious, was caused in procuring a conveyance to take her to hospital: eventually she was removed in a taxi.

When told of this, I said surely this was a case for the motor ambulance, but upon enquiry, I find the police could not requisition it, as they do not know where it is kept.

I need scarcely say how pained and upset I was to hear this. The police should have been the first to be acquainted with its whereabouts, and I have drawn the attention of Mr Magnus to it.

I hope soon the whole business will be placed on a proper basis: I can assure those friends who supported me, that I am not at all satisfied with the present arrangements.

Yours faithfully,

(Mrs) S. A. Hatcher.
26 Ranelagh-gardens, Ilford

The editor of *The Recorder* had obviously contacted William Magnus to afford him the opportunity to reply. His response was reported, as follows, in the same edition of the paper. Superintendent Magnus writes as under in reply to the letter from "A. Ingram," referred to in "Editorial Gossip"-

I do not think that very many people in Ilford are under the wrong impression as to the Motor Ambulance in question, as a whole the appeals that have been issued to the press or by letter have contained the phrase "A Motor Ambulance for use in connection with transport of wounded from Ambulance Train to Hospital." And this was the sole reason for the fund being instituted by those concerned. As a further proof of intention. I would refer you to the "Flag Day" bill, which distinctly stated "Fund to provide a Motor Ambulance for the conveyance of wounded soldiers from Ambulance Trains to Hospital."

Having obtained the motor, the division are quite prepared to undertake the transport of cases requiring the use of a stretcher, either from home to hospital or hospital home without cost to those requiring it: and the car has been used for such cases since the dedication.

With regard to the dedication ceremony which was essentially a religious service, the committee felt that speeches would be entirely out of place, and this is borne out by the fact that a very large number of the invited subscribers have commented favourably on the wisdom of the decision.

Further, and it may not be generally known, it not being the practice of the local brigade to seek cheap advertisement, they being quite satisfied to do their best in the alleviation of suffering without shouting it from the housetops, more than half the money required was contributed by the members and their friends before any public appeal was made.

With regard to the non-use of the device (mentioned in Mr Ingham's letter) this has quite a simple explanation. A regulation that the crest was not to be used for street collections and that the uniform of the member must not be used for such, had been made by our headquarters authorities, but a copy had not been received by me. As soon as this was pointed out, I took steps to put matters right, not by going around and posting slips over the bills, as suggested by your correspondent, but by issuing slips in the case of about 20 bills that had already been distributed and by arranging of all other bills sent out to be correct before issue.

The Recorder 29 June 1917 carried further news on "The New Motor Ambulance". The report was as follows -

The New Motor Ambulance

Councillor Sheat, under the item "questions" said he had been waited upon by several ladies and gentlemen with regard to the motor ambulance given to the town. There seems to be a little uneasiness in the minds of those who had been working for this worthy object. He asked the following question: Is it correctly described as a motor ambulance for Ilford? Was the fund instituted as a war charity and registered as such as under the War Charities Act? What arrangements has been made for the ambulance to be immediately available in case of need? What restrictions, if any, are made by the user?

Amplifying these questions, the speaker said the minute referring to the dedication of the ambulance spoke of it as having been purchased "for use in Ilford district." The ladies and gentlemen who waited upon him wanted to whether that was so. He recalled the recent accident when a women was run over by a motor-bus and the ambulance had disappeared. The next Sunday night a wounded soldier had arrived at Ilford railway station to be taken to the Emergency Hospital, and the attendant was there to receive him, but there was no motor ambulance. On the previous night a curious accident happened outside his house, three children being injured, one of the being taken to hospital, and the police were asking "Where is the ambulance?" He suggested the clerk made enquires with regard to the matter.

The chairman said at the dedication ceremony it was never clearly explained what the ambulance was for. He suggested the clerk see Mr Magnus and have a word with him.

Sir Peter Griggs said that Mr Magnus came to a meeting of the hospital governors a few days ago and explained that the new ambulance was for Ilford, first to take wounded soldiers to the hospital and after that for general hospital work. Mr Magnus also said his committee would meet again in about a week's time. If people had a little patience he thought all reasonable demands would be met.

Included in *The Recorder* on 29 June 1917 was a piece headed Ilford Hospitallers A-Z by an Onlooker. It was basically a list of prominent citizens of Ilford involved with the Ilford Emergency Hospital. Listed under 'M' was William Magnus recorded as "*Magnus the great.*".

His efforts had not gone unnoticed and perhaps, the above phrase, is a true reflection of the esteem in which he was held by the community in June 1917.

Also, in June, in fact on 18 June the Ilford Education Committee met to consider what lesson could be learnt from the raid on 13 June. The day light raid inflicted a grave loss of life at one London County Council school[81] and this caused significant concern at many schools in the

---

[81] Upper North Street, Poplar was bombed by one of Germany's new long-distance Gotha aeroplanes. The plane was part of a squadron targeting the city in the first daylight air raid of the First World War. Eighteen children were killed – most just 5 years old. At least 37 others were seriously injured.

Ilford and wider Essex area. The Education Committee Secretary intimated that he had received a petition from a number of parents of children attending Valentines School to ask that children be realised from school in case of future air raids. This led to a meeting of Headteachers in Beckton. On 22 June notices were sent out to parents regarding conduct during air raids.

Photograph Credit *Portsmouth Evening News* 14 October 1940 - A German Gotha Bombers of the type used in 1917 -1918.

The Recorder 6 July 1917 reported –

> Imposing Military Review.
>
> In honour of receiving their new hon. colonel, Colonel H. Day, for the first time on parade with his Battalion, and the first to be officially inspected by Colonel Brooker Ward, V.D.,T.D., Deputy Lord Lieutenant of the County, and Colonel Commandant of the Essex County Cadets, accompanied by his Staff Major Hudson and Captain Gilchrist. The 3rd Cadet Battalion turned out on Sunday morning in fine strength in the command of their popular and energetic commanding officer, Major F. Leighton, and great credit and praise is due to him for giving some 4,000 people who witnessed the inspection such a fine and impressive ceremony.

From a St John Ambulance perspective, the information below concerning Cadets will be of interest, as officially it was 25 May 1922 before the first St John Ambulance Cadet Division was formed. The above article concluded as follows -

> The commanding officer is pleased to receive the services of Mr Magnus, of the Ilford St. John Ambulance Company, who is taking a commission and will have charge of the Cadets Ambulance Section. This gentleman stands out in Ilford second to none in untiring energies to render every assistance to the sick and wounded in uniform or civilian, and his work with the Battalion is hoped to be a long and lasting one. This staff of both men and lady nurses were on the ground in true support of a local enterprise.

The Globe on 10 July 1917 carried a reported

> Air Raid Inquests. Dr King Houchin held inquests on 12 persons whose deaths occurred in consequence of Saturday's raid." The inquest was as a result of a large air raid on East London and the City on 7 July 1917 when 22 German Gotha Bombers carried out an attack. In total 57 people were killed.

The Recorder 17 August 1917 reports

If there are people who think that the town ought to be provided with a motor ambulance, instead of the one drawn by a horse – and there are – their obvious duty is to approach the Council with representations on the subject, and I have no doubt our representatives would give the matter sympathetic consideration. It is grossly unfair, signally ungenerous, and mischievous waste of time to attempt to jockey Mr Supt. Magnus and the St. John Ambulance Brigade into virtually making over to the Urban Council a motor ambulance which was honourably obtained through their own enterprise and largely by their own efforts, for their special and always beneficent work in the town.

1918

Ilford Fire Station, Lay Street, Ilford c1918 shown with Fire Appliances and Ambulances Authors Collection – Photographer unknown
The Ambulance under "Ilford' is thought to be that of Ilford Division St John Ambulance.

Funds were still needed for the Hospital and Mrs Magnus was a very active fund raiser for them. *The Recorder* of 4 January 1918 ran the following article under the headline

> Pound Days for Ilford Emergency Hospital". It continued "The pound days arranged by Mrs Magnus on December 14th and 15th, on behalf of the Ilford Emergency Hospital, entirely eclipsed the efforts of the previous year, notwithstanding the difficulty of procuring supplies. The number of pounds was about 1,400, or about 2 ½ cwt., more than last year, which total doubled the number of pounds of the previous year, the first of its kind on behalf of a local institution.
>
> Mrs Magnus desires to express her gratitude to all those who kindly helped towards this magnificent result, also to Mr Longman, of Messrs Upson's for the use of the shop as a receiving depot, and to the 1st Seven Kings Boy Scout's for kindly conveying the goods to the hospital – no mean undertaking, looking to the total weight, well over half a ton.
>
> Should there be any who inadvertently overlooked this even, goods can still be received at 51, Stanhope-gardens, Ilford. The money received, which amounted to nearly £10, has been spent on purchasing goods wholesale, and is included in the total number of pounds given.

Tragedy hit the Dr and Mrs King Houchin on Good Friday 1918.

> The memorial notice read "HOUCHIN.-In unfading memory of darling Vi, eldest daughter of Dr and Mrs King Houchin, who passed to her rest so suddenly on Good Friday, 1918.[82]

---

[82] 30 March 1923 - Eastern Counties News

Also, in April 1918 another member of the Ilford Division was killed in action - Henry Shenton. He had been present, with the Division, at the 1912 Royal Review.

The Commonwealth War Grave Commission details are as follows -

> In Memory of Private HENRY SHENTON Service Number: 30216 10th Bn., East Yorkshire Regiment who died on 12 April 1918 Age 29 Son of Joseph Thomas and Isabella Shenton, of 57, Argyle Rd., Ilford; husband of Kathleen Lily Shenton, of 14, Bathurst Rd., Ilford, Essex. Remembered with Honour PLOEGSTEERT MEMORIAL Panel 4.

Fundraising was also to the fore and the Divisions fundraising concert was held in October, 1918. *The Eastern Counties Newspaper* dated 18 October, 1918 reported the following –

> The concert in aid of the funds of the No. 46 (Ilford) Division of the St John Ambulance Brigade realised a profit of £50. 0s. 0 ½d. The £50 has been duly credited to the fund, the balance being divided in equal proportions and presented to the organisers as a souvenir of the occasion.

The very next paragraph mentioned the opening of the Valentines Mansion as a Military Hospital. It read

> The formal opening of the Valentines Mansion as a Military Hospital is to take place of Saturday afternoon, October 26th, by Lieut-General Sir Francis Lloyd. This is in connection with the splendid effort of the Masons to provide funds for furnishing the wards. Masonic ritual will be observed. Outstanding subscriptions and donations should be sent in without delay, either to Mr W. Hare, the treasurer, at the bank, High-road or to Councillor J. Lowe, hon. secretary. "Edgebaston", Belfour-road, Ilford".

In June 1918 the District Order Reported on an Air Raid Casualty. The report read –

> The Deputy Commissioner announces with deep regret that Private White, of the No. 4 Division whilst preparing to proceed on air raid duty, was killed together with his wife, by a bomb from hostile aircraft on May 19th, 1918. The funeral took place on the following Wednesday, and was attended by an escort form the Division, the special permission having been obtained from General Sir Francis Lloyd that the coffin should be draped in the Union Jack.
>
> Air Raids
>
> Reports have been received from various Divisions showing that members of the Brigade did excellent service in each part of London where bombs fell on the occasion of the air raids on Whit Sunday, May 19th.

J.R.F.A Rymer, Jim, certainly did not have an easy time whilst serving in Basra, in modern day Iraq and located on the Shatt al-Arab. On the 17 June 1918 he was in the care of the RAMC and was operated on for "Scraping sinus in the abdominal wall". The anaesthetic used was "C&E" Chloroform and Either. The Anaesthetist was Lt McCormick and the Surgeon was Lt McDonal.

British Armed Forces Medical WWI Soldiers Medical Records - Find My Past website accessed 20 June 2022

It appears that Jim survived the operation, however, two months later he was ill again. *The Recorder* dated 16 August 1918 reported the following news

> Mr Jim Rymer (Eldest son of Mr F. J. Rymer, of 8 Belmont-road), has many friends in, Ilford, and these will be sorry to hear that he is down with dysentery in a hospital in Basra, Mesopotamia. He is very cheerful, and the last news of him was favourable. Mr Rymer, Sent., is a great worker at the High-road Congregational Church, and a prominently connected with the I.M.M. As young Jim Rymer has many chums, in the town, some of them may perhaps like to send the boy a word of cheer, and so we give his address, viz., Sergt J. F. Rymer, 9874, R.A.M.C., Indian Expeditionary Force D., 33rd B.G. Hospital. C.o Casualties, Basra, Mesopotamia.

Further information on WWI appeared in 1931 when the Ilford Division published a leaflet to mark the Order of St John Centenary it included the following comment –

> Of the original members, 31 went on active service in the Great War, two were killed in action, several missing and not heard of since, one gaining Military Medal. Those not going overseas, being for various reasons exempt, carried on handling a great number of convoys of wounded (totalling several thousands of cases) between London and Colchester, at all hours, many times throughout the night, as well as being on duty for air raids, all without pay, but bearing their own expenses.

Chapter Eleven - VAD Records and Post War Events

The British Red Cross hold the records of the Voluntary Aid Detachments from WWI. The following information has been extracted from them with additional material incorporated that has been found.

Williams Magnus's record shows service from May 1915 within the Essex 27 Detachment. He was Commandant of the Oakwood VAD Hospital in Chigwell, Essex. Additional information on his service card records "Organised whole of Ambulance Transport in connection with Ilford Emergency Hospital[83], also assisted in connection with Oakwood Red Cross Hospital, Chigwell - a total of 84 convoys - and 1500 soldiers.

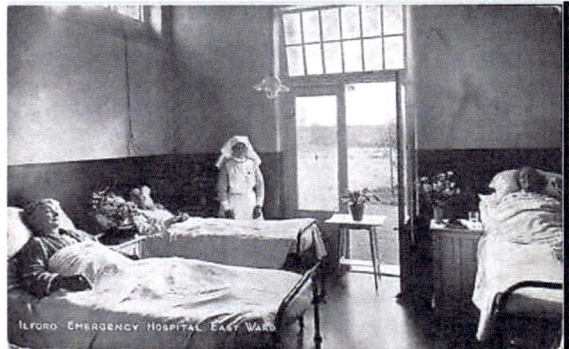

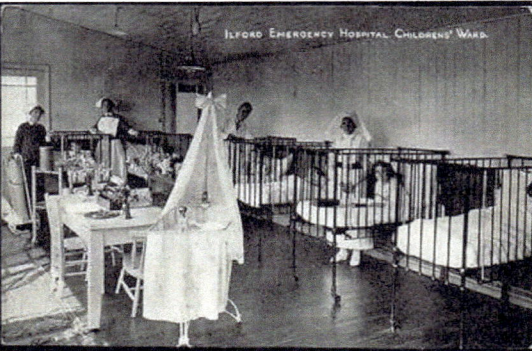

Ilford Emergency Hospital, East Ward.   Ilford Emergency Hospital, Children's Ward.

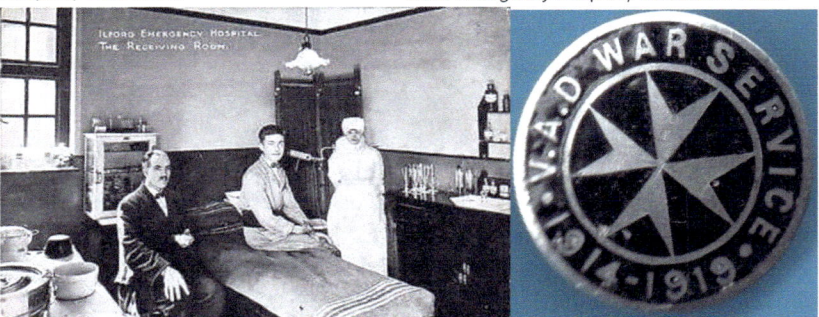

Ilford Emergency Hospital, Receiving Room and St John VAD 1914-1919 Badge

In addition, 44 journeys were arranged to various London & provincial Hospitals with transfer cases, over 100 wounded were transferred involving journeys varying from 10 to 110 miles. Personally, driven car 6000 miles. - Air Raid duties of detachment arranged also"

His services were recognised with a 'B' Mention in Despatches (N.B. – A List for publication in the Press only, and will not be gazetted).
The names of the undermentioned have been brought to the notice of the Secretary of State for War by the Chairman of the British Red Cross Society and Order of St John in England for valuable general Red Cross service during the War: -
England & Wales -Essex

A Communique Issued by the "War Office – 21st April, 1920.
Magnus, Mr W. R., Ilford

---

[83] Ilford Emergency Hospital. This hospital, funded by local charities, was opened in 1912. It became a military hospital in May 1915 with 56 beds and provided intensive care for wounded troops until March 1919. The hospital buildings later became part of the King George Hospital, Eastern Avenue, opened in 1931.

Mrs Maud Beatrice Magnus's record is equally impressive: -
Maud's record shows service from 3 May 1915 within the Essex 114 Detachment. She was Commandant of Valentines Mansions Hospital[84], Ilford. Additional Information on her service card records.

Equipped first 20 beds for Military. Organised all the Voluntary Nursing Staff working at Ilford Emergency Hospital, & did a considerable amount of night and day duty myself, 9106 hours. From July 1918. Prepared Valentines Mansions, Ilford for Military & had sole charge of same until demobilised March 1919. Served for over a year on the Executive Committee of the Essex Branch, British Red Cross Society and the Order of St John of Jerusalem in England.

Her services were recognised with a 'B' Mention in Despatches (N.B. – A List for publication in the Press only, and will not be gazetted).
The names of the undermentioned have been brought to the notice of the Secretary of State for War by the Chairman of the British Red Cross Society and Order of St John in England for valuable services rendered in the connection with the establishment organisation and maintenance of Hospitals:-
First mention in a Communique Issued by the War Office – 12th January 1918.
Second mention in a Communique Issued by the War Office – 8th April 1919.

Magnus, Mrs M. Ilford

Dr Edmund King Houchin's record
Name	Edmund King Houchin
Address	Cranbrook Road, Ilford
County	Essex
Service from:	05/1915
Rank at engagement:	Medical Offr.
Date of engagement:	05/1915
Particulars of duties:	Stood by for Air Raid duties & assisted 6 convoys of wounded
Commission:	Essex 27

A record is also on file for Edmund's son, Mr Victor S Houchin who served in the VAD, serving as a Dentist. [85]

---

[84] By 1912 this time the Council had already purchased even more of the parkland and then in 1912 bought the remaining 37 acres and the Mansion. The council were unsure what to do with the house once they had bough itt. The farm buildings and stables just north of the house were demolished to make way for tennis courts and the house was used to accommodate Belgium refugees during the 'Great War'. It was also used as a hospital as the conflict progressed. In 1925 the Council's Public Health department moved into the Mansion on a "temporary" basis but its occupation of the house lasted 40 years. BBC web page accessed 14 January, 2022
https://www.bbc.co.uk/london/content/articles/2008/10/23/redbridge_valentinesmansion_feature.shtml

[85] Red Cross Record for Victor S. Houchin, LDS.,DDS., Etc. 45 High Street, Orwell, Burland Road, Brentwood. Served from 11/1914 to 03/1919 Coombe Lodge, Great Warley. Dentist at Army rates for first year then nil. Paid several visits to the Hospital to extract teeth etc. & patients visited him at his house whenever required. Coombe Lodge Primary Auxiliary Military Hospital Mr Houchin did valuable work, assisted at several facial operations, besides extracting teeth & prescribing for toothache.

Valentines Mansion Correspondence

An exchange of correspondence took place between 12 June 1918 and 15 August 1918 which related to No 15 Ilford Nursing Division (Voluntary Aid Detachment Essex114) taking over the running of Valentines Mansion as an Auxiliary Hospital to the Ilford Emergency Hospital.

This information is held in the archives at the Museum of the Order of St John and is reproduced at Appendix No 9 courtesy of the of the Museum which holds the copyright.

Nursing Officer Appointments

Promotions in No 15 Ilford Nursing Division were approved by the Chief Commissioner and promulgated in District Orders of November 1919.

> Mrs Mary Waldron to be Nursing Officer, 13.11.19. Miss Annie Jessie Rymer to be Nursing Officer. 14.11.19. Nursing Officer Miss A. H. Law resigned her appointment, 14.08.19.

Mrs Maud B Magnus appointed Serving Sister of the Order

On 20 February 1920 Mrs Maud B Magnus (Ilford Div. and VAD) was appointed a Serving Sister of the Order of St John.

William Magnus and the Great Eastern Railway

During the First World War Magnus was selected to undertake important duties in connection with a special organisation which was set up at Liverpool Street, and for a lengthy period he acted, alternately with another, as acting night superintendent.

It should be borne in mind during this period of the increased demand on the Railway, with increased freight, troop trains and ambulance train movements.

The Annual General Meeting of the Great Eastern Railway[86] report for 1918 contained the following details covering 1917. Whilst not mentioned by name it is safe to assume that William Magnus and his team were directly responsible for this effort. The report read: -

> Since the commencement of the war they had provided on the Great Eastern Railway over 10,000 special trains for the conveyance of troops. Last year the number of military special trains run exceeded 2,000, and the traffic conveyed included approximately 16,000 officers, 1 1/4 million men, 33,000 horses, about 6,000 military vehicles of different descriptions, including guns, 10,000 cycles, and over 8,000 tons of baggage. In addition, last year over 4,000 special trains, principally of a merchandise character, were run for the purpose of conveying Government traffic of different descriptions, largely consisting of military horses, baggage, meat and other stores. The number of ambulance trains passing over the system during year 1917 was 289, conveying 45,000 patients. Considering the many difficulties to be contended with, the general traffic working for the year 1917 was very satisfactory.

---

[86] Great Eastern Railway Magazine. Volume 8 March 1918 Page No 46

A comparative statement as to the punctuality of passenger trains running into Liverpool Street Station showed that whereas in 1916, 74.12 per cent, of the trains arrived not more than 2 minutes late, in the year 1917, whilst working under even worse conditions than in 1916, the percentage had improved to 83.29.

The report also stated that -

Since the commencement of the war they had completed at Stratford seven ambulance trains and have another one under construction.

Perhaps some of William Magnus's work on traffic movements is reflected in the following extract from 1919 Great Eastern Railway Report, particularly that referring to the "*Great War*". It also reflects on their role in previous conflict. The section of the report referred to is headed "*Ambulance Aid*". It continues -

Two of the company's restaurant cars, with staff completed, were running on ambulance trains. Started at Stratford in 1879, the Great Eastern Ambulance Corps fulfilled an extremely useful function. Thirteen G. E. Ambulance men volunteered for the South African War, and one went on ambulance duty to the Balkans in 1912. The Great War stimulated still further the interest of the employees in the movement, and down to the end of 1918 the number of occasions on which first aid was available during big movements was 2,918, and the cases dealt with included 220 officers and soldiers, 143 of the company's servants, seven other persons and one horse. The Ambulance men also assisted in detraining from ambulance trains of wounded soldiers and sailors at many places on the company's system.

His efforts were rewarded. *The London Gazette* Birthday Honours list of 1918 shows that William Robert Magnus — Chief of the Train Control Section, Great Eastern Railway was awarded an MBE, which was conferred on him by HM the King in person.

15 June 1918 the *Railway News* published the honours list, and showed the many railway employees. It is described as the Order of the British Empire. Railwaymen Second List. The award on an MBE to Magnus is recorded as follows: -

Magnus. Wm. Robert. Esq., Chief of the Train Control Section. G.E.R.

William Robert Magnus – Photograph Credit: *The Great Eastern Railway Magazine*

Chapter Twelve - Ilford Emergency Hospital

The Recorder of 5 March 1920 carried a lengthy report on the Annual Meeting of the Ilford Emergency Hospital. It is worth recording this report in full as it deals with Voluntary Aid Detachments and has several mentions of the Magnus family.

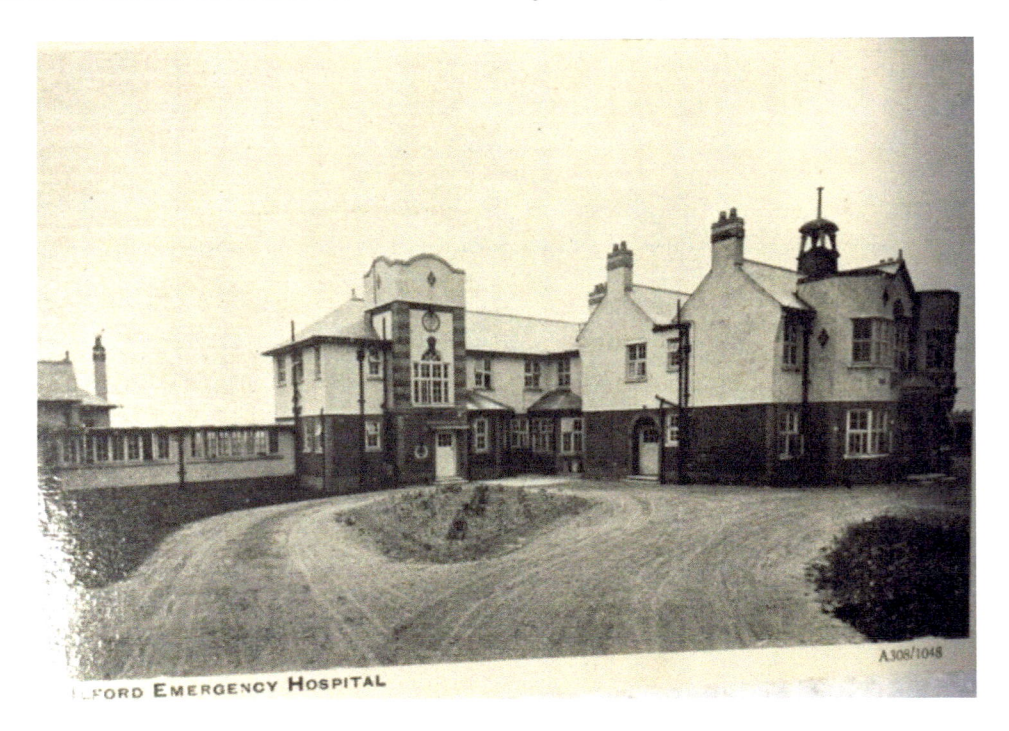

C 1919 Postcard of Ilford Emergency Hospital
Photograph published by Time News and book Supply Seven Kings

Annual Meeting and Presentations for 1919 and 1920. These reports are included in detail as they show they key role played by St John Ambulance and the VADs in the hospital's first years. They also give insight into the social history during these formative years.

The Recorder dated the 5 March 1920 reported on the Ilford Emergency Hospital Annual Meeting and a Presentation.

> The annual general meeting of the Ilford Emergency Hospital was held on Friday evening, in one of the halls associated with the High-road Congregational Church. Sir Peter Griggs, M.P., chairman of the Board of Governors, presiding. There was a crowded attendance. The hon. secretary, Mr G. J. Maggs, announced letters regretting inability to attend from Mr W. Page, Miss J. Dar[ling] – latter gentlemen being absent on the Continent.
>
> The Annual Report.
>
> The report of the Governors for 1919. The report expressed the Governors sincere thanks and congratulation to the Hospital Saturday Committee, and said it was extremely gratifying to know that as a result of their splendid work the hospital funds would ultimately be enriched by a sum of £2,075.
> The governors again beg to place on record their sincere thanks to the Honorary Consulting Staff and x-ray operator for their valuable assistance, and desire to acknowledge the debt due to those of our local practitioners who have formed the Honorary Medical Staff. They are also deeply indebted to the Ilford Ambulance division of the St John Ambulance Brigade, Essex

V.A.D. No. 114 (Lady Superintendent and Commandant, Mrs Magnus), and the V.A.D. Essex 130, British Red Cross (commandant Mrs E. Mary Hewitt), who have gratuitously rendered increased service to military wards; also, to the members of the Ilford Ambulance Division, Essex, V.A.D., No 27 (superintendent and commandant. Mr W. R. Magnus, ambulance officers, M. G. Matthews and F. G. Grayson) for their assistance at all times in connection with the transport of the sick and wounded.

The number of patients admitted during the year was 525, being made up as follows: Civilian 380, Military 132, pensioners 13. Although the hospital's work for our soldiers did not stop with the armistice, every week a steadily increasing number of war pensioners are treated, 3,311 treatments having been given during the year.

The hospital was closed for treatment of Military on March 17th last, and from May, 1915 to the date previously mentioned, 1,429 cases had been admitted, and the governors have been pleased to receive the thanks of the officer commanding, General Military Hospital, Colchester, "for the very excellent work that has been carried out at your hospital." With the release of the beds reserved for the military, attention was then directed to re-arranging the wards and increasing the number of beds available for the civilian population of Ilford, with the result that there is now accommodation for 42 patients, as against 18 last year.

With increased wages, and the enormous rise in the cost of living, the average cost per patient per week shows an increase, being £2 15s 4 ½d against £1 18s 2 ¾d.

Despite the heavier expenses, although the income and expenditure account show an adverse balance of £650 8s. 11d., there is a set off against this of £1,600 on deposit, and an anticipated balance of £1,826. 16s from the Hospital Saturday Committee. The governors therefore beg to congratulate the members, subscribers, and friends on this usefulness of the hospital, records its thankfulness to all who have made such a result possible.

The income derived from private and public wards shows a marked increase, which may be attributed to the increase in the number of patients, 380, as compared with 150 in 1918, whilst the receipts for treatment have increased with the number of treatments.

The Sunday School Cot, for which the Ilford Auxiliary of Sunday School Union generously provided £30 per annum, has been in considerable demand throughout the year.

The Congregational collections have excelled, as also the collecting boxes, while the results from the special appeal are very gratifying and commendable to the Collecting Committee and its hon. secretary, Mr W. Brazier Martin.

The efforts of Mrs Hatcher in organising "Alexandra Day" in Ilford resulted in the receipt of £100 from the "Alexandra Day" Committee.

Exceptional sources of revenue have proved of the utmost help, for instance, the "Harold Wadham" Memorial £260, Special Constabulary £212. 0s 11d., the Valentines Masonic Fund £64 1s 11d. Cots have been named in respect of the first two items, and a tablet relating thereto affixed to the wall of the Ingleby Ward. The board of Governors, in view of the excellent support derived from the Masonic Fund propose to pursue the same course to perpetuate their good work. Under the will of H. J. Stone, Esq., late of Geyshafin Lodge, High Road, Ilford, a legacy of £100, free of duty, has been left to the hospital.

Part of the equipment and furniture of Valentines Mansion was transferred for use at Newbury Park, while the superfluous portion was disposed of by sale to hospital workers, etc.

The governors desire to place on record their sincere thanks to Lady Griggs for presiding on the fifth anniversary of the Pound Day, which took place on December 18th, this being the first occasion of its being held at the hospital; thanks are due to the matron and nursing staff for the arrangements made and results attained.

The Board of Governors have under consideration plans for enlarging the hospital accommodation of 80 patients, and it is hoped with the settlement of the preliminaries, to commence building in the near future. The purchase of a further piece of land adjoining the hospital grounds in Hatch-lane has been made, and the governors desire to place on record their grateful thanks to the hon. solicitor. Mr H. Foden Pattinson for having so ably conducted and carried out the negotiations.

The governors are pleased to record that many gifts of vegetable seeds and plants have been received, also that the weekly gifts of goods, periodicals, etc., have been well maintained, and they tender their sincere thanks to the donors thereof. They also desire to thank those who have provided entertainments at the hospital or elsewhere, especially to Miss Hiles and friends who have rendered faithful service in this direction since 1915. Also, to the matron, the sisters, and all the staff for their loyal co-operation in carrying out the arduous work performed during the year with much success.

H.M. the King invested the matron (Miss L. E. Green) with the Royal Red Cross on April 12th, 1919, and the honour thus conferred reflects great credit on her personal work and standing of the hospital.

Matron Miss L. E. Green

Since the closing of the year the hospital has sustained a very severe loss by the death of one its oldest worker and supporters, Mr H. Gilbey. The work was dear to his heart, and it is impossible to state how much he will be missed.

In conclusion the Board of Governors look forward with pleasure to the coming year, with the remembrance that "The smallest act of charity shall stand us in good stead."

The Governors retiring by rotation are Sir John H Bethell, M,P., Miss Darling. Messrs W. Taylor, T. Gibson, T. A. Richardson, and two vacancies by the retirement of Mr Magnus and the decease of Mr Gilbey.

The Medical Committee's report showed that 380 civilians, 132 soldiers, and 13 pensioners were treated as in-patients during the years. Besides these 390 casualties were attended to without admission, 194 cases examined by the x-rays, and pensioners aggregated about 3,311 attendances.

The Chairman moved the adoption of the report and accounts, and said that economy had been considered as far as possible, prices having gone up for food and everything else, and he thought they might congratulate themselves upon the present position. Expressing the opinion that the hospital site buildings and equipment could not be replaced under a cost of £10,000. Sir Peter emphasised the need of the proposed additions, and the difficulty of providing them, in view of the disclosures as to the cost of the new building. The plans had been approved, and the governors hoped before long to make a start. Having warmly acknowledged the handsome results of the Carnival Committees work, which had been a great encourage to the governors, Sir Peter said that with perhaps one or two exceptions, all the governors wished the hospital to continue on the present voluntary basis, and not placed upon the rates to become a burden to the town. (Applause.)

Mr Hawkins seconded the adoption, and the hon. secretary, in reply to criticisms by Dr. Drought, as to the spelling of certain technical terms in the report of the Medical Committee explained that they were simply printers' errors. Questions by others gentlemen present were satisfactorily answered, and the report and accounts were adopted.

Election of Governors
Five retiring governors were re-elected (there being no other nominations), viz., Sir John Bethell, Miss Darling, Mr W Taylor, Mr T. Gibson, and Mr T. A. Richardson. In place of the late Herbert Gilbey and Mr W. R. Magnus (retired), Mr John Harris and Mr Sidney A. Hatcher were elected. The three governors representing the Ilford Medical Society were re-appointed, viz., Doctors Coleman, O. E. Powell, and J. E. Price Watts.

Thanks
Mr Magnus moved and Mr Brazier Martin seconded a vote of thanks to the honorary consulting staff, the hon medical officers and the hon. x-ray operator, Mr B. V. Storr. This was seconded and unanimously agreed.

Dr J. Ross Steen, in moving a vote of thanks to the matron, sister, and staff, said the matron had been with them ever since the hospital was opened, and he did not think by any possibility they could have better. (Applause.) She had made the hospital a success in every way, and soldiers who had been treated there testified that in no hospital where they had been previously, either abroad or in this country, had they been made to feel so happy and comfortable as in the Ilford Hospital. (Applause.) Dr Steen testified that the new sister was doing very well indeed, as also were the nursing staff. It was a great credit to the matron. That she had been able to secure a supply of nurses, in view of the great shortage of nurses, and of the fact that the salaries offered none too high. (Hear, hear.)

Mr E. R. Fyson, in seconding, emphasised the points made by Dr Steen, and said that no matter what might be the shortcomings of the governors, the matron, sister, nursing staff and the medical staff did their duty exceedingly well, and were the backbone of the hospital. Having quoted the figures given in the report of the medical committee to show the immense amount of work that had been done, Mr Fyson said it was part of the policy of the governors to treat the nurses a little better than they were dealt with in some hospitals. Nurses were wretchedly paid –(Hear, hear) – and the profession ought to be recognised and placed on a much more generous lines that it was a present. It was worthy of considerably better pay and better conditions. (Hear, hear.) The governors had given their nurses one day off in seven, and the fact was commented upon in one of the hospital journals, and Ilford was complimented upon having taken the lead in this matter. He hoped that the policy would extend to other hospitals. (applause.) The resolution was carried.

The chairman alluded to the splendid work of the Hospital Saturday Committee, which raised, last year, a net sum of £2673. That represented a vast amount of work and energy, and the committee deserved the congratulations of the governors and support of the hospital. (Applause.) He moved a hearty vote of thanks to the committee.

Councillor F. D. Smith, C.C., in seconding, said that but for the Hospital Saturday Committee there would be no hospital to-day. He eulogised the committee for the splendid contributions of the past, and expressed the hope that they would reach the figure of £3,000 this year. (Laughter and applause.)

Mr J. E. Holloway, organiser for South Hainault, acknowledged the vote at the suggestion of Mr Fyson, who pointed out that the ward was at the top of the collection of over £500.

Mr Merchant, organiser for Loxford complimented South Hainault upon having beaten Loxford this year. Replies were also made by Mr Hawkins (Park Ward), and Mr J. Harris (Cranbrook), and the letter mentioned that last year Cranbrook reached its highest total, and he felt convinced they would near £500 this year.

Mr A. W. Hare proposed a vote of thanks to the auditor, Mr R. Barlow Tyler, who had carried out the duties faithfully and well for a good number of years. (Applause.) Mr Hall seconded the resolution, which was supported by Mr Brazier Martin, and carried.

Mr L. J. Burke moved a vote of thanks to the secretary, Mr G. J. Maggs, expressing high admiration for his conscientious, enthusiastic, and systematic services. He did as much good work the hospital as would be done by a competent secretary who was receiving a good salary. (Applause.)

Mr Ainsworth seconded, and described with pleasure the hearty way in which Mr Maggs took up the position of secretary when Mr Hare resigned, and also alluded to improvements he had been the means of bringing about at the hospital.

The Chairman warmly endorsed these compliments, and the vote was carried with applause.

Mr Maggs, with characteristic modesty, replied, speaking of the pleasure with which he acted as organiser for four years of the Seven Kings Ward, and adding that he had been working for the hospital from its inception, and had been pleased to do so, not for charity but in the scared cause of humanity. (Applause.)

At the call of the chairman a hearty clap was given for Mrs Maggs.

Presentation to Mrs Magnus. The chairman mentioned that Mrs Magnus had done magnificent work for the hospital, and it was proposed to show the appreciation of the governors and subscribers by making her a small present of an illuminated address and a gold watch. The address, which was nicely lettered and framed, read:

"Presented to Mrs Maud Magnus, lady superintendent and commandant of the Essex V.A.D. 114, together with a gold watch, as a token of our esteem from the Board of Governors and subscribers, for services rendered with great devotion and fidelity from May, 1916 to April 1919."

On coming to the table to receive the gifts, Mrs Magnus was loudly cheered, and the chairman observed that Mr Magnus ought to have come forward as well, for he had done good work in the past, which that all appreciated. (Hear, hear.)

Addressing the lady, the chairman said they were delighted to do honour to whom honour was due. She had won golden opinions from all associated with the hospital by her service, and by her V.A.D. work. He then handed her the gifts, amid enthusiastic applause.

Mrs Magnus said she accepted the gifts not only for what she had done, but for what her loyal members had done. (Applause.) How could she have gone on without the support of those members. Few in the room had any idea what this voluntary work at the hospital meant. Her part was to ask the members to do it, and they did it cheerfully, turning out at 7.30 in the morning or at 8.30 in the evening for night duty, often going through Lay-street with shrapnel bursting over-head and watching all night with sisters and nurses at the hospital during air raids. The gifts would remind her of the past. The work was first started, not to help the hospital, but with the intention of helping the country. (Applause.) She was glad that their efforts also helped the governors of the hospital in time of stress, when it was badly needed. Mrs Magnus closed by thanking Sir Peter and the governors, and coupling with it thanks to her members who worked so loyally with her. (Applause.)

Thanks to the Chairman.
Councillor Lowe moved a vote of thanks to the chairman, not alone for presiding at this meeting, but for all his past service to the hospital. (Applause.) No word of his could adequately express all that he desired to convey of the public appreciation of what Sir Peter Griggs had done for the hospital, and for the town. When the speaker had come to Ilford, 29 years ago, Sir Peter's work thrust it-self upon him, his development of an estate that did credit to the town – and his love for Ilford itself. (Applause.) He alluded to the fountains and other memorials of Sir Peter's generosity in the public parks; to his establishment of soup kitchens for the poor during those dark days of distress and unemployment, and his services to education, and other causes in the town's municipal life. Regretting Sir Peter's health had not been good during the past six months, the speaker hoped for his recovery, and that he and Lady Griggs might be able to take a journey round the world. (Applause.)

Mr Charles Smith seconded in a couple of sentences, heartily endorsing the compliments paid by the mover, and the motion was put by Mr Fyson, and carried with acclamation.

The chairman returned thanks, mentioning that he had worked in Ilford between 20 and 30 years, and for nearly the whole time had worked 18 hours a day. As to his public work, he felt he had only done his duty. Alluding to his indifferent health, Sir Peter said he would die in harness, but he was not one of those who could stand down and look on, and do nothing, and so he had got the run down, as was the case a year ago, when he took a rest and rallied again. The speaker enlarged upon the strenuous character of his Parliamentary Work, combined with county and local work, and showed how impossible it was for him to attend all meetings and functions promoted by his constituents with the freedom of his old days before his election as a member for the borough. Concluding, Sir Peter said he thought he might fairly claim that he had done his full share of the town's work for many years. (Applause.)
On the motion of Mr Ainsworth, seconded by Mr C. Smith, a hearty vote of thanks was accorded for the free use of the room.

Meeting of Governors
Following the annual meeting, the governors assembled for the appointment of officer. Sir Peter Griggs, M.P., was unanimously re-elected chairman, and on his nomination, Sir John Bethell. Bart., M.P., was with equal unanimity re-elected vice-chairman. To preside in the absence of these gentlemen, on Parliamentary and other business, Mr E. R. Fyson was re-elected deputy-chairman. There was a general desire to elect Dr Coleman and Mr A. W. Hare (manager Barclay's Bank, High-road, Ilford) as joint hon. treasurers, but as the article provided for election of "a treasurer" it was held that two gentlemen could not legally be appointed to office. In the result, owing to the undoubted convenience of appointed the bank manager to the position, Mr Hare was unanimously elected Hon. treasurer. Mr J. G. Maggs by acclamation was re-elected hon. secretary. And the next meeting of the governors, when the various committees will be appointed was fixed for Saturday afternoon, March 27th, at the hospital.

At the close of the War the Commissioners of the City and Metropolitan Police and the Secretary of the London County Council tendered their grateful thanks for this service on the part of No. I District, while similar expressions of appreciation were received by the Deputy Commissioners in charge of the other Districts concerned. Also, many Divisions presented their members with illuminated Air-Raid Certificates which were produced by the proprietors of the journal First Aid and provided an interesting souvenir of many hundreds of hours' voluntary service. [87]

Fundraising in 1920

"The Mutual Friendly Aid Society" was the headline of an article in *The Recorder* dated 26 March 1920, recorded

> A boxing entertainment, in aid of the hospitals of London, is to take place in the Queens Hall, People's Palace, Mile End, E., on Wednesday, April 7th, under the direction of the Mutual Friendly Aid Society.
>
> This society had recently contributed £21 to the Ilford Emergency Hospital, £21 to the Ilford War Memorial, and £5. 5s to the Ilford St John Ambulance, and nearly £2,000 to different hospitals in London during the past three months. Tickets for the boxing entertainment are obtainable from the president, Mr Chas. Mead, 117, Lansdowne-road, Seven Kings or from the secretary, Mr, W. Prior, 42 Hazeldene-road, Goodmayes."

The Recorder dated 26 March 1920

> "Ilford St John Ambulance and Nursing Division. Sale of Work Opened by Lady Warwick – In aid of the funds of the St John Ambulance Brigade (Ilford division) there was a sale of work in the Baptist Lecture Hall., Cranbrook-road, Ilford on Friday and Saturday, under the personal supervision of Supt. W. R. Magnus (ambulance division), and Lady Supt. Mrs Magnus (nursing division), assisted by members of sections of the local brigade The object of the sale was to raise funds to carry on the work of the division in the district; to keep in practice a body of men and women, ready at all times to attend any public function to render first aid in cases of accident or sudden illness, and to provide the necessary dressings and nursing requisites for voluntary work amongst the sick poor of the district.
>
> The ambulance division was formed in 1903, as a result of first aid and home nursing classes arranged under the auspices of the Ilford Men's Meeting. From that year on it has carried on its humanitarian work by some of its members being present at practically every function in the Ilford district or in London, where their services were likely to be appreciated. Nor have its services been confined to these efforts. At the outbreak of the great war nearly half of their members volunteered for service with the colours, and since then the strength of the division has been augmented, and from time to time others have been transferred to regular army and navy. In all 23 members served in the war, and of this number one member paid the greatest sacrifice, another was awarded the meritorious service medal, whilst another was mentioned in despatches. In nearly all other cases promotion was obtained while serving with the forces. Nor is this the only conspicuous service the Ilford division rendered during the war, for in May, 1915, when the Ilford Emergency Hospital, was first used for wounded soldiers, the members undertook the whole of the transport work in connection therewith, and dealt with about 1,300 cases, in addition to which assistance was also rendered to the Oakwood Red

---

[87] Fletcher, N.C. The St John Ambulance Association: Annals of the Ambulance Department. (Hertford: Stephen Austin & Sons, Ltd. 1949), Page No 128

Cross Hospital at Chigwell, and during the whole of this period the civil work was also efficiently continued.

The Ilford nursing division has a history no less distinguished since its establishment in 1911. When, during the war, the governors of the Emergency offered the War Office a portion of the building, the division tendered its services, and was mobilised as a voluntary aid detachment under the Territorial Forces Association.

When the Ilford Urban Council granted use of Valentines Mansion as an annexe military hospital to the Emergency Hospital, Mrs M. B. Magnus and her staff took charge, and the whole of the nursing duties were carried out by the members of her division, with the exception of those of the trained sister and trained night and day nurses, the whole of their services being voluntary. From May, 1915 to March 1919, the members of the division worked no less than 75,638 hours.

The building in which the sale of work was held was beautifully decorated for the occasion, and heavily-laden stalls were artistically arranged and were in charge of the following ladies:-
Needle-work (No. 1),   Lady Supt. Mrs Magnus assisted by nursing sisters Miss Stenning and Miss Baker, Mrs Drayson, Mrs G. W. Smith, and Mrs Swinchat.
Needle work (No. 2),   nursing officer. Mrs Waldon, assisted by nursing sisters Mrs Rymer and Mrs Bernard, Mrs Andrews and Mrs Friedrichsen.
Needle work (No. 3)   nursing sister Miss Robinson, assisted by nursing sisters Miss Erwood, Mrs King, and Mrs Robinson.
Needle work (No.4)   nursing sister Miss E. Smith, assisted nursing sisters Miss Joy and Miss Goodwin, Mrs Webb and Miss Gregory.
Pottery stall, nursing sister Miss Haslam, assisted by Miss Cunningham, with Mrs A. V. Pitcher, and Miss Wetton.
Sweet and Cake stall, nursing sister Miss White, assisted by nursing sister Miss Avery, and Mrs F. E. White.
White Elephant and bookstall, Nursing office Miss Rymer, assisted by nursing sisters Miss Jenks, Mrs Long. and Mrs Betty Haddon.
Household Stall, nursing sister Miss Lawson assisted by Miss Vaughan and Miss Rowe, with Mrs Warner and Miss J. Lawson.
Flower and Fruit Stall, nursing sister Miss Skinner, assisted by nursing sisters Miss Cunningham, and Mrs Luck, and Mrs Skinner.
Refreshments, nursing sister Miss Symonds, assisted by nursing sister Miss Willmott and Miss Glanville, Miss Oxer, and Mrs Pratt, Miss. W Symons and Miss Gibson.
There was a lucky well under the care of Miss Magnus, Miss D. Rymer, Miss Waldron. Mr Reg. Ostime, magical entertainment and ventriloquist, among the slide shows, presented his popular entertainment each evening with his partner "Ginger" Wilkins.

The opening ceremony, on Friday afternoon, was performed by the Countess of Warwick, in the presence of a large gathering. Major-Gen. Sir H. W. Thornton, K.B.E., had been announced to preside at the interesting ceremony, but at the last moment he was summoned from town on important and imperative business, and asked Mr S. A. Parnwell (assistant general manager of the Great Eastern Railway) to occupy his position. In opening the proceedings, he paid high tribute to the useful work carried on by the Ilford Ambulance and Nursing Division of the St John Ambulance Association, and paid a high tribute to Mr and Mrs Magnus, and he (the speaker) spoke feelingly, inasmuch as that gentlemen had rendered him personal service, for which he would be ever feel grateful. The speaker also spoke of the demands the Ilford Division had upon the public, and expressed a hope that they would thoroughly appreciate on the present occasion, that Mr and Mrs Magnus would realise their fullest expectation. (Applause.)

Countess Warwick[88], rising to pronounce the sale open, was received with hearty cheers. She thanked Mr and Mrs Magnus for giving her the opportunity of being present, and proceeded to speak of the admirable work they were carrying on in the district. They were old friends of hers, she added, and nothing she knew could give her greater pleasure than being able to support them in their great and beneficent work, (Hear, hear.) She knew that in Ilford their work was enthusiastically carried on, and she could testify to the value of their labours, and all those associated with them during the war. (Hear, hear.) The war having passed, it was necessary to keep up their tradition for usefulness, and benefit from the experience gained in during that terrible time. Referring more particularly to the nursing division, her ladyship said it becomes every women to know something of nursing and hygiene, especially regards children. All that tended to improve and strengthen and improve the race, and it benefits would reflect in future generations. (Hear, hear.) There was always with us, she continued, the continuous presence also of illness and disease, but much could be combated by such institutions as this. The work that Ilford had done in the respect was very encouraging. And she felt certain that efforts that were being made that day to enable the ambulance and nursing local divisions to be better equipped for the work that lay before them would have a permanent and beneficial effect upon the future. Nobody knew how soon they may need such service as this institution could render, and it was absolutely essential that it should be thoroughly equipped so that its efficiency should always be of the highest. Her ladyship then declared the sale open, amidst the plaudits of her hearers.

Mrs Magnus proposed a vote of thanks to the Countess for her presence and hopeful words of encouragement. This was briefly seconded by Mr Magnus and carried with acclamation.

On the motion of Colonel A. J. Challis, a vote of thanks was accorded the chairman for presiding. Before the commencement of "business" the result of a home baking competition was announced as follows; 1 Miss. M. A. Morgan; 2 Miss I. B. Lawson: three 3rd prizes Mrs E. M. Swinchat. Mrs E. Lanworth, and Mrs P. King: Certificates, Miss Elsie Eales, Mrs A. Eales and Mrs A. H. Wright.

The opening ceremony on the Saturday afternoon was performed by Lady Perrott, R.R.C.,[89] Col. A. J. Challis presiding. The attendance was good, and business continued brisk until a late hour in the evening.

---

88 Frances Evelyn "Daisy" Greville, Countess of Warwick (*née* Maynard; 10 December 1861 – 26 July 1938) was a British socialite and philanthropist. She established a needlework school and employment scheme in Essex as well as using her ancestral homes to host events and schemes for the benefit of her tenants and workers. Greville was a long-term confidant to the Prince of Wales, who later became King Edward VII. During WWI she became the President of Essex Red Cross and Voluntary Aid Detachments in Essex. She was also said to be referenced in the popular music hall song "Daisy, Daisy", owing to her rather unorthodox conduct.

89 Ethel Lucy (née Hare), Lady Perrott (1875-1939), Royal Red Cross; wife of Sir Herbert Charles Perrott, 1st Bt; daughter of Marcus Hare First Lady Superintendent-in-Chief of the St John Ambulance Brigade. She held this office for 29 years. During her time, she did much to re-organize the nursing service and improve its efficiency. During the First World War she was the key coordinator of St John nurses both at home and in Europe, and she mobilized many nursing staff at short notice. She was made a Dame Grand Cross of the Order of St John in 1928, its highest recognition for voluntary service.

On both days the Grange String Band was in attendance under the leadership of Mr F. T. Kennedy, and played choice selections at intervals. Concerts were also given at frequents intervals each evening.

Lady Ethel Perrott RRC– Superintendent in Chief. St John Ambulance Brigade. This portrait was taken three days after this event.
Photograph by Bassano Ltd 23 March 1920 – Photograph Courtesy NPG (x120383) License 24674 30 April 2022

The case of a strange item being sold for St John Ambulance. *The Birmingham Gazette* on 25 March 1920, reported *"A cigarette made by the Rev. C. Spurgeon many years ago has been sold at Ilford on behalf of St John Ambulance." It is* likely it relates to the above event.

Other events were recorded: William's service was acknowledged, by the Secretary of State for War ("B" Mention in Despatches) along with that of Mrs N Harrop (Manor Park) who was Superintendent of No8 East Ham Nursing Division. This was reported in *The Recorder* of 30 April 1920.

The Great Eastern Railway Magazine, 1920 Volume, Page 87 reported that the Mr F. J. Warner was awarded a War Service Badge for duty with Ilford Division, St John Ambulance Brigade.

The St John Ambulance Brigade Ilford

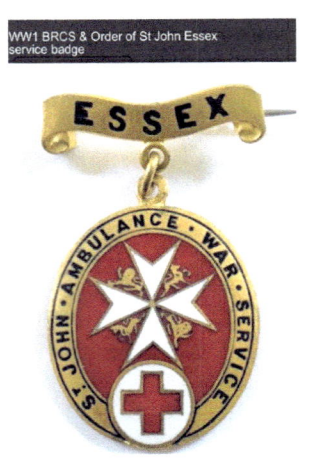

30 July 1920, *The Recorder reported a special award* -

The St. John Ambulance Association.
Dr Drought receives "Special Thanks".

To the Editor of the "recorder."

Sir, - As it may be of interest to many of your readers of your paper who were formally members of the Ilford and Chadwell Heath sections of the Metropolitan Police Special Constabulary, I take this opportunity of stating the Dr P. J. Drought, the surgeon-instructor to the first aid sections, was awarded for service the "Special Thanks" of the Order of St John.

The emblazoned vote of thanks engrossed on vellum has now been received from the Order, and duly presented to Dr Drought. I enclose a copy of the text. –
Yours truly,
H. W. Apling.
Late sub-inspector Metropolitan Special Constabulary (Ilford) and Branch hon. sec. St. John Ambulance Association[90].

Henry W. Apling. c 1920 Photographer Unknown

---

90 Henry W Apling lived at 11 Ruskin Avenue, Manor Park. He was married to Florence (née Wainwright). His occupation was a solicitor's managing clerk, he was also a Freeman of the City of London. In 1904, his family moved to 212 Thorold Road, Ilford. Henry and Florence's first son Stanley Herbert Apling was born on 4 May 1899 in Manor Park. (Stanley's First World War experiences are related in John Barfoot's book, *Over Here and Over There: Ilford's Aerodromes and Airmen in the Great War* (Ian Henry Publications, 1998) Stanley began a life-long career in insurance. Another son, Harry, 1904 -1990. He moved to Norfolk and during WW2 was in the Dereham Home Guard. When the Home Guard stood down he was a Lieutenant. In later life he was regarded as an expert on Corn Mills and published a definitive book on the subject in 1985, It was titled *Norfolk Corn Windmills. Norwich*. ISBN 10: 0950979309 and published by Norfolk Windmills Trust, 1985.

> The Grand Priory of the Order of the Hospital of St John of Jerusalem in England
>
> "Extract from the minutes of the meeting of the Chapter-General, held at St. John's Gate, Clerkenwell, London:
>
> "Resolved: That the Special Thanks of His Royal Highness the Grand Prior be hereby conveyed to Percy James Drought, of the Ilford Branch St. John Ambulance Association, for distinguished services rendered in furtherance of the work of the Order in connection with its ambulance department.
> Dated this 17th day of October, 1919.
> Arthur, Grand Prior;
> J. P. Hewett, Chancellor;
> Evelyn Cecil, Secretary General."

The Chairman of Governors of Ilford Emergency Hospital, Sir Peter Griggs, JP. MP, who had only recently paid tribute to Mr and Mrs Magnus, at the Ilford Emergency Hospital AGM died on 11 August, 1920. His funeral was recorded on 27 August 1920 in *Eastern Counties News*.

Still the courses and recruiting continued. This short piece appeared in *The Recorder, 15 October 1920*. It took the form of a letter headed-

> First Aid to the Injured". It read " Sir, I should be glad if you would call the attention of your readers to the fact that classes in "First Aid to the injured" for men and women will commence on 21st inst., and that I should be pleased to send all details to intending students on hearing from them. –
> Yours faithfully,
> W. R. Magnus
> 51, Stanhope-gardens,
> Cranbrook Park, Ilford,
> October 10th, 1920

When Dr Edmund King Houchin was nearing the end of his career, he was acting coroner for East London, his old district of Stepney, where he held two inquests.

The first was another notorious case in which a Jewish man murdered his daughter, tried to commit suicide by cutting his throat, but was unsuccessful and was taken to the London Hospital for "repair." He too, suffered the death penalty.[91]

---

[91] 13 October 1920 - *Leicester Daily* reported on what was known as Black Fast Murders. This followed the "death of Fanny Zeitoun (23), the wife of a Jewish tailor, named Sion Zeitoun, who on September 23, the day following the Jewish Black Fast, or Day of Atonement, was found dead across a bed in the room she occupied with her husband at 17, Grove-street, St George's-in-the-East, while by her side lay her father, known as Marks Goodmacher, but whose real name was now stated to be Gutmacher, also with his throat cut. He was removed to hospital in a critical condition, but recovered. The jury returned a verdict of " Wilful murder "against Marks Goodmacher, the father, who was accordingly committed for trial upon the Coroner's warrant. Later he was found guilty and hanged at Pentonville – said to be only the second Orthodox Jew to be executed. He was Russian and had served in the Tzar's army from 1898-1899 before moving to England. He pleaded insanity, but the defence failed.

The second was on the tragic deaths of three London firefighters[92] who died as a result of a fire on 1 November 1920 at Lower Oliver's Wharf in Wapping. On 04 November, 1920 the *Pall Mall Gazette* carried the following report headed

> Wapping Fire. – Stepney Mayor Criticises L.C.C [London County Council] Action." It continued, "There was an unusual incident today at the inquest, by Dr King Houchin, acting coroner, on three firemen who were killed at the Wapping fire.
>
> Major Attlee[93], Mayor of Stepney, rose in the body of the court, and stated that when the old fire station was abolished and the present Shadwell created, the Stepney Council protested to the L.C.C. against the removal of the station., on account of the danger there would be to the Wapping area from a fire owing to its very congested condition.
>
> Albert Sidley, Superintendent of the Eastern Fire District, attributed the fire to escape of gas, whether coal gas or from rubber in the building he was unable to say.
> The coroner commended Station Officer Moore for his promptitude in withdrawing his men when he smelt gas, and a verdict of "Accidental death" was recorded.

Dr King Houchin attended a presentation to a colleague who had achieved fifty years of service his name being Mr Thomas Chivers. The event was marked on 7 October 1921 by a report in the *Daily News*. The headline read

> 50 Years of Tragedy. London Officials Association with Famous Crimes.
>
> Fifty years' service as coroner's officer in East London was recognised yesterday, when Mr Thomas C. Chivers was presented by the members of the medical profession in the Tower Hamlets with an address on Vellum and a cheque.
>
> Dr R. L Guthrie, the coroner, who made the presentation, said the Mr Chivers had been associated with many tragedies. He commenced about the time when Henry Wainwright was executed, and, in fact, before the crime, Wainwright slept at the house of Mr Chivers for one night. Then there were the "Jack the Ripper" crimes, the tragedies associated with the Sidney-street siege, and the inquest on the spies shot at the Tower during the war.
>
> Dr King Houchin said that Mr Chivers's winning smile and his snuff-box – something as familiar almost as the man himself – were alone sufficient to perpetuate his memory for a long time to come.

In January 1921 Corbet Fletcher records that

> *The* British Red Cross Society this month issued a Badge (the 1921 first ever issued by it) in recognition of voluntary services rendered by members of the Society and its Voluntary Aid Detachments between 4th August, 1914, and 31st December, 1919, who had not received any British award, decoration, or any existing military medal for services rendered in respect of Red Cross war work. Among those eligible were members of Voluntary Aid Detachments who had done 1,000 hours of unpaid work, ambulance drivers or bearers who had done 500 hours, and those who had incurred personal risks while doing air-raid duty.

---

92 The three firefighters killed at Lower Olivers Wharf were John Coleman, Alfred Best and Harry J. Green

93 Major Clement Richard Attlee was a Major with the South Lancashire Regiment in First World War and served in Gallipoli and Mesopotamian Campaign and Western Front. He went on to serve as Deputy Prime Minister during the World War Two Coalition under Churchill and was Prime Minister from 1945 -1951. He was created 1st Earl Attlee, KG, OM, CH, PC, FRS

Chapter Thirteen – Magnuses and the Houchins - Time to Move On

At the time of the 1921 Census, William and Maud were still living in Ilford but in 1922 following the promotion of William within the GER, the Magnus family moved to Norwich. This resulted in St John affairs in Ilford being passed on to new leadership. William handed over the role of Divisional Superintendent of Ilford Division to a new Superintendent Frederick G Drayson.

Whilst Maud had handed over the reins of the No 15 Nursing Division, formed on 1 May1911, to Mrs Waldron and Miss E Stenning[94].

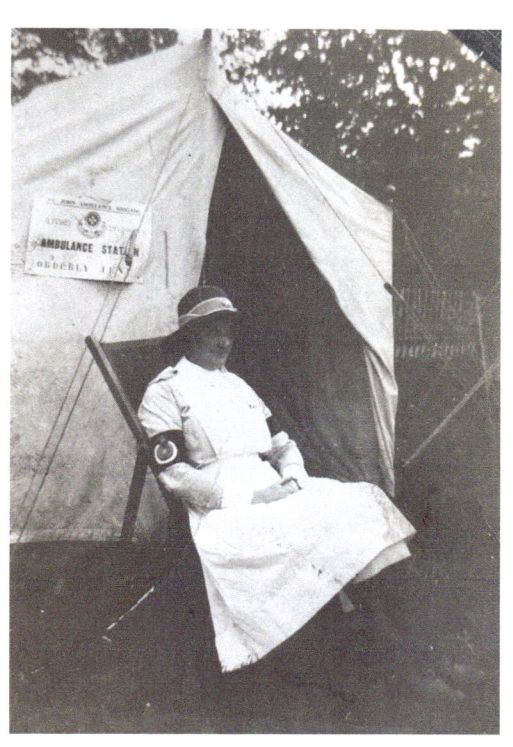

Miss E Stenning Photograph from G.C Everitt's Collection -Courtesy of Redbridge Museum and Heritage Centre

The Recorder dated 31 March 1922 carried an article regarding Ilford Division AGM it recorded –

> Congratulations were tendered to Ambulance Officer F. G. Drayson on his official appointment as superintendent of the 46 Ilford Division.

A report in *The Recorder* dated 28 July 1922 covered the wedding of Mr A. Connolly and Miss A. J. Rymer and it read: -

> Local Weddings
> Mr A Connolly and Miss A. J. Rymer
>
> A wedding, in which considerable local interest was evinced, was celebrated at the High-road Congregational Church on Saturday, in the presence of a large gathering of relatives and friends.

---

[94] Miss Stenning was awarded the King George V Jubilee Medal, as reported in *The Recorder* 16 May 1935

The bride was Miss Annie Jessie Rymer, eldest daughter of Mr and Mrs Fred J Rymer, 8, Belmont-road, Ilford, and the Bridegroom was Mr Alexander Connolly, eldest son of Mr and Mrs J. H. Connolly, of Lafond, Alberta, Canada. The Revs. C. H. Vine, B.A., and J. Boden officiated, and Mr Leonard C. F. Robson presided at the organ.

The Bride was an original member of the Ilford Nursing Division of the St. John Ambulance Association (Prince of Wales' Corps), and has for some time been its first officer, under Mrs Magnus and Mrs Waldron. A detachment of men and nurses from the Brigade attended the service in uniform, and formed a guard of honour at the church.

Miss Rymer was a volunteer nurse when the Ilford Emergency Hospital undertook the nursing of the wounded in the war, and continued until the institution ceased treating them. It was there that she met her future husband, who as Private Connolly, of the Canadian Imperial Force, was brought to Valentines seriously wounded. Afterwards he returned to Canada and was disbanded and spent some time on his farm. Then he came back to England to seek the hand of his nurse. After again going to Canada, where he built a new house, he started once more for England, on June 30th, leaving Montreal on the "Canadian Commander."[95] but three days later the vessel was wrecked on the rocks of an island at the mouth of the St. Lawrence.

Fortunately, no lives were lost, and the passengers were taken back to Montreal.

Mr Connolly, however, elected to catch the "Empress of France" sailing from Quebec, on

July 11th, and reached this country in time[96] to claim his bride on the 22nd. Mr Connelly is a native Canadian, but of Scotch descent. His father was originally in Ontario, but migrated west many years ago.

During the service the hymns, "O. love divine," and we come unto our Fathers' God" were sung. The bride, who was given away be her father, wore a cream gabardine frock, trimmed with silk embroidery and pearls, cream crinoline hat, underlined with drawn georgette, and trimmed with ospreys to match. She also wore a necklace of pearls, and carried a bouquet of cream roses. The bridesmaids were Miss Dorothy E. Rymer (bride's sister), and Miss Cissie Vowles (bride's cousin). The former's dress was pale pink crepe de chine trimmed with silver flowers: she wore a pearl and diamond brooch, the gift of the bridegroom, and had a bouquet of pale mauve sweet peas. The latter was attired in white crepe de chine frock adorned with lace, and hair band of white satin trimmed with forget-me-nots. Her jewellery consisted of a gold initial brooch, she carried a basket of pale pink sweet peas. The Bride's mother was dressed in deep mauve chiffon rave, trimmed with black and gold hand-made embroidery, with a black georgette hat trimmed with a white osprey. Sergt. James F. A. Rymer, of the St. John Ambulance Brigade, was best man. (See Appendix 2)

After the service a reception was held in the lecture hall adjoining the church, through the courtesy of the minister and deacons. The guest numbering 65 included the following:-

Miss Dorothy Rymer, bridesmaid; Miss Cissie Vowles, bridesmaid; Rev. C. H and Mrs, Vine, Rev. J and Mrs Boden: Messrs Dav. B. Murray, and Walter Tyrrell (of Southwark); Mr and Mrs James F. Q. Rymer, Master Jammie and Miss Nancy Rymer, Mr and Mrs A. W. Haddow

---

95 *Canadian Commander* was launched in 1920, with completion in April 1921. Her port of registry was Montreal, under the British Flag. On 3 July 1922, *Canadian Commander* ran aground at Saint Pierre and Miquelon, she was re-floated on 16 July. She was then sold to an Italian firm in 1932 and renamed *Giaocchino Lauro*. She was seized by the United Kingdom in 1940, passed to the Ministry of War - Transport and renamed *Empire Engineer*. She served until 4 February 1941 when she was torpedoed and sunk by U-123.

96 Empress of France arrived at Southampton on 26 July 1922 *The Times*, Wednesday, 26 Jul 1922; pg. 2; Issue 43093; col A

(Sunbury-on-Thames), Mr and Mrs, Peter Clark (Sunbury-on-Thames), Mr and Mrs Lionel Oakley (Gipsy Hill), Mr and Mrs Percy Oakley (Muswell Hill), Miss Oakley (Wimbledon), Mr "Bill" Peckham (Dulwich), the Misses Cissie and Lilly Peckham. Master James Vowles, Mrs Marks (Southend), Miss Emmie Philbrick (Southend), Mr Frank Macey, Mr Bert Macey, Mr and Mrs Cornwall (Balfour-road), Miss Norah Hepburn (Rayleigh), Mrs E. J. Beal (Forest Gate), Mrs Earnest Long, Miss Long (Rayleigh), Mrs Wilson, Divisional Superintendent [Name corrected, should read 'Drayson'] and Lady Divisional Superintendent A. E. Waldron[97], with men and nurses of the St. John Ambulance Brigade.

Later in the day the happy couple left for Harlow for their honeymoon, the bride travelling in a tailor-made costume and a golden-brown hat.

The wedding cake was supplied by Mrs Wheeler, the carriages by Wheal and Crane, and the flowers by N. and W. Toole. The Church was decorated by Mr W. Harvey and Messrs N. and W. Toole. The bride and bridegroom received many handsome presents.

Mr and Mrs Alex Connolly's future address will be: St. Paul de Metis, Alberta, Canada, where they will always be pleased to hear from old friends.

The Recorder dated 11 August 1922

First Aid Station for Barkingside

Thanks to the generosity of an honorary member of the Ilford Division, St John Ambulance Brigade, will be enabled to establish a first aid station at Barkingside.

Plans are in hand, and it is expected that early autumn will see the scheme in working order with telephone installed, medical and surgical appliances, motor ambulances and driver, together with a squad of trained ambulance men on Saturday afternoons during the football season ready and prepared to deal at once with casualties should they occur on the outlying and scattered playing fields. This is an important step in the right direction.

Several serious accidents occurred last season which caused a little storm of protest and adverse comment at the lack of suitable arrangements for dealing with such emergencies – some even suggesting it was the duty of the St John Ambulance Brigade to provide the trained staff. This is, of course, an entirely erroneous attitude.

St John Ambulance work is carried on entirely by Volunteers and Voluntary contributions – the scope of the work is limited primarily by number of active members – secondly financial considerations.

The officers of the Ilford and District Amateur Football League were quick to realise the immense importance of having trained men to deal with casualties, and to Mr S. G Jones in particular is due the thanks of the footballing fraternity of the district.

In conference with those responsible for the local division St John Ambulance Brigade this scheme has come into being – the St John Ambulance Brigade are to be congratulated on the

---

97 *11 April 1924 - Eastern Counties' Times - London, London, England – The District Nursing Committee noted the* "Resignation of Mrs *Waldron* as representative for the *St. John Ambulance* Division for *Ilford*, and on behalf of the committee desired to welcome Mrs Barnard. who had been nominated by the St. John Ambulance Brigade vice Mrs *Waldron*. *It was unanimously resolved that a letter of thanks be sent to Mrs Waldron for her services to the committee*".

initiative and energy with which they have evolved this scheme, from which it is probable further developments will follow.

To have immediate aid available on the fields a course of lectures on first aid to the injured will be commenced on August 24th by Dr Edger W. Whiting who, from long personal experience, is able to deal with those injuries which occur most frequently on the football field.

It is up to the football section of this community to do their share. This is a special summer course at a most unusual season of the year. It is suggested that every club in the district send at least two -either players or supporters – to pass out, and then, if desired, to form a football section of Ilford Division, thereby enabling each certificate holder to keep in touch with the work. This is specially recommended to the club secretaries for Ilford Division, thereby enabling each certificate holder to keep in touch with the work. This is specially recommended to the club secretaries for wholehearted support.

The Recorder dated 10 November 1922

St John Ambulance Brigade
A Super Donation

The greatly increased activities of the local division are of importance and considerable interest to the town.

In common with kindred organisations it suffered during the days following the armistice from loss of members, local apathy and financial difficulties. Those who have been responsible for carrying on the good work are to-day finding those difficulties slowly but surely disappearing, and there is promise of a brighter future in social service, additional help for those stricken by accident and sudden illness, and in revival of those social functions which were familiar and popular in this district in pre-war days.

It is gratifying to learn that membership is increasing, thanks to energetic publicity methods, and to notice in these columns which have stimulated the interest of many in this useful and necessary subject.

The medical and surgical and other stores and equipment used in rendering first aid to the injured are costly nowadays to replace, and is more or less a tax on the individual pockets of the members. They receive no grants, are self-supporting, and pay their own expenses in most cases. The workers are all volunteers, and give their services without pay or reward.

It was recently announced that the chairman and directors of the Ilford Super Cinema, opposite the railway station, proposed to devote the proceeds of the opening ceremony to the funds of the 46 Ilford Division St John Ambulance Brigade and the Ilford War Memorial; and Mr H. Sheffield has handed to Supt. F. W. Drayson a cheque for the substantial sum of £50 to carry on Brigade work in the district.

This public-spirited generosity deserves the thanks of the town inasmuch as it enables a voluntary public work to be carried on more effectively, and with a wider sphere of usefulness. Accidents are sudden, and all too frequent. The importance of first aid work is daily becoming more apparent. The St John Ambulance Brigade throughout England and Wales is doing its utmost to give all who are willing to learn the knowledge of what to do and what to avoid doing in the emergencies of daily life. This knowledge has proved of inestimable benefit to hundreds of thousands of people. The Ilford Division ask for greater co-operation in order to provide a more extensive and efficient ambulance service for the town. Volunteers will receive a hearty welcome. Dr Edgar W. Whiting is conducting a course of instruction on first aid to the injured every Tuesday evening, at 8 p.m., at the United Methodist School, Ilford-lane, opposite the end of Albert-road. It is not too late for those desirous of attending to join the next lecture on November 7th.

The sportsmen of the district especially those who play on the Fairlop Grounds, gain direct benefit from the contribution by the directors of the Ilford Super Cinema now that arrangements have been completed. First aid, medical, surgical and transport equipment will be provided in the central pavilion of the London Playing Fields, Fairlop. A flag staff is also to be erected, and when the flag with the eight-pointed cross is flying all and sundry will know that members of the St John Ambulance Brigade are on duty, and that help is available in case of need. The ambulance service available, not only for the Playing Fields, but also the Ilford Council and adjoining grounds. Given the increased membership, and other circumstances permitting, it is hoped to extend the service the ambulance service to the cricket season. Members on duty on Saturday next. This will be in addition to the other regular duties at the Ilford Football Ground and Ilford Super Cinema.

Photograph c1920 Ilford Station on left and Ilford Super Cinema on left of picture Photographer unknown.

It is also an open secret that Dr Edgar Whiting[98], of Woodlands-road, has accepted the honorary position of senior officer of the Ilford Division as divisional surgeon. Dr Whiting is a well-known sportsman and popular lecturer, in whom ambulance workers in the town have an invaluable supporter.

A whist drive was held in aid of divisional funds on November 2nd. The next social evening will be held on December 7th and all who wish to join these popular gatherings are advised to book early with Mr Fred Palmer, 2 Albert-road, Ilford.

The Ilford Division will be on duty at the Ilford War Memorial ceremony on November 11th.

---

[98] 1923 & 1935 Medical Register carried the same entry. Dr Edgar William Whiting, 51 Woodlands-road, Ilford. Date of Registration was 14 February 1913 in England. MRCS England 1913., LRCP London 1913., MB.,BS 1913, U. London.

The Recorder dated 30 March 1923.

> Success of Late Ilford Resident – Hastings Music Festival. Miss Lena Magnus, late of Ilford, daughter of Mr and Mrs W. R. Magnus, has been awarded two first prizes for singing at the Hastings Musical Festival, one in an open class, and one in a local class for mezzo-soprano solos.
>
> Miss Magnus is a pupil of Miss Alice Norton. L.R.A.M., A.R.C.M., and was until her removal from Ilford studying under Mrs Kennedy, of Mayfair-avenue.
> The adjudication, Captain Halford, complimented the singer on her excellent interpretation of the songs "Orpheus and his lute," and "The Knight of Bethlehem," and congratulated her upon gaining two successes in one season."

The next year *The Recorder* dated the 18 April 1924 recorded another success for Lena, the article read

> Further Musical Success of Former Ilford Resident. At the Hastings Musical Festival, held during last week, Miss Lena. E. Magnus daughter of Mr and Mrs W. R. Magnus, late of Ilford, was the winner of the gold medal for solo singing in a class open to all comers who had previously obtained first prize at and earlier festival.
>
> It will be remembered that Miss Magnus was the recipient of two first prizes in the 1923 festival.
>
> Miss Magnus is the pupil of Miss Alice Norton, of Hasting, and when in Ilford was under the tuition of Mrs Kennedy, of Mayfair-avenue."

Dr Edmund King Houchin's retirement followed several years after resignation and move from Stepney in 1899. He certainly had a fully and varied life, and one that was surrounded by historic events in the East End of London.

What follows are two reports that covered his retirement and departure from Ilford in 1924. On 11 January, 1924 *The Recorder* reported the following; -

> Presentation to Dr Houchin.
> "An Ideal Family Doctor"
> "Thanks, from Patients and Friends"
>
> At the former residence of Dr Houchin (who has now retired from practice), in Cranbrook-road, Ilford, on Tuesday Evening, a number of the principal residents and friends of the doctor, met to wish him farewell and fear [fair] practical testimony to the esteem in which he is held.
>
> Among those present were Councillor J. W. King (Vice-Chairman of the Urban District Council). Mr and Mrs Catto, Mrs Crown, Mrs and Miss Haslam, Mr and Mrs. King, Mrs Waldron, Messrs, R Kennedy, C. P. Wootton, A. S. West, B. N. Goodman, J. Bowmer, A. Sampson, R. H. M. Green, etc.
>
> Councillor King occupied the chair, and said they had met there for a special purpose, and that was to present to their dear old friend, the doctor, with a souvenir on his retirement. He had known him for more than 50 years, and more intimately for at least 25 years, as his own medical man, and he was convinced that those present know that no man that had ever come into their house in times of sickness had been more kind and sympathetic than he (Applause). It was not too much say that the

doctor, on entering a sickroom, was a comfort to the soul as well as the body.(Hear hear)

A Notable Personage

Mr Wootton remarked that he deeply regretted Ilford was losing the doctor, who had for so many years been such a notable personage in the town from its very foundation. (Hear hear) When Dr Houchin came to Ilford the population was much below 25,000, and now it was approximately 100,000, so he has seen the town grow up from its infancy to its present dimensions.

Dr Houchin came here to retire in the country, but he had not been here long before he was prevailed upon to carry on again. (Hear, hear). At that time, he was not a young man by any means, and they could understand that his bed had not been a bed of roses, but in the midst of it all kindly manner and sympathetic ways had been endearing to everybody, and ever since he had been here his presence has been a tonic to his patients, almost as good a tonic he could prepare in his surgery. (Hear, hear and laughter.) He hoped that his retirement he would have happiness and comfort, and have many years of peace and rest in which to enjoy them (Hear, hear.)

The Gift

Mr Catto was then asked to make the presentation. He expressed the regret at Dr Houchin leaving Ilford, but at the same time he hoped he would have rest and enjoyment in his retirement that he had so richly earned. Addressing the doctor, he added:- "In giving you this little gift, doctor, we ask you not to consider its intrinsic value. It does not represent all the feeling behind it. (Hear, hear.) Behind it all there is a great deal of respect of what you have done for the town and your patients. (Applause.) We hope you will have a real happy time in Clacton with Mrs Houchin in your retirement. We all wish you God-speed." (Loud cheers.)

Mr Catto then handed a handsome and massive solid silver tea and coffee service of the Queen Ann pattern to Dr Houchin, together with the following illuminated address in an album, also containing the names of the subscribers:

" Presented to Dr E. King Houchin by a few of his patients and friends as a small memento of his twenty-five years' residence in Ilford.

" His geniality and good humour his unique personality as an ideal family doctor, and above all, his untiring attention on behalf of the sick have endeared him to everyone who had the privilege of his friendship, or being ill were fortunate enough to depend on skill.
" We realise that during all that time he had been actively assisted by Mrs Houchin. To her and the doctor we would express the hope that they may enjoy many happy days in their well-deserved retirement. – January 1924".

The Doctor's Response

Dr Houchin, who was visibly touched, said they could hardly expect him to be able to give utterance to what he was feeling at that very moment. He was, however, very much obliged to all who had expressed such sentiments towards him. Of course, it was a very matter for a man to retire from active life into inactive life, and it was a question whether a man after so many years' service as he had had, should not take up a hobby. He though he must take up something. He did not mean with partner or practice in the ordinary way. If he could not do anything else he might in some way attach himself to a public body. (Hear, hear.) He thanked the organisers of the testimonial because it enabled him to retire with dignity. He had always tried to bear a good name, and thought their testimony that night showed he had succeeded.

Mrs Houchin's Help

He also thanked them for including Mrs Houchin in their appreciation for she had not been only a wife, but had ever been a great help to him in his profession in time of great pressure. He was proud, therefore, that they had included her in this splendid souvenir.

He would prize it during the whole of his life, and when the end came he would hand it down with pride to those who might follow. (Applause)

Councillor King said he would have pleasure of presenting Dr Houchin with ten guineas, the balance of the testimonial fund, after cost had been met.

It may be mentioned that the silver service was supplied by Mr T. Gibson, jeweller, High-road, Ilford, and the Illuminated address was executed by Mr W. Spooner, of Grosvenor-road, Ilford".

The Second report was published on 11 January 1924 in the *Eastern Counties News*.

" A DOCTOR LOOKS BACK - TALK WITH Dr E. KING HOUCHIN
BIOGRAPHICAL SKETCH.

After many years of valued work in Ilford, and formerly in the East End, Dr E. King Houchin, of Cranbrook-road, retires this month from practice, and will make his home in Clacton-on-Sea. Coming to Ilford 25 years ago, he has made a wide circle of friends to whom his going will occasion much regret.

Dr Houchin, who is 76, was born at Colchester. He was apprenticed to a local chemist, qualified in that profession, then left for London, whence the eyes of youth were always turned. His first position was that of a dispenser to a doctor in Stepney. He took it because it gave him time for reading, and the doctor at once remarked to him "Why don't you go in for physic?"

"I hadn't thought of it," answered the young dispenser, but he took hold of the idea, and to that end entered the London Hospital, where he passed his examination and qualified for the L.S.A.[99] His next step was to go to Edinburgh. He studied there for some time and took double qualification, and then returned to Stepney as assistant to the doctor, whose friendly advice had proved so practical and so wise.

Sometime later Dr Houchin was able to buy the practice, also succeeded to the appointment of Police Surgeon, first to the K Division, and then to the H Division, which he held for 17 years. He was asked by the then coroner, Mr Wynne E. Baxter, to act as his deputy, and although a busy man at that time he accepted the offer. With a view to qualifying himself for the post he entered Middle Temple as a law student, read for the Bar, and practised as deputy-coroner for some years. In addition to being deputy-coroner for the Eastern Division of the County of London, he was deputy-

---

[99] Licence of the Society of Apothecaries (L.S.A.)

coroner for the Liberty of the Tower of London[100], and in that capacity, it fell to his lot to conduct the inquests on the spies who were shot at the Tower[101].

A WHITECHAPEL MURDER

Naturally his work as deputy-coroner brought him in touch with many interesting phases of life. Several murder cases came within the sphere of his investigation, notably the Whitechapel case some 30 years ago, in which a seaman[102] murdered an old Jew in Turner-street. The murderer was hunted and finally "run to earth" by detectives on the roof of a three-storey building from which, with the motive of defeating justice, he threw himself headlong. As luck would have it, his only really injury was a broken arm. He was taken to the London Hospital, and his arm repaired and allowed to get well, after which he stood trial and was sentenced to death.

Dr Houchin also held enquiries into the explosion at Silvertown during the war.

Ilford Crime recalled.

Many Ilford People will still have recollections of the ghastly affair of Cocker, the Cranbrook-road chemist, who murdered his wife and children. From a point of view of criminology, his terrible plan was extraordinarily well conceived. He first rendered his wife and Children unconscious by giving them hyoscine, after which, to make death certain, he gave them each a teaspoon-full of strong prussic acid. The bodies lay in upper rooms for something like sixteen days, during which time, it being summer, they decomposed rapidly. Cocker used to lock up the shop at night, go up town and sleep at some temperance hotel, returning to open the shop in the morning. Although he had a dispenser, no one was aware of the tragedy that had occurred above. His wife and children were supposed to be away at a cottage that he had provided them near Brighton. Ultimately, he committed suicide by taking prussic acid.

A DREADFUL CONFESSION.

One bright morning Dr Houchin received a letter from Cocker making the whole dreadful confession. The doctor took the letter to the police, with whom he went to the house, and following the instructions given in the letter, found a hidden key which

---

100 The Liberties of the Tower, or the Tower Liberty was an area adjoining the Tower of London, which was outside the jurisdiction of either the City of London or the County of Middlesex. The liberty originally consisted of the area inside the walls of the Tower and immediately outside it, including Tower Hill. The limits were set out in the sixteenth century. The liberty continued as a franchise coroner's district until the Coroners (Amendment) Act 1926. This provided that the district could be dissolved when a vacancy arose; when a vacancy occurred on 10 May 1939, an order was made on 30 November 1939 combining it with the east district. This came into effect on 1 January 1940.

101 During the First World War eleven German spies were executed at the Tower of London, but surprisingly some were not German nationals and included Latvians, two Dutchmen, a Swede, a Turk and three South Americans who decided to work for German intelligence.

102 On the 8th May 1896. William Seaman (46) was indicted for the wilful murder of John Goodman Levy. On the evidence Stephen White (*Inspector H*). On May 1st, on the prisoner's discharge from the hospital, I told him I was a police officer, and that I should take him into custody upon a charge of wilfully causing the deaths of Annie Sarah Gale and John Goodman Levy, at 31, Turner Street, on April 4th, and also for stealing a quantity of jewellery at the same time and place—he said, "Yes; very well"—at the Police-station, when the charge was read to him, he said, "Yes.". The Verdict was "Guilty". Internet accessed 20 April 2022 Old Baily online records. oldbaileyonline.org/print.jsp?div=t18960518-407.

admitted them by the scullery door. In the first room they entered was the body of Cocker[103]. The curtains were drawn, and a night light was still burning, while the vessel from which he had taken the prussic acid was thrown over the coverlet. In other rooms they found the bodies of the victims in such a decomposed state of decomposition that the sexes could only be determined, on cursory examination, by hair of the head. Dr Houchin was of course the chief witness at the inquest, at which the verdict was one of murder against Cocker and suicide whilst of unsound mind.

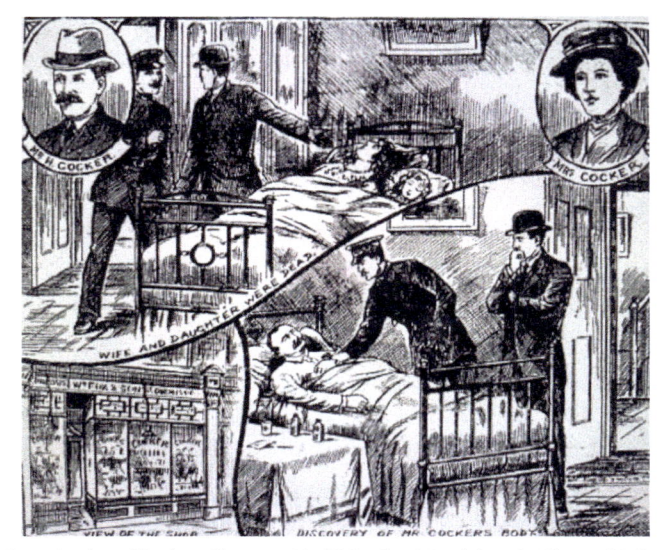

"The Ilford mass murder, and a view of the shop of horrors at No. 23 Cranbrook Road, from the Illustrated Police News, 8 August 1918."

Ilford Broadway - showing Village Pump and original entrance to Station. 104, 105.

STUDIES IN GERMANY.

But we pass on from the recollections of such gruesome things. Dr Houchin spent some time studying in Germany, where he investigated the treatment by inunction [106],

---

103 These events were reported in the press even reaching New Zealand where the Dominion, Volume 11, issue 269, Page 5 of the 2 August 1918. Reported at follows:- *"London, July 31. An Ilford chemist, named Harris Cocker wrote to a local doctor revealing a terrible tragedy. He stated he had murdered his wife and four children a fortnight ago, and intended to commit suicide last night. The police found the six dead bodies in the house this morning. Cocker feared being called up for the Army."* – Aus.- N.Z. Cable Assn.

104 Photograph from *Potted History of Ilford* by Norman Gunby, privately Published in 1997.

105 In the book *Murder Houses of Greater London* by Jan Bondeson, published by Matador, ISBN 978 1784623 333. She noted "this shop and the maisonette flat above it stood for decades to come, until it was an unlamented victim of the expansion of Ilford Station in the 1980s". The 1980 rebuild was also closed on 25 January 2020, when site was remodelled as part of the Crossrail Project.

106 The rubbing of ointment or oil into the skin.

and on his return to England practised it in the West End of London. One of the professional organisation to which he belonged was the Medical Society of Weisbaden.

Later he went to Copenhagen and spent what he described as "a delightful week" with the late Professor Fynson, and was the first to bring over to this country the Fynson Lamp for the treatment of lupus and skin diseases.

Medicine and surgery have both very much advanced, Dr Houchin remarks, so much so that the General Practitioner of today is a good man as the consultants of yesterday. In both medicine and surgery. In fact, the consultant feels a special draught; he gets fewer cases for the simple reason that the general practitioner is able to deal with the majority of them. In passing, Dr Houchin pays a high compliment to his professional brethren in Ilford, from whom, he says he has always received the greatest courtesy.

A SMART BRIGADE

Dr. E. KING HOUCHIN.

Photograph taken from Eastern Counties News 11 January 1924

Dr Houchin had the honour of establishing the Ilford division of the St John Ambulance Brigade, which at its zenith was one of the smartest, and used to attend all big functions in London, such as the Lord Mayor's show and Opening of Parliament. He was lecturer and examiner in first aid for the Brigade and Association, and instructed most of the men of the Great Eastern Railway Company by lectures at Liverpool Street, and also the local fire brigade. He was never on the staff of the Ilford Emergency Hospital, although he adds that he has many patients there, and can speak very highly of the management and general conduct of the institution by the matron and sisters and nurses.

Dr Houchin was a colleague and personal friend of the late Sir Frederick Treves [107], and also of Lord Dawson, of Penn.[108]

THE SMALLPOX EPIDEMIC.

It may be also of interest to recall that the doctor was in East London during smallpox epidemic of nearly 40 years ago, when he had 800 cases in his own practice. It occurred coincidently with the time when authorities were contemplating the removal of infectious
Cases, and the public mind was so opposed to it that people used to hide their cases away, so that often when called to a case that was supposed to be dead – and very often was - the doctor found six or eight cases under one roof, everybody being down with the disease and receiving no treatment.

Dr Houchin's only hobbies are sea-fishing and – a game of bowls! "

Photograph of Dr Edmund King Houchin - Photographer Unknown c 1924

---

107 Sir Frederick Treves, 1st Baronet GCVO, CH, CB, FRCS, KStJ [Knight of Grace] (15 February 1853 – 7 December 1923) was a prominent British surgeon, and an expert in anatomy. Treves was renowned for his surgical treatment of appendicitis, and is credited with saving the life of King Edward VII in 1902. He is also widely known for his friendship with Joseph Merrick, dubbed the "Elephant Man" for his severe deformities.

108 Bertrand Edward Dawson, 1st Viscount Dawson of Penn, GCVO, KCB, KCMG, PC, FRCP (9 March 1864 – 7 March 1945) was a physician to the British Royal Family and President of the Royal College of Physicians from 1931 to 1937.

And finally, on retirement Edmund King Houchin gave notice on 2 January 1924 that he had dissolved his partnership with Dr Archibald Romanes, of 66, Cranbrook-road, Ilford, who will carry on the practice in his own name.

On the 12 September 1924 the *Recorder* announced that Ilford Division's arrangements for first aid courses, were now being finalised for the autumn season. It noted in part –

> The importance of first aid knowledge is now universally recognised. We would recommend these lectures to all affected by the Workmen's Compensation Act, 1921, both employers and employees, as a sound investment.

Chapter Fourteen - Dr Wynne Baxter – Dr King Houchin's Boss

The Globe on 1 October, 1926 carried news that Edmund King Houchin's former boss, as Coroner for East London had passed away. Perhaps to give a feel of the work under taken by the coroner's team in East London it is worth reproducing the report.

> Famous Coroner. – Death of Dr Wynne Baxter, who held 38,000 inquests. – "Jack the Ripper" Memories. A romantic figure is removed from the ranks of London coroners by the death of Dr Wynne Baxter, who presided over the East London Court.
> Dr Baxter, who lived at Stoke Newington and was 76 years of age, had a heart seizure while holding a court at Poplar a fortnight ago, and although he rallied for a time he had a relapse in the early part of the week. He died at his residence to-day.
>
> Among the 38,000 or more inquests which Dr Baxter held during the period of about 35 years during which he was coroner for East London, he had to inquire into all the "Jack the Ripper" Murders, and many other well-known crimes.
>
> Air Raid Victims.
>
> He also held inquests upon scores of people who were killed in the air raids during the war, and also upon all the spies who were shot in the Tower of London.
>
> On one day alone at the London Hospital he held inquests upon over 60 of the victims of the Silvertown, explosion, on which occasion not only were the ordinary mortuaries filled, but also bodies had to be laid in rows on either side of the corridors.
>
> Before coming to London Dr Baxter was coroner in Sussex, where he held the inquest on Mr Gold, who was murdered by Lefroy.[109]
>
> Dr Baxter was a native of Lewes, and was trained as a solicitor. He was a D.L. and J.P. for London and Chairman of the Licensing Bench in Stoke Newington.
>
> He also served as Under Sheriff of London and Middlesex High Constable and first Mayor of Lewes, and was vice-president from 1871-1876 of the Provincial Newspaper Society."

On 4 October *The Globe* recorded

> Dr Wynne Baxter. Funeral of famous coroner this afternoon.
>
> The funeral took place at Lewes, Sussex this afternoon of the late Coroner of East London, Dr Wynne E. Baxter.[110]
>
> A Preliminary service was held at St Mary's Old Parish Church, Stoke Newington, of which for many years Mr Baxter was Churchwarden.

---

[109] Percy Lefroy Mapleton (also known as Percy Mapleton Lefroy; 23 February 1860 – 29 November 1881) was a British journalist and murderer. He was the British "railway murderer" of 1881. He is important in the history of forensics and policing as being the subject of the first police composite picture to appear on a "wanted" poster and in a newspaper.

[110] On 3 December, 1920 his will was proved and he left £29,319. The report, in *The Globe,* also stated his father was the proprietor and editor of the "Sussex Express".

The Rev. J. Le Couteur officiated, and a crowded congregation included the Mayor of Stoke Newington, Councillor F. A. Dod, J.P., many aldermen and councillors, and representatives of many public bodies throughout the district.

After the service the remains were conveyed in a motor funeral car by road to Lewes, where the interment was made.

Dr Wynne Baxter 9 October 1920, London Illustrated News

Chapter Fifteen - Ilford Division and the Upminster Section.

A short report in *The Recorder*, dated 13 December 1929, announced the appointment of a new Divisional Surgeon for No 15 Ilford Nursing Division.

> St John Ambulance Brigade
>
> In a report of a presentation to Dr R. Boyd Robson, on his retirement as divisional surgeon of the 15th (Ilford) Nursing Division, St John Ambulance Brigade, the name of his successor was inadvertently given as Dr J. A. Dawson, M.A., M.B., Ch.B.

Ilford Division Ambulance c1930 at Hainault Forest Lt to Rt. J.C. Raith, W. R. Gander and G. C. Everitt. Photographer Unknown. Body of Ambulance constructed by W. R.Gander at his residence in Barkingside 1929-1930 Courtesy of Redbridge Museum and Heritage Centre

The St John Ambulance Brigade Ilford

Ilford Division and Ambulance c1930 at Hainault Forest Photographer Unknown Courtesy of Redbridge Museum and Heritage Centre

Ilford Division Ambulance c1930. Location and Photographer not known. Courtesy of Redbridge Museum and Heritage Centre

A regular feature of the Divisions activities was a fundraising concert, this was part of the 1930 programme.

Two photographs from the 1930 Ilford Division Evening Concert Programme and the Arterial Road Service Dressing Station.
Courtesy of Redbridge Museum and Heritage Centre

The 1931 Centenary Leaflet mentioned a major initiative with the provision of a Road Service Dressing Station the opening described as follows -

> Road Service Dressing Station, opened on April 4th, 1931 at Little Heath on
> The Southend Road, has already passed our record of service for the short period it
> has been in use.
>
> It was opened by Ilford's "First Citizen," Alderman H. G. Odell. J.P. fifth Mayor of the Borough together with the Lady Mayoress, supported by the Deputy Mayor (Ald. Smith. CA., E.C.C.), Lieut.-Colonel Francis Brooks, M.D. (Commissioner of No. 1, Prince of Wales's District). Captain Goodley, M.C. (Assistant Commissioner for Public Duty), Dr Edgar W. Whiting (Divisional Surgeon), District Officer C J. Fitch, Divisional Superintendent Andrews, Lady Superintendent Miss H. Stenning, Rev. Frank Smith who in his temporary capacity as Chaplain, dedicated station, Mr. Councillor C. W. Clark, District president, conducting the proceedings.

Opening of the Ambulance Station by the Mayor of Ilford (Ald. H. G. Odell, J.P.) *

Some Members of the Local Division grouped in front of the Ambulance Station, Barley Lane and Eastern Avenue Corner *

Two photographs from the 1931 Ilford Division Centenary Leaflet covering the opening of the Ambulance Station
Courtesy of Redbridge Museum and Heritage Centre

The Division also had opened a Medical Comforts Depot, the report noted -

> Our service 26 Clements Road known as "Medical Comforts Depot for supplying sick room appliances has now passed its 300-case mark.

Upminster Section of No 46 Ilford Ambulance Division.

In 1929, Ilford formed a Section of the Division to cover Upminster and Hornchurch. The 1931 leaflet carried the following information.

> The Upminster Section of Ilford Division is now after two years hard work, making good progress and should be up to strength in a few weeks time, thanks being due to Divisional Surgeon Dr A. Alastair Bain for the time given and trouble and patience taken in training to

attain this satisfactory end. As a result of this, a Dressing Station is about to be placed at Hall Lane (Upminster) crossing of the Southend Arterial Road, where members have also been doing duty for the past two summers.

The Upminster, Hornchurch and District Section, with Ambulance purchased mainly from the proceeds of the 1933 Concert. Courtesy of Redbridge Museum and Heritage Centre

Evening Concert at the Capitol Cinema, Upminster 29 April 1934 attended by Sir George Gillett. JP., MP.

The Dedication of a new Ambulance Upminster June 1935

The Essex Chronicle dated 21 June 1935 reported on the arrival of the new Ambulance the report read –

> Ambulance Dedication – The new motor ambulance of the Upminster and Hornchurch section of the St John Ambulance Brigade was dedicated at a ceremony held in the Recreation Ground on Sunday. Ald. C. W. Clark, ex-Mayor of Ilford, presided, and the dedication ceremony was conducted by the Rev H. H Holden (rector). Among those present were the members of the Hornchurch and Upminster VAD's, Boy Scouts, Girl Guides, Mr F. H. R Davies, JP (chairman of Hornchurch Council), and Capt. Dr G. W. Kendall commissioner for Eastern Area. The ambulance, a handsome vehicle, with a cream body and Green interior, is thoroughly up-to-date. It was examined by the company present, and afterwards Ald Clarke commented upon the value of the work of the St John Ambulance Brigade. He said he hoped that the Hornchurch Council would continue to subsidise the ambulance as it had done in the past. During 1934 the men of the section had put in over 2,300 hours of voluntary work in dealing with over 200 cases. The Upminster and Hornchurch section would soon become a division on its own. – About two hours after the ceremony the new ambulance was called out to carry its first patient, the victim of an accident on the arterial road being conveyed in it to Oldchurch Hospital, Romford.

No 46 Ilford Division's Silver Prize Band

The Recorder carried a letter on 12 October 1933 from Divisional Superintendent James Andrews[111] regard the Prize Band. It gave some background to the Band and its history.

It read –

> Ilford Silver Prize Band.
>
> Dear Sir – May I be allowed to correct the Social Column paragraph in last week's "Recorder" referring to the new band for Ilford. The writer is in error in mentioning the "Late Silver Prize Band." This band has never ceased to exist and is still so

---

[111] *The Recorder* 15 December 1932 Assistant Commissioner Goodley MC presented James Andrews with the Service Medal of the Order of St John at the Divisions Concert the previous week.

registered with the National Brass Band Association it only having added "St John Ambulance" to its title. It has full membership and is doing exceedingly well, is highly popular at concerts and with football enthusiasts, and in fact, from what one hears, is as much a feature nowadays as the match.

Mr E. H. Allder was its conductor up to early 1933 when he resigned. The band did not automatically cease to exist, which seems to be inferred. It will be recalled that this band won third place in the Section C Junior Shield A contest at Crystal Palace, 1932, this under Mr E. H. Allder's leadership. As a result, it should have moved up to Section B but miss this section and was put up to Section A instead. This speaks very highly for the band's ability and also for the enthusiasm and team work of the members.

I am delighted to say, and our many supporters will be pleased to learn, that under the conductorship of Mr T. Doughty. ANCM., the band only just missed being placed in prize position, this against 23 other bands, many of whom were past Shield Champions.

Ilford will definitely be represented, at the East Ham Band Festival, by the Ilford St John Ambulance Silver Prize Band. –
Yours faithfully
James Andrews
Div. Supt St John Ambulance Bde.,
No 46 Ilford Division
38 Charlbury-Gardens,
Seven Kings.

The Ilford Division Silver Prize Band c1933
Courtesy of Redbridge Museum and Heritage Centre

Chapter Sixteen – William Magnus MBE and LNER Ambulance Corps

The Great Eastern Railway, following a re-organisation of the Railways had now become part of the new London North Eastern Railway Company.

William remained active within the first aid competition world, as evidenced by the *Chelmsford Chronicle* who carried the following report on 15 February 1924, which in part read -

> Ambulance Tests. Good Work at Parkstone. At the Parkeston Railway Club on Saturday members of the Parkeston and Harwich Division of the L. and N. E. R Ambulance Corps held some highly interesting and valuable competitions. The judge was Mr Magnus of the St John Ambulance Brigade, London.

On 18 February 1927 William Magnus was promoted by The Order of St John to the Grade of Officer.

The London & North Eastern Railway Magazine on March 1928 reported on what appears to be a much larger event at Parkeston. The report reads: -

> "Parkeston. The Railway Club, Parkeston, was a hive of industry on February 11, when the ambulance competitions of the Parkeston Divisions were held, Messrs W. Magnus and T.O Mein being the judges. A tea followed at which Mr C. Keep (assistant marine superintendent) presided, supported by Mrs R Davis, Mrs Keep, Mr and Mrs E. Smith, Mr and Mrs J. H. Child, Mr and Mrs E. W. Tyzack, Mr and Mrs J. L. Meadowcroft, Miss Regina Evans (Commandant, V. A. D.) Miss Sable, Miss Watts and the Rev. W. Harling.
>
> The Secretary in his report said that there were now 38 active members. Next autumn it is hoped to run a class so as to augment the numbers. For the year 1927: 5 serious cases were treated and sent to hospital, 5 cases taken home on wheeled litter, and 1,357 miscellaneous case. In the competition they had two teams in the G. E. Sectional competition. The "A" team, captained by Mr H. Burrows took first prize. The team "B" under Mr Birch took 5 place.
>
> Mr H. Burrows proposed a vote of thanks and Mr Lemm seconded. Mr Tyzack, replying, said it was the seventh occasion on which test had been held in the hall, and it was up to all to follow the advice given and so benefit.
>
> He presented two wallets to Messrs. Mein and Magnus as a token of regard from the Parkeston Division.
>
> Mr Tyzack also said it was a pleasure to see how well the division was officered, especially in the secretary, Mr Geo. Peck, who had filled that office for many years, also Mr H. Burrows, who had done excellent work as first officer, and a wallet was presented to each of these gentlemen.

In the June 1928 edition of the *London & North Eastern Railway Magazine* the reported:-

> "L.N.E.R. Group Competition." was reported as follows "On April 27, at Liverpool Street Station, a competition was held between the premier Ambulance teams of the Great Central, Great Eastern, Great Northern and North Eastern Sections of the London & North Eastern Railway for the Ambulance Competition of the St John Ambulance Association which was to take place in London on May 16. Mr Alex. Wilson, Mr T. Smith (G.N. Section Secretary), Mr

> T. O. Mein (Great Eastern Section secretary), Mr H. Higson (Great Central secretary), and Mr G. Jackson (North Eastern Area secretary), Mr Mangus, Mr Wardale, Mr Goodley and other watched the competition.
>
> "G.E. Sectional Final Ambulance Competition 1929" The LNER report showed "The final ambulance competition with this Section's centre was held at the G. E, Mechanic's Institution, Stratford New Town, on April 17, when the seven teams mentioned in the April issues were subjected to most interesting tests set by judges, Lieut.-Colonel Brooks, M. D. ., and Dr. A. C. White-Knox.
>
> Mr T. O Mein (hon secretary of the G.E. section centre) announced the result of the competition as follows: -
>
> | | | Marks (Maximum 305) |
> |---|---|---|
> | 1 | Parkeston "A" team | 222 |
> | 2 | March | 221 |
> | 3 | Stratford | 217 |
> | 4 | Liverpool Street | 196 |
> | 5 | Ipswich No. 2 Division | 186 ½ |
> | 6 | Bishop's Stortford | 182 |
> | 7 | Kings Lynn | 162 ½ |
>
> The prize for best individual work was won by T. Lemm, of Parkeston "A" team, with 42 ½ out of a possible 50 marks.
>
> The prizes were then distributed by Lord Ailwyn (a director of the Company). Also, on the platform were Mr Alex. Wilson, Colonel H. H. Mauldin, Mr Magnus, Mr T. O. Mein, Colonel F. A. Brooks, and Dr White-Knox (judges in the competition).
>
> Mr Alex Wilson proposed a vote of the thanks to Colonel Brookes and Dr White-Knox. This was seconded by Mr Magnus and carried by acclamation."

04 January 1929 - *Eastern Counties News*. Devastation for Dr King Houchin who placed a memorial notice in the newspaper which read

> Amy Elizabeth Houchin, who died suddenly at the residence of her daughter, 489, Princess-avenue, London, Ontario, Canada, December 31st, 1926 [Error. Date should read '1928'], the beloved wife of Dr E. King Houchin, 26, Valkyrie-road, Westcliff-on-Sea. "Hand across the sea, good-night my darling

In May 1929 the London and *North Eastern Railway Magazine* reported

> The annual general meeting of the Norwich Social and Athletics Club was presided over by Lord Ailwyn[112] and recorded another year of progress.

---

112 Edward Fellowes Ailwyn, 1st Baron Ailwyn of of Honingham, KCVO, KBE, PC, DL (10 November 1855 – 23 September 1924), was a British businessman, farmer and Conservative politician. He was a member of Arthur Balfour's Cabinet as President of the Board of the Board of Agriculture between March and December 1905. Fellowes was also director of the London and North Eastern Railway (LNER), Norwich Union and the National Provident Association and deputy chairman of the Great Eastern Railway prior of the 1923 grouping with LNER.

What was noted was the fact that Mr W. Magnus was the secretary of the club.

In November 1929 the *London and North Eastern Railway Magazine* reported

> Great Eastern Railway Old Comrades' Association.
>
> Liverpool Street Memorial.
> On June 22, 1922, Field Marshall Wilson, Bart., G.C.B., D.S.O., M.P.,[113] unveiled the memorial at Liverpool Street to men of the Great Eastern Railway who fell in the war. Two hours afterwards he was assassinated. On the seventh anniversary a wreath was placed before the tablet to his memory which adjoins the larger monument.

The report continued with Branch news, on Hotels, and then gave news on Norwich.

> Norwich. H.R.H. Princess Mary, on June 29, opened the new wing of the Jenny Lind Hospital, of which the stone laying ceremony was mentioned in the September, 1928, number.
>
> On the following day, which was the eve of the 13th anniversary of the commencement of the battle of the Somme, the Norwich Branch arranged a memorial service to fallen railwaymen.
>
> A parade of about 100 members was organised by Messrs, Bush and Crane, and Lieut.-Colonel Lord Ailwyn, D.S.O., M.C., led the, to Thorpe Station, where the Bishop of Norwich conducted the service, assisted by the Rev. E. T. Keyden, Vicar of Thorpe Hamlet, and the Rev. G. E. Stone. Others present were Mrs Pollock, Lady Ailwyn, Mr H. C. R Carver, Mr G. B. Hennesy, Mr W. R. Magnus and Mr J. B. Willis.
>
> The singing was led by the choir of Thorpe Hamlet, and accompanied by the Norwich Railway-men's Band under Bandmaster Burges.
>
> About 400 people attended the service, and the collection resulted in a further generous contribution to the hospital funds.

A second report appeared in the *"Norwich Social Club,* it read: -

> The literary and debating section opened their season on October 7, when a lecture on "Our Docks, Staiths and Quays" was given by Mr R. Bell, Assistant General Manager. Mr H. W. C. Drury was in the chair, and the lecture was illustrated by slides shown by Mr W. R. Magnus. The lecture, although somewhat of a technical character, was made clear to all, owing to Mr Bell's gift of lucidity. He disclosed the fact that although the L.N.E.R. had sunk 24 ½ million pounds in dock property, there was no direct return on the money.

In 16 May 1930 William Magnus was appointed to Assistant District Superintendent of the L.N.E.R. at Norwich which was announced and reported in the *Essex Chronicle*.

---

113 Field Marshall Sir Henry Hughes Wilson, 1st Baronet, GCB, DSO (5 May 1864 – 22 June 1922), was one of the most senior British Army Officer of WWI and was briefly an Irish Unionist Politician. Wilson served briefly as a Member of Parliament, and also as security advisor to the Northern Ireland government. He was assassinated on his own doorstep by two Irish Republican Army gunmen in 1922 whilst returning home from unveiling a war memorial at Liverpool Street station.

> The L.N.E.R. announce that Mr F. C. Wilson, stationmaster at Liverpool Street, has been appointed District Superintendent, Norwich, and Mr W. R. Magnus, Assistant District Superintendent."

On 24 May 1930 at St Peter Mancroft Church, which has stood in the heart of Norwich for almost 600 years, saw the marriage of William and Maud's daughter, Lena, to William Ernest Heighton.

The Signature of W R Magnus from his daughter's Marriage Certificate

William had other interests outside the Railway and Ambulance world. The following article shows he was a member of the Norwich Hospitals Contributory Scheme Committee. On this occasion Mr Magnus gave a lantern lecture, at Bressingham, on the history and work of the Norfolk and Norwich and Jenny Lind Hospitals which was reported in *The Diss Express* of 20 March 1931

On 17 March 1933, *The Diss Express* reported another event this time at the Corn Hall in Diss.

> Norwich Hospitals Contribution Scheme. Contributory Scheme. – Cinematograph Exhibition and Concert at Diss."

> Under the auspices of the Diss and District Branch of the Norwich Hospital Contributory Scheme, a cinematograph exhibition and concert took place in the Corn Hall, Diss, on Tuesday evening, when the spacious building was well filled with an interested and appreciative audience.

> The films shown depicted the various department of the Hospital under actual working conditions, together with scenes taken during the Queen's visit in October. Mr W. R Magnus (a member of the Hospital Board of Management and Contributory Scheme Committee) explained the pictures and also paid warm tribute to the magnificent work of the nurses and medical staff.

A report published in the *Journal* on 30 December 1933 showed Magnus continuing in his role on the Executive Committee of the Norwich Hospital Fund and Contributory Scheme Committee.

Chapter Seventeen - Superintendent A. A. Atkins Retirement

In the Friday 26th January 1934 edition of the *East Ham Echo* there was a report about the retirement of Superintendent A. A. Atkins.

The article has been edited to show Superintendent Atkins service, purely as he was the Superintendent with responsibility for the Ilford Section of East Ham Division when it was first formed. The salient point of the article are as follows:-

"Ambulance Work

Local Brigade loses its "Father" and "Mother"

APPRECIATION OF RETIRING OFFICERS

East Ham Division of St John Ambulance Brigade is now an "Orphan." Its "father" and "mother" have gone.

For these were the terms affectionately given to Supt. A. Atkins and Lady Ambulance Officer Mrs Read respectively, who have decided to retire from active service.

On Thursday evening (18th January) a farewell gathering of officers and members of the Ambulance and Nursing Divisions was held at Lathom-road School, when the Commissioner, Capt. W. Goodley, presented each of them with a divan chair, and a fireside chair for Mrs Atkins.

Supt Atkins' Record

Capt. Goodley said that Supt Atkins's whole career could be looked upon by every member of the Brigade as one of which a man might be proud. He has done volumes of work and volumes of good, and, if it had not been for "dear old Atkins" the present Commissioners name would not have been Goodley.

"He leaves the Division a credit to him-self, to the area, and to the district to which we belong," he said.

The presentation then took place.

Replying, Supt. Atkins said he would like to thank them most heartily for the compliment they had paid him. His work in the past had been one of love stimulated by kind devotion and assistance from all with whom he had come into contact.

Mr M. Harris, the President, presided over the gathering, and among those who came to give farewell greetings were:- District Surgeon Capt F.E. Bendix; District Officer C.J Fitch and Mrs Fitch; District Officer A. Bowers. and Mrs Bowers; Lady District Officer Miss Curtis; Divisional Surgeon Dr McKettrick; Lady District Superintendent Miss. Rideout; H. Lessman, Vice-President; Supt. Gray, of Beckton Division. Lady Supt. Mrs E.M.Morrish (Nursing Division); Ambulance Officer A.E. Ambler; Ambulance Officer T.E.Walsby (Acton Division).

A number of former members of the Division were also present.

Supt. Atkins obtained his First Aid Certificate in May 1894, became attached to the old Oxford House Division and did street duties with the organization before making one of the original members, who inaugurated the East Ham Division in April 1895.

He was also a dual member of the Bethnal Green Division from June, 1894-1901. He was a member of the G.E. Railway team that helped win the G.E.R Cup in 1896. In 1899, he led a team of his new Division at East Ham to victory in the "Dewar Shield" against all England and Wales in ambulance competition. Again in 1901 it was won under his leadership, and one of the most important trophies in the ambulance world rested in East Ham for three years. Was appointed Superintendent in November 1901. He conducted over 2,000 students in ambulance work over the Royal College of Surgeons in London, and organizer of all ambulance work in East Ham during the air raids, which East Ham experienced during the war.

Chapter Eighteen – The Death of William R Magnus

Only weeks after Atkins retirement came the news that William Magnus had died on 1 April 1934 in Norwich. A report of the funeral was published in *The Journal* on 14 April 1934.

> Railwaymen's Tribute.
> At Funeral at Norwich of Mr W. R. Magnus
>
> Railway officials and workers and others, attended in large numbers the funeral service at Norwich on Thursday week, of Mr W. R. Magnus, of Kett's Castle Villa, St Leonard's Road, Norwich. Assistant Superintendent of the Norwich District of the L.N.E Railway.
>
> The service was held at St Peter Mancroft. Lining the pathway of one of the entrances to the church were a number of ticket collectors, goods guards, porters, cleaners, and others engaged in the service of the L.N.E.R.
>
> The body was met at the church door by the vicar, the Rev High McMullan, and a surpliced choir. After the chanting of the 23rd Psalm, the lesson was read by the vicar. There were two hymns. "On the resurrection Morning and Abide with me" As the coffin was being carried out of the church the Nuno Dimittis was chanted, and the organist played "O Rest in the Lord." (Elijah).
>
> The remains were conveyed to Ipswich for cremation.
>
> Among the members of the family were the widow, Mr and Mrs W. E. Heighton (daughter and son in law). Mr Gill (Uncle). Mr G. J. Selby (brother-in-law) and Misses G and F. Selby (sisters-in-law), Mr C. J. Fitch, Sister Clarke.
>
> Many Officials.
>
> Other present included Col. H. H. Maudlin (Superintendent Eastern Section L.N.E.R). Mr E. F Greenfield (District Superintendent, Norwich), Mr F. C. Wilson (District Superintendent, Stratford). Mr Thos. R. Buck (District Police Inspector representing R. R. Buck, Chief of Police), Mr G. B Hennessy (District Loco Superintendent, Ipswich), and Mrs Hennessy, Mr P. S. Ludlam (District Goods and Passenger Manager, Ipswich), Captain W. Goodley (Commissioner No 1 District) Mr H. R Statham (District Good and Passenger Manager Norwich) and Mrs, Statham.
>
> The list continued with further railway officials and mention of Lowestoft Ambulance Division and a long list of Hospital Representatives from the Norwich and Norfolk Hospital Management Board and the Hospital Contributory Scheme. The Sincerity Lodge of Freemasons of which Mr Magnus was a member. Mr T. O. Mein (Hon Secretary of the G. E. R Ambulance Centre), Mr R. D. Brown (Secretary of the L.N.E.R Ambulance Division), C. J. Fitch (Ilford) [Already mentioned with the family above].

On 21 April 1934, *The Journal* reported on a First Aid Competition held in London. It is pertinent to note the following

> Congratulations to Yarmouth team on attaining second place in the railwaymen's St John Ambulance and first aid competition held in London last week. They had to compete against thirty-five teams from the largest places in the Kingdom, and actually, on points, came within two points of winning the highest award. It was their best performance. At the tea following

the competition the chairman paid a unique tribute to the late Mr W. R. Magnus, of Norwich, L.N.E.R., by reciting the whole of chapter XXV, of St Matthew's Gospel. Mr Magnus had been at the heart and soul in ambulance and first aid work.

Probate index 1934

> William Robert Magnus Thorpe Hamlet Norwich died 1st April 1934 Probate 10th May 1934 to Maud Beatrice Magnus and Charles Joslin Fitch, assistant Manager estate value £1146.0.2d.

Charles J Fitch[114] was another prominent St John Ambulance Officer and he also was a president of The Hospitallers' Club in 1932 and Honorary Treasurer from 1928-1930.

---

[114] Charles Joslin Fitch was born to Charles William Fitch, a cooper, and Elizabeth on 23 August 1875 in Kennington. He attended Bellville Road School in 1887. At the time of the 1901 census he was living at 28 Nuffield Road, Leyton. Charles Joslin was a commercial clerk. In 1909 he married and the 1911 census shows he, and his wife Amy lived at 170 Hampton Road. Ilford. In 1925 he became Divisional Superintendent of No 4 Leyton and Leytonstone Division and later in 1927 promoted to District Officer and in 1940 Assistant Commissioner Eastern Area. In 1939 he was appointed Assistant Controller of Essex VAD. In 1933 he was admitted as an Officer of the Order of St John. He died in Rush Green Hospital on 27 January 1941.

Chapter Nineteen - A. A. Atkins and Dr King Houchin Pass Away

In 1936 came the loss of two key members who had supported Ilford Division from its early days. First there was the news of Dr King Houchin in February and later in August saw the loss of Mr A. A. Atkins, who was in charge of the East Ham Division when Ilford was a Section of his Division. So, between 1934 and 1936 all the founding fathers of Ilford Division had passed away.

On the 22 February 1936 the *Essex Newsman* reported in its

> "Brentwood Section – Former Coroner's death at Shenfield, - Mr Edmund King Houchin died at Oaktree Cottage, Shenfield, on Monday, at the age of 88 years. Formally coroner in the East End of London. Mr Houchin, as a police surgeon had to do many well-known cases. He retired about 15 years ago, and lived at Kelvedon until a short while since."

Dr King Houchin was last recorded in the 1935 Medical Register as follows:-

> HOUCHIN, Edmund King (retired), 1, Knights Templars, Kelvedon, Essex--L.R.C.P.Ed. & L.M., L.R.C.S. Ed. 1880 ; L.S.A. Lond. 1875; (Lond. Hosp. & Ed.); Fell. Hunt. Soc.; late Dep. Coroner E. Lond. & Liberty of the Tower.[115]

He was survived by his son and a daughter who lived in Canada.

In August 1936 the news of the death of Mr A. A. Atkins the former Superintendent of No 15 East Ham Division was recorded in the *London & North Eastern Railway Magazine, (Volume 26 page 617)* reported that:-

> Mr A. A. Atkins, formerly an assistant in the Engineer's Office at Liverpool Street, died on August 1, at the age of 80. He served for 42 years and retired at the end of 1921. Mr Atkins was a member of the Geological Association and for many years was the curator of the G.E.R. Museum in the Board Room at Liverpool Street. Other activities included the office of superintendent, East Ham Division, St John Ambulance Brigade with whom he had a long period of continuous service.

His home and occupation shown in various Censuses as follows

> 1881 Census Living in Battersea - Occupation Draughtsman
> 1901 Census shown living at 41 First Avenue Manor Park - Occupation Draughtsman
> 1911 Census shown living at 41 First Avenue Manor Park - Occupation Assistant (Drawing Office) Engineer's Dept GER

---

[115] The Liberties of the Tower, or the Tower Liberty was an area adjoining the Tower of London, which was outside the jurisdiction of either the City of London or the County of Middlesex. The liberty originally consisted of the area inside the walls of the Tower and immediately outside it, including Tower Hill. The limits were set out in the sixteenth century. The liberty continued as a franchise coroner's district until the Coroners (Amendment) Act 1926. This provided that the district could be dissolved when a vacancy arose; when a vacancy occurred on 10 May 1939, an order was made on 30 November 1939 combining it with the east district. This came into effect on 1 January 1940.

Chapter Twenty - Mrs Maud Magnus

Mrs W. R. Magnus presented prizes at the Norwich First Aid Competition. The following is a short extract taken from *Yarmouth Independent* 01 February 1936 (edited).

> Rail Ambulance Contest
> Yarmouth Team Win Norwich District Officers Shield
>
> L.N.E.R Norwich District Officer Shield was won by the team from – Yarmouth (South-town), (leader, Mr W. Page) at the seventh annual ambulance competition, at Ailwyn Hall, Norwich on Saturday. The runners-up team were the Norwich Team (leader, Mr H. G. Lindens).
>
> The shield was given by the District Officer [Given by W.R. Magnus in 1930] to encourage ambulance work among the members of staff under their supervision. On four occasions Lowestoft has had the distinction of holding the shield, Norwich having succeeded twice. On Saturday, competing teams came from Yarmouth, Lowestoft, Norwich, Brandon, Thetford, Attleborough and Wymondham.
>
> The judges were Capt. W. Goodley, Commissioner, London District, St John Ambulance Brigade (team test) and Mr C. J. Fitch, District Officer, London District, St John Ambulance Brigade (individual tests).
>
> At the close Mrs W. R. Magnus (Serving Sister of the Order of St John), whose late husband inaugurated these competitions, presented the shield and prizes to the winning teams, the first prize, in addition to the honour of holding the shield, consisting of cake-stands, and the second fruit spoons.
>
> Proposing a vote of thanks to Mrs Magnus, Mr H. R. Statham said that the sprite of the work that Mr and Mrs Magnus had done for the ambulance movement in Norwich would live.

In 1938 Maud Magnus was again invited to be present at the Norwich District Competition. The following is a report taken from the *Yarmouth Independent* 29 January 1938 (edited).

> SHIELD WON FOR THE FOURTH TIME
>
> Norwich Success in Railway Ambulance Contest.
>
> For the fourth time Norwich Railwaymen's ambulance team won the District Officers Shield Competition at the Ailwyn Hall[116] on Saturday. They thus equal the record of Lowestoft. Yarmouth have won the shield once, and on this occasion, they were runners-up.
> The team test was watched by an interested gathering. A man was assumed to have been knocked down by a van and the patient had been moved to the pavement outside a shop. The supposed injuries were on the arm, ribs and knee-cap.

---

116 Ailwyn Hall was used for First Aid Competition by the GER and LNER, and named after a former Director of the company. The building has fallen into disrepair and has been derelict since 2005. By November 2020, the building has decayed further, and is now without a roof. The historic hall in Lower Clarence Road, Thorpe Hamlet, was widely known as the venue of the Norwich branch of the Federation of Railway Clubs. For more than 80 years it has been a favourite haunt for past and present railway workers and their families and in its heyday had more than 800 members.

The test was judged by Captain W. Goodley, M.C.,Kt.St,J., Commissioner of London District of the St John Ambulance Brigade, who was in charge of the First Aid Organisation for the Coronation celebrations in London. Individual Tests were conducted by Mr C. J. Fitch, a district officer of the London District

The arrangements for the competition were ably carried out by Mr R. D. Brown, secretary. Result: Norwich 321 marks, Yarmouth 305, Thetford 260, Lowestoft 247, Attleborough 245, Brandon 225.

The shield and prizes, consisting of cut-glass sugar basins, were presented to the winning team by Mrs W. R. Magnus, S.S.St.J., whose late husband inaugurated the competition in 1930.

Mr H. R. Statham, district goods and passenger manager, who presided, was supported by Mr H. G. Fish (district loco superintendent) Mr H. O Rampling (assistant district superintendent), and Mr Ainger (Stationmaster at Norwich Thorpe). Mrs Statham, Mrs Fish, and Mrs Fitch were also present.

"Work in Rail Disaster"
The Chairman said he was glad to see six teams competing again and welcomed the return of Attleborough. It was essential that ambulance work should be 100 percent everywhere. He appealed to the womenfolk to encourage their husbands and sons in this important work. After the presentation of the shield Mr Fish thanked Mrs Magnus mentioning that she was a Serving Sister of the Order of St John and during the war she not only served in a war hospital but rendered valuable service at the great Ilford rail smash.

Mrs Magnus recalling that disaster, which happened in 1915, said that she had never felt so tired in all her life as she did when they finished attending to the injured. If they were called upon only once in a lifetime to help in an emergency like that, all their training and study would have been worthwhile.

Responding to a vote of thanks from the Captain of the Norwich team, Captain Goodley thanked the "Patient" for his services in the test.

Mr Fitch reminded the losing teams that most marks were lost over lack of knowledge over subjects in the Black Book. This could be remedied by Individual study.
The Chairman was thanked by Mr Rampling and Mr Statham thanked the Secretary Mr Brown and Mr Fayfield for the use of the hall and Mrs Tallent at the tea table.

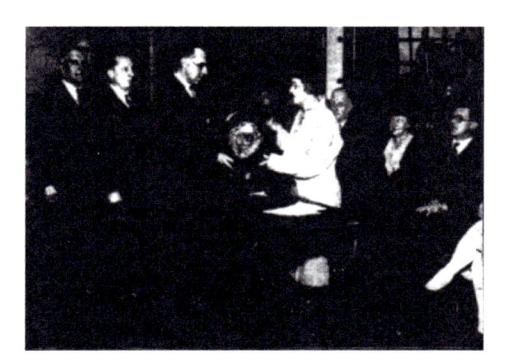

Mrs W. R Magnus, whose late husband inaugurated the L.N.E.R. Ambulance Competition, presenting the shield to the Norwich team, who have won the competition for the fourth time.

After 1938 I could find no further record of Maud Magnus until 1961, a year before her death, when she was invited to the No 15 Ilford Nursing Divisions Golden Jubilee and a letter was received by the then Divisional Superintendent. Mrs. A. M. Walker. It was reported in *The Recorder* on 12 October 1961

> A letter was received from the first superintendent, Mrs. Magnus, now living in Norwich, she was unable to attend the celebration through infirmity. Instead, she sent a plaque which during the First World War was hung over a bed in France in 1915. The bed was subscribed for by Ilford [for] the St. John Hospital at Etaples. The plaque is now in the keeping of the superintendent pending the acquisition of a permanent headquarters by the division in which it can be housed[117].

She was born in 1878, having survived her husband by 28 years and died on 16 September, 1962, at the age of 84 years and left her estate of £3084. 8s, to her daughter Lena Elsie Heighton.

William and Maud's Daughter and Son-in-Law

William and Maud's example of public service was passed on to their daughter and son-in-law who both played their part in Voluntary Service during World War Two. Lena and William Heighton married on 24 May 1930 in Norwich.

William Heighton was a shop keeper. He was also a Red Cross First Aider according to the 1939 Register. William Ernest Heighton, died in late 1973 in Norwich, Norfolk, when he was 69 years old. Lena Heighton was a member of the WVS Civil Defence again as detailed in the 1939 Register. Lena Elsie Heighton (née Magnus) survived her husband by 12 years and died in Sexlingham Nethergate, Norfolk on 1 February 1985. Sadly, there was no issue from their marriage. Probate was granted, in Ipswich on 2 May 1985, with an estate worth £46705.

Perhaps Maud Beatrice Magnus's words at the 1938 Norwich Competition are a fitting tribute to her and her husband William and Dr Edmund King Houchin. Mrs Magnus said in recalling the Ilford Railway disaster of 1915: -

> **If they were called upon only once in a lifetime to help in an emergency like that, all their training and study would have been worthwhile.**

---

[117] Divisional Superintendent G. C. Everitt, came into procession of the plaque and was part of a collection of items he handed to the Redbridge Museum and Heritage Centre.

Appendix No 1 The Cases of Dr Edmund King Houchin

Dr King Houchin Police Surgeon
A Dickensian Case

The first case has all the hallmarks of a tale from Charles Dickens. It appeared initially in the *Tower Hamlets Independent* on 19 January 1884. The paper reported -

> The Charge of starving a child. In this case one William Weston, 40, a glass pillar maker and Emma Burton, 40 of 4, Lydia-street, White Horse-lane, Stepney. They were both placed in the dock charges, on a final remand with cruelly treating and neglecting to provide proper food and nourishment for Charles Holmes Joyce, a little boy aged 7 years, and nephew of the defendant Burton. Inspector Young of the H. Division prosecuted for the Police. The prisoners were undefended. The court was densely crowded. Amongst others Dr Edmund King Houchin was called in his capacity as Divisional Surgeon for the Police, High Street, Stepney. He testified as to the terrible state of starvation and ill-usage in which he found the child whom he was called to examine. Dr Anson Atkins, Jun., medical superintendent of Mile End Town Infirmary, said that he received the child when it was brought in on the 24 November. It was in a most pitiable state. Witness heard Dr Houchin's evidence, and agreed with it in every particular. For some time after the child was admitted it suffered from convulsive fits and syncope's being due to its debilitated condition and at times, its recovery appeared doubtful. It had however, got on very well with careful nursing. When admitted it only weighed 24 lbs., but it now weighed 25 lbs., and was progressing favourably. The Prisoners then, in answer to the charge made some rambling remarks, denying that they had been unkind to the boy. Mr Sanders, the Magistrate, then committed them both for trial as the next Middlesex Sessions.

The Standard of 8 February 1884, took up the story when the case against Emma West, alias Burton and William Weston, was heard at the Middlesex Sessions when the case was heard before Mr Edlin, QC, Assistant Judge.

> Constable Crabtree said he was called to the "house where the prisoners lived, when he got there he heard moaning from a room upstairs. He went up and knocked on the door, but received no answer, he entered the room, he saw the female prisoner standing up and the little child sitting in a chair, a rope tied five times round his body, and fastened to the back of the chair. There was another rope tied around his wrists in front of him, As the child was moaning loudly, and appeared greatly distressed, witness cut the ropes and the child, who was in fainting condition, fell into his arms. Having placed the child on the bed, he turned to the female Prisoner, and asked her what was the meaning of all that, and she replied that she had tied him in the chair to keep him out of mischief, upon which he took her into custody. When the child recovered his senses, he was asked who had tied him in the chair, and he said his auntie. The child was at first taken to the station and afterwards the infirmary. Mr Edmund King Houchin, divisional surgeon, said he examined the child at the station. He was about eight years of age, and was in a very weak and emaciated condition and weighed only twenty-four pounds. There were ulcers, bruises, and scratches all over him. The child was only about half the proper weight for a child of his age. – The jury found the women Guilty, and said they regretted to acquit the male Prisoner. The Assistant Judge sentenced her to be imprisoned and kept to hard labour for nine months.

Houchin's and the possible 'Jack the Ripper' Case

Dr King Houchin also had connections with some cases which are often linked with and around the time that the Jack the Ripper murders occurred in the Whitechapel area.

One case is that of Aaron Kosminski formerly Kozminski who was born on 11 September 1865 in Poland.

Mr Kosminski became a prime suspect in the Whitechapel murders – which took place between 1888 and 1891 – when the head of the CID at the time, Sir Robert Anderson, published his memoirs in 1910 which claimed that the police knew the identity of Jack the Ripper.

In July 1890, Aaron was taken to Mile End Old Town Workhouse because he was exhibiting signs of mental instability. He was discharged on 15 July 1890. Following a gap of just over a year we find that on 5 February 1891 he was readmitted to Mile End Old Town Workhouse. He was examined by Dr Houchin on the 6 July 1891 and declared insane.

Dr Houchin's report on Aaron gives his views about the patient's mental state, and says specifically -

> He declares that he is guided and his movements although controlled by an instinct that informs his mind; he says that he "knows the movements of all mankind" and "Compulsively self-abused himself".

When Kosminski was admitted to Colney Hatch, it was said that, 'He goes about the streets and picks up bits of bread from the gutter and eats them, he drinks water from the standpipe and refuses food at hands of others, he is very dirty and will not be washed.' Kosminski died as a patient at Leavesden Asylum in 1919 after being sent there in 1894 from Colney Hatch Lunatic Asylum. [118] He was buried in East Ham, this was confirmed when it was stated by "The United Synagogue can confirm we have an Aaron Kosminski buried in East Ham Jewish Cemetery in London."[119]

Sadler and The Whitechapel Murder

The Times (London) on 17 February 1891 reported on the Whitechapel Murder.

> The police, after detaining the man James Thomas Sadler upwards of 40 hours in the Leman-street Police-station, considered that they had then sufficient evidence to charge him with the wilful murder of the young woman, who has now been positively identified as Frances Coles. On Sunday Sadler complained of a pain in his side, and on being examined by the divisional surgeon he was found to be suffering from a broken rib. Yesterday Dr Houchin visited the Arbour-square Police-station and treated the injury.

---

[118] https://www.watfordobserver.co.uk/news/9996344.jack-the-ripper-suspect-buried-in-jewish-cemetery-in-east-ham-claim/ accessed 25 April 2022.

[119] Ibid www.watfordobserver.co.uk

Sadler, was not able to give any coherent account of his movements after an early hour on Thursday night, owing to the condition he was in from the effects of drink. He stated that he met the deceased woman on Wednesday and passed that night with her at a common lodging-house. During the greater portion of Thursday, he was in her company and gave her money. He strongly denies having had anything to do with her death.

The police still incline to the belief that the prisoner has had nothing to do with the previous murders in Whitechapel, and, in fact, one or two of his discharges prove that he was away at sea at the time some of them were committed.

It has been ascertained that the woman Coles was the daughter of an old bootmaker, who is now an inmate of the Bermondsey Workhouse. She was 25 years of age, and at one time was engaged in an East-end bottling warehouse.

Sadler was placed under arrest, and a mob almost lynched him at the exit of a police station. Eventually, he was dismissed by police for having a solid alibi, and obtained compensation from a newspaper that had branded him as Jack the Ripper.

No one else was charged with the killing of Frances Coles.

Emma Dorcy – The strangest case that had ever come to the Coroner's notice.

The Standard dated 30 April 1892 carried a report of an inquest held by Dr Wynne Baxter at which Dr Houchin was a witness.

> Mr Wynne E. Baxter, Coroner for East London held an inquiry yesterday at the Seaman's Chapel, Ratcliffe, into the death of Emma Hannah Dorcy, aged 40, the wife of a blacksmith residing in Belgrave-street, Stepney, who died on Wednesday under the following circumstances – Ambrose Dorcy, the husband, deposed that on his return home on Easter Sunday, about three o'clock, he was informed that his wife had gone to the doctor's as she had swallowed a piece of bone whilst eating her dinner. When she returned she said "Ambrose, this is my death blow," and added Dr Houchin had passed an instrument down her throat but was unable to find anything. At ten o'clock Witness went for the doctor again, and he advised the deceased be taken to the London Hospital. Witness conveyed her there in a cab, arriving at the hospital about a quarter past ten p.m. She was taken and the card which was given by Dr Houchin was handed to a porter, who went in search of a doctor, but after a lapse of half and an hour he returned and said he could not find one. Some little while afterwards two doctors arrived and used an instrument, afterwards which they said they had cleared the obstruction, but as they could make the deceased understand it, they would keep her in for a day or two, she stayed there till the Tuesday, and then left.
>
> At home she was attended by Dr Houchin till her death on Wednesday morning. Alice Wilson, the wife of a shop-man, said that the deceased was her mother. On Easter Sunday they were having dinner, which consisted of rib of beef, greens and potatoes. They were eating rather hurriedly, as they wanted to get out, when the deceased suddenly said she had swallowed a piece of bone. – Dr Houchin deposed that he examined the deceased throat and gullet, but could not discover any foreign body. The same day that she came out of the hospital he found her suffering excruciating pain in the back. She went on fairly well for two days, and then the pain became more intense, and extending lower down. Death took place from exhaustion, the deceased having vomited a quantity of blood and mucous membrane, which had coughed away from the gullet. The deceased was under the impression that she had swallowed a piece of bone or skewer. The post-mortem examination had shown that a piece of lamp-glass, about an inch in length, with jagged edges, had become embedded in the gullet, having cut through the windpipe to the extent of one and a half inches. Being concave

on one side and convex on the other, it would adapt itself to the walls of the gullet, and Witness did not think it could have been extracted by any means during life. It was a marvel how the deceased swallowed so large a piece of glass. – Mrs Wilson, recalled, stated that about a fortnight before Easter a large lamp-glass exploded in her room, the pieces being scattered all over the place. A basket which was laying there was subsequently used to bring home the greens which they had for the Sunday's dinner, and the probability was that the piece of glass was put in the saucepan with them. – The Coroner remarked that it was one of the strangest cases that had ever come to his notice. With regard to the alleged delay at the hospital, he suggested that the Jury should leave this matter in his hand, and he would communicate with the House Governor. -The Jury returned a verdict of Accidental Death.

Death from Anthrax

On 17 November 1899 *The Monmouth Beacon* reported on a case of "Death form Anthrax." On Saturday Dr King Houchin (deputy coroner) held an inquiry at the London Hospital respecting the death of Edward Brandon, a horsehair-currier, who died on Wednesday last from anthrax.

> On the Saturday previous Brandon went to work in perfect health, but returned later complaining of severe pains at the back of the neck. Witness then noticed a small pimple, in the centre of which was a little black spot like a small piece of black horsehair. The following day it became inflamed, and the deceased said that the pains were spreading all up the back of his head. On Monday he was too ill to go to work, and his throat began to swell. On Tuesday he went to work, but the pain was so intense he had to leave, and on the way home he called at the London Hospital, where he was detained and died the following day. Deceased in his duties used English and American hair, but he had nothing to do with Russian hair, though Russian tails were on the premises. Notices as to cleanliness were hung prominently about the premises and appliances supplied.
>
> Mr Clement White (house surgeon) stated the deceased was admitted suffering from anthrax, and an operation was deemed necessary. The patient was placed on the operation table, but as soon as chloroform was administered he expired. The autopsy showed death to be heart failure, the result of the weak condition to which the anthrax had brought the patient and to the fact that the deceased was an alcohol subject.- The jury returned a verdict of "Death by Misadventure."

Needle Prick Causes Death.

Within a week or so another case was reported on 25 November 1899, in the *East London Advertiser*.

> Needle Prick Causes Death. At the London Hospital, an inquest was held by Dr King Houchin concerning the death of Amelia Such, 45, the wife of a furrier, living at 85, Campbell-road, Bow. The evidence showed that a fortnight ago the deceased pricked her finger with a rusty needle while sewing. No notice was taken of the occurrence until the finger began to swell. A doctor was called in, who advised removal to hospital, and death ensued form blood poisoning. A verdict of "Accidental death" was returned.

Ilford Builder's sad suicide.

Another case came to light on 06 December 1902 when the *Essex Newsman* reported

Ilford Builder's sad suicide. Dr Ambrose held an inquest at the Town Hall on Thursday on Chas White, 40, a builder, of Valentines-road, Ilford. – Mrs White said her husband had suffered for some years from nervous disability and dyspepsia. On Monday, at 6.40 a.m., he said he would wash himself, and entered the bathroom. She heard a thud, and found her husband lying on the bathroom floor, bleeding from a wound to the throat.- The police produced a bottle labelled "poison" and a razor which were found in the bathroom. – Dr King Houchin said the deceased's windpipe was severed. The deceased died at three a.m. on Tuesday, from shock due to haemorrhage. – Mrs White, recalled, said the deceased had apparently taken the poison bottle, which was empty from the cupboard. -A verdict of "Suicide while temporarily insane" was returned.

24 July 1903 *Essex County Chronicle*. It reported on the death of a docker.

"Death from a Mosquito Bite". "Dr King Houchin held an inquest on Saturday on Robert Sutton, 40, dock labourer, of Pennington-street, St George's, E., who died on Tuesday from the effects of a mosquito bite. – Three weeks ago, the deceased was working at Tilbury Docks, and returned home with his eye greatly swollen. He said that he had been bitten by a mosquito, and the pain was dreadful. On the 3rd inst, he obtained some lotion from the parish doctor, but on the following day was admitted to the infirmary, where he died on Wednesday. – Dr Bowlem, medical superintendent, deposed to finding the deceased's face very red and swollen. There were marks on the forehead and eyelids consistent with mosquito bites. Deceased was suffering from erysipelas supervening on mosquito bites." – Verdict, "Death by misadventure."

Appendix No 2 The Rymer Family - A new life in Canada

Founders of Edmonton Division, Alberta, Canada.

The following accounts appeared in the press following the family's move to Canada.

On the 31 August 1928 the *Eastern Counties News* announced :-

> Births
> Connolly. – To Annie (née Rymer), wife of Alex Connolly, 11522 - 85th Edmonton, Albert, Canada, on August 25th – a daughter (cable message).

The Rymer's sent the following to *The Recorder* who published it on 10 July 1931.
> We have been very pleased to receive this message from two old Ilford residents who are now happily settled in Edmonton, Alberta, Canada. "At the close of their first year's residence in 'The Golden West,' Fred J and Mrs Rymer send hearty greetings and kindest regards and remembrances to all old friends and neighbours, and they are glad to say that they are now comfortably located in the house next to their eldest daughter, Annie (Mrs Alex. Connolly), at 11520-85th Street, Edmonton. The home is large enough to accommodate them and their youngest son Alfred, together with their youngest daughter, Dorothy (Mrs Dan Connolly) and her husband. Their eldest son James F. Q. Rymer, his wife and two children are also living in the city just a street car journey away. Climate and conditions generally in Western Canada have so far agreed with all the family, that apart from the effects of 'Anno Domini,' continues good. They find it impossible to write to all their old friends but are always glad to hear from them, if only a few lines, occasionally.

The Recorder published information from the Rymer family on the 8 June 1933, it read-

> Ilfordians in Canada.
>
> News of old Ilfordians abroad is welcome by the "*Recorder*," and so I was particularly interested in a copy a copy of the "*Edmonton Journal*" sent by Mr Fred J. Rymer, formerly managing director of Sampson Low, the publisher, and now residing at Edmonton, Alberta, Canada. Mr Rymer lived in Ilford for many years and was a valued member of the Ilford Men's Meeting. When he retired from business to or three years ago he decided, much to the regret of his many friends in this country, to make his home in Canada, where many members of his family had already settled.
>
> From the "*Edmonton Journal*" I gather that Rymer is a name that carries distinction in that part of the world. On the front page is a picture of two groups of fine upstanding men, rival teams in a first aid contest between Edmonton and Calgary. St. John Ambulance Brigades. The chief point of the story from my point of view is that the captain of the Edmonton team is Mr Rymer's eldest son Supt. James F. Q Rymer, who recently founded and organised the Edmonton Division of the Brigade. Also, in the team (and the tallest member of it) is Mr Rymer's youngest son. Alfred, who has followed in his brother's footsteps by becoming an ambulance enthusiast.
>
> Although the Edmonton Division did not win the report says that they lost by only a small margin of points and the Calgary superintendent paid a "high tribute to their ability and sportsmanship."

A good many people will remember Supt. Rymer as one of the founders of the Ilford St. John Ambulance Division, Prince of Wales Corps, when it came into being through the agency of the Ilford Men's Meeting. By the way he is still and overseas member of the I.M.M.

I am glad to learn from Mr Rymer's letter that both he and his wife are in good health – "keeping fairly well for two old people," as he puts it. His two daughters Mrs Annie Connelly and Mrs Dorothy Connolly, have both been under serious operations at the chief hospital in Edmonton but are now convalescing. He concludes by sending regards to all old friends in Ilford.

The Recorder 14 June 1934 carried the news that

Mr F. J. Rymer. Death of Former Ilfordian in Canada.

News has been received from Canada of the death of Mr Fred J. Rymer, of Edmonton, Alberta, formerly of Ilford.

Mr Rymer, who was in his 75th year, was for many years managing director of the well-known publishing house of Sampson, Lowe Marston & Co. Ltd. He joined the company nearly fifty years ago, and in the course of business made the friendships with famous authors. He was intimately acquainted with Oliver Wendell Holmes, H. M. Stanley, William Black, R. D. Blackmore (Mr Rymer's house in Canada was named "Lorna Doone") and among more modern writer, Jeffrey Farnol and Dona Byrne.

Until he retired from business four years ago, Mr Rymer lived in Ilford, where he took a great interest in the work of the Ilford Men's Meeting. His children having made their homes in Canada., he and Mrs Rymer decided to spend their leisure years near them. It was characteristic of Mr Rymer, however, that he never forgot his friends in Ilford and from his letters, which he sent fairly frequently it seem that he had settled happily in his new home.

A card from him always reached the "Recorder" office at Christmas, and the last bore quotations from Dickens: "May the wing of Friendship never moult a feather" (Dick Swiveller [120]) "God bless us every one" (Tiny Tim [121]).

Mr Rymer was a member of the Edmonton Club, the Optimist Club and the McDougall Men's Association of Edmonton.

The *Recorder* 9 August 1934 noted the death of Mr F. J. Rymer, of Edmonton, Alberta, formerly of Belmont-road, Ilford, and died also on June 8th, at the age of 74, left £8,408.

---

120 Richard 'Dick' Swiveller is a fictional character in the 1841 novel The Old Curiosity Shop by Charles Dickens.

121 Timothy "Tiny Tim" Cratchit is a fictional character from the 1843 novella A Christmas Carol by Charles Dickens.

The St John Ambulance Brigade Ilford

Appendix No 3 A Fine Romance

A wounded soldier finds romance in the hospital, the story of Ruth Gilham and George Jack.

Ruth Victoria Gillam was born in Ilford in 1899, then aged 11, she was shown on the 1911 Census for England and Wales as living at the Old School House, Horns Road, Barkingside Ilford. Her Father was Walter George Gillam, aged 41 and her Mother was Sarah Graydon Gillam, aged 45.

George Lindsay Jack was born in 1897 in Craigiemore Lathen Nairn, Scotland

The WW1 Pension Record Cards and Ledgers, Reference 1/MJ1157 showed George was recorded as having a "Disability" and was discharged from the Army on 8 October 1918. The Roll of Individuals for 1919 showed that George was awarded the Victory Medal and the British War Medal.

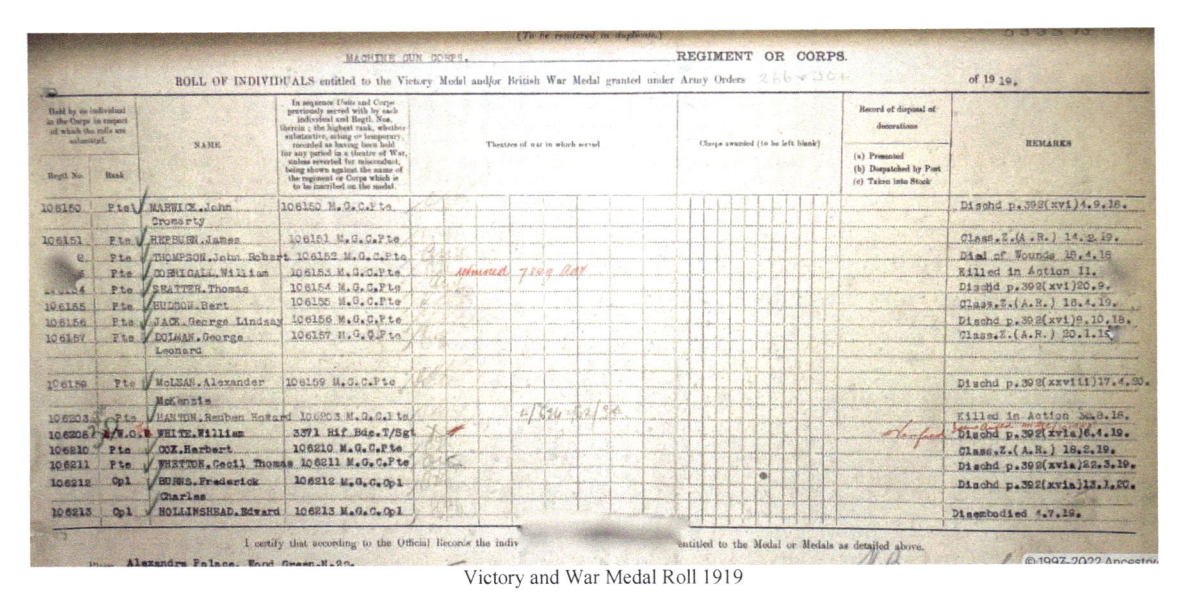

Victory and War Medal Roll 1919

George Lindsay Jack was a Private in the Machine Gun Corps, Regimental No 106156. In 1920 he was awarded War Service Badge No 516629.

War Service Badge Roll

Ruth V Gillam was married in 1925 to George L Jack in the Romford Registration District.

After their marriage they move to Scottish Highlands and lived at 5 Glebe Cottages Auldearn,- Spysar Lethen.

Ruth died on the 3 September 1967, aged 69, and was laid to rest in Auldearn & Dalmore Kirk Burial Ground, Highland, Scotland.

George, survived Ruth by 15 years. He died on 21 October 1982, aged 84, and was also laid to rest in Auldearn & Dalmore Kirk Burial Ground, Highland, Scotland.

These comments were written by George Jacks daughter.

George Lindsay Jack was a Private in the Seaforth Highlanders, Machine Gun Corps. Amongst the family items are

1. Snapshot Album of Ilford Emergency Hospital containing 12 views in sepia. Printed for
fundraising. 7 images.

2. Autograph book kept by Ruth Gillam, Ilford Emergency Hospital. Mainly 1918. 17 images.

Story

George Jack was my father. He was the eldest of 5 brothers. My parents met when my father was wounded (Ypres 1917) and returned to England - to Ilford Emergency Hospital. He served with Seaforth Highlanders and was chosen to serve in Machine Gun Corps. 106156 was his regimental number. George Lindsay Jack. My mother, Ruth Gillam, nursed him in Ilford Emergency Hospital. The small book of photos of this hospital was sold to raise funds for an extension to the hospital.

My mother, Ruth Gillam, nursed him in Ilford Emergency Hospital. The small book of photos of this hospital was sold to raise funds for an extension (due to W WI casualties) though the hospital was only built in 1910.

My parents did not marry until 1925 and I recently discovered that this was due to his "flash backs" causing his mother to remark (so I am told) that "He's not well enough to take a wife yet.

They moved from England to the Highlands.

Several soldiers (patients at the hospital), family and friends wrote in her autograph book and some drew! [122]

---

[122] 27/02/2019, Gordon Highlanders Museum, LWF, Aberdeen.

Ruth Gillam nursed George Jack at the Ilford Emergency Hospital. The following are photographs from the Snapshot Album of Ilford Emergency Hospital containing 12 views in sepia. Printed for fundraising. 7 images.

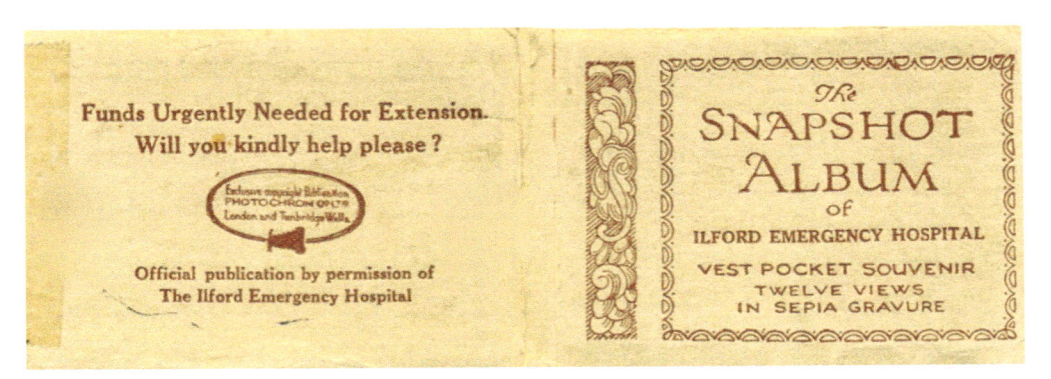

The Board Room

The Verandah King Edward Ward

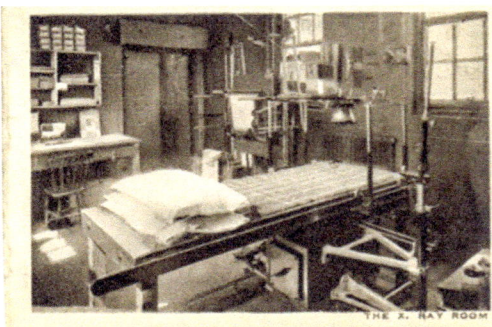

The X-Ray Room

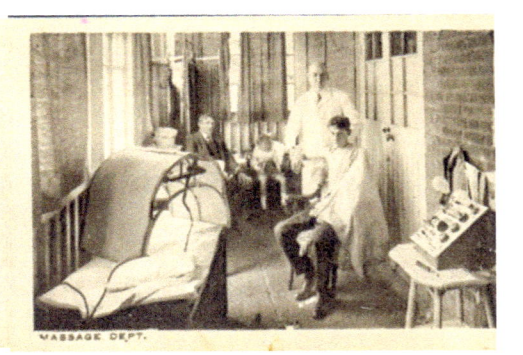

Massage Room

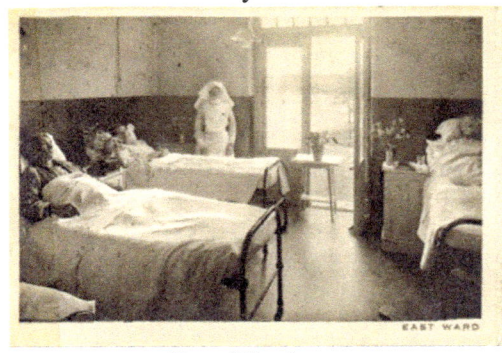

East Ward

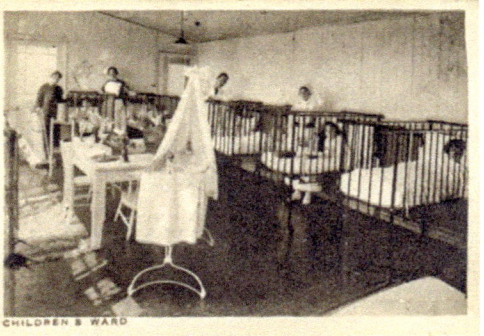

Children's Ward

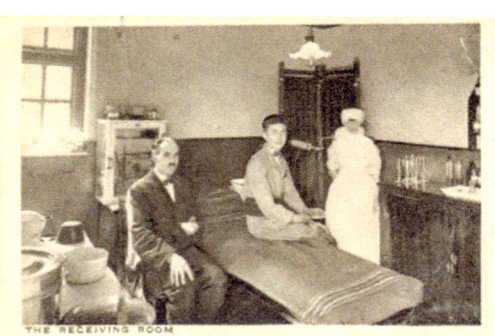

Entrance Hall   Receiving Room

Front View   Back View

Ruth Gillam nursed George Jack at the Ilford Emergency hospital. This is from her autograph book. [123]

> Keep your face always to the sunshine and the shadow will always fall behind you.

Comments on a post[124] indicate

> She was only 18 at the time so I don't think she was a trained nurse but I cannot find her Red Cross record.
>
> The hospital, funded by local charities, was opened in 1912, it became a military hospital in May 1915 with 56 beds and provided intensive care for wounded troops until March 1919[125].

As a maid, as indicated in the Autograph book she may not have been part of a Voluntary Aid Detachment and was possibly employee or a volunteer at the Hospital.

Autograph book kept by Ruth Gillam, Ilford Emergency Hospital. Mainly from 1916 to 1918 contains 17 images. Some of the entries are from soldiers recovering at the Hospitals are identifiable as being form 43rd Battery, Australian Field Artillery and the 38th Canadians Infantry Battalion.

---

[123] Internet access Facebook page of "Remembering British women in WW1 – The Home Front and Oversea" 14 May 2019
[124] Ibid

Whoever has ought to love &
lives aright, will never in the
darkest hour despair.

———

Disappointments should always be
taken as stimulants & never
viewed & discouragements.

Treat your friends for what
you know them to be
Regard no surfaces
Consider not what they did
but what they intended.

With kind regards
from Pte O H Pearse
43 Battery 40th
A.I.F.

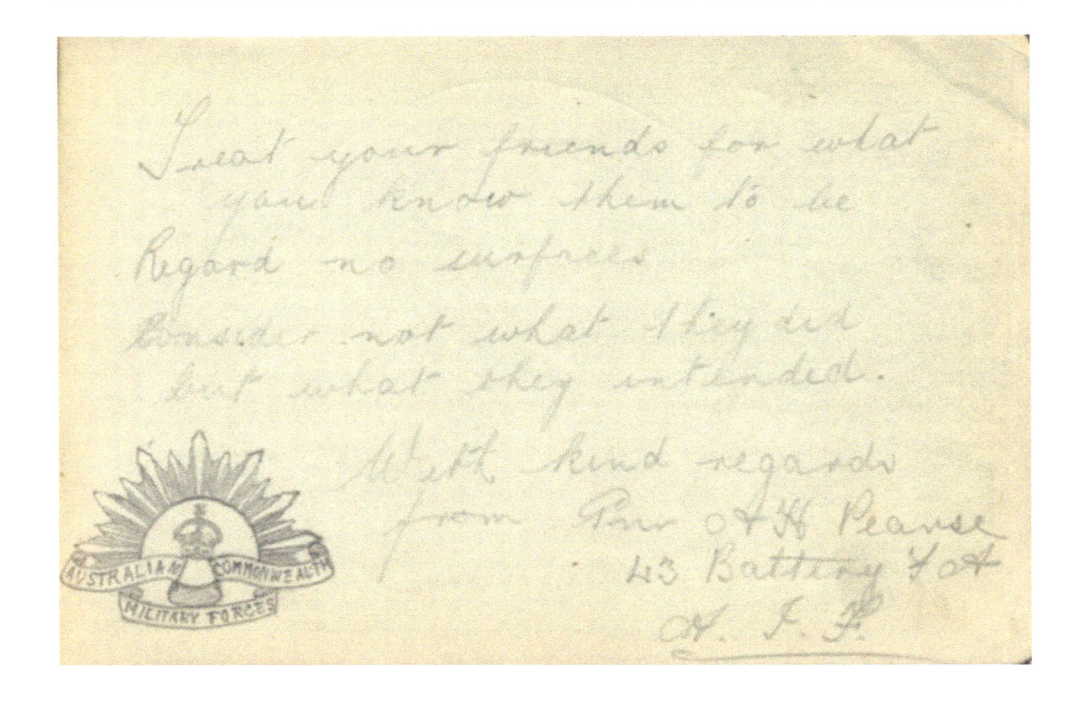

May Good Luck Attend You

Will Savill
28 A.T.S.

ILFORD MIL HOSPITAL
ESSEX
FOR SOLDIER'S ONLY

GEE WHIZZ. A DUD!

Dec. 31st '16.

"If we do our best, if we do not magnify trifling troubles, if we look resolutely, I do not say at the bright side of things, but at things as they really are; if we avail ourselves of the manifold blessings which surround us; we cannot but feel that life is indeed a glorious inheritance." Sir John Lubbock.

Yours sincerely, E. Anderson.

"Smile a little
  & Don't Worry."

                    Motto for 1917.

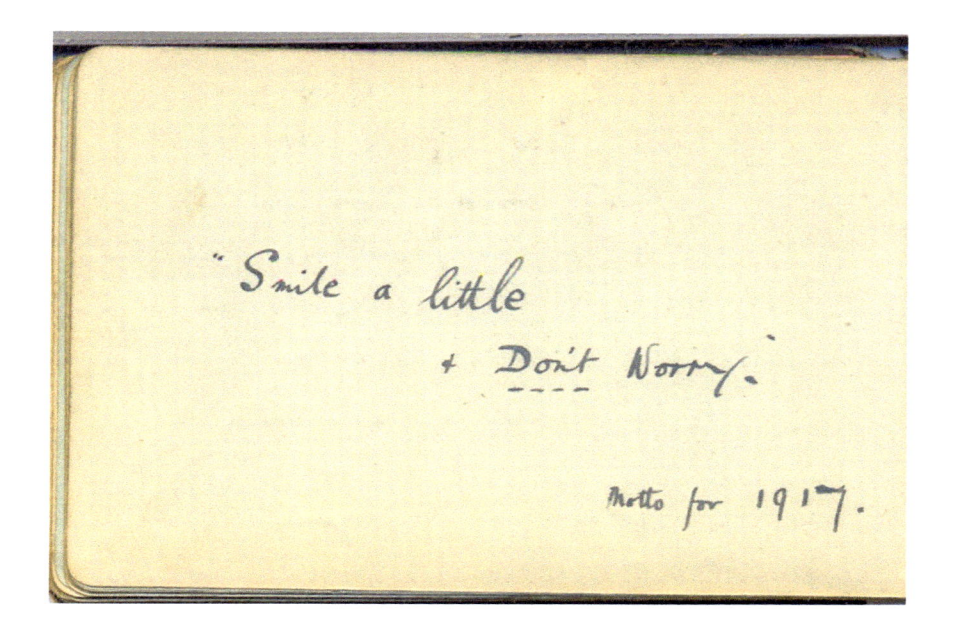

There is so much good in the worst
    of us,
And so much bad in the best of us,
That it ill behoves any of us,
To talk about the rest of us.
                    ―――――
                              A. Frost.
                              25/3/17

Be good sweet maid & let who will
    be clever,
Do noble deeds, not dream them all
    day long.
And so make life, death, & that
    vast forever
One grand sweet song.

                              A. Simmonds
                              6/5/17

The St John Ambulance Brigade Ilford

To Miss Gillam
Feb 18
With kindest regards
Ernest Wardsley

Emergency Hospital
Ilford. Apr. 6, 1918

Keep your face always to the sunshine,
And the shadows will always fall behind you.
Sincerely yours,
Melvin J. O'Reilly.
38th Canadians

Wounded at Passchendaele
Ridge-Ypres- Oct. 31st 1918.

A man may drink & no be drunk
A man may fight & no be slain
A man may kiss a bonny lass
And be welcome back again.
Very Sincerely Yours
Alfred E. Stote
Tank Corps

April 6th 1918.

Lifes Book.

Life is a story, in volumes three,
The past the present, and yet to be,
The first is written, and laid away,
The second we are writing every day,
The third and last of the volumes three
Is locked from sight, God keeps the key.

R.V.S.   G.W. Holmes

"Who did this?"

Many a Ship is lost at Sea.
Through want of tar and Rudder
Many a boy has lost his girl"
Through flirting with another?

Mary had a Harem Skirt
My word it made you laugh
Who cares a d— for Mary's lamb.
When you can see her calf"

The Wages of Sin is Death"
But the wages of the army
Is a D— site worst!"
By one Who Knows

A.W. Savill
28th R.A.F.

Hearts are light. When the Sun is
Shining.
Clouds may darken silver sky.
Every cloud has a silver lining.
It will be brighter by & by.

E. Owen
I.F.H. 14.12.1917

The St John Ambulance Brigade Ilford

Appendix No 4 Ilford VAD Members

The Recorder 04 November 1921

> Recognition of War Service
>
> Mrs W.W. Fish of Auckland, New Zealand, a daughter of Mr and Councillor Mrs Whitten, of Ilford, has been awarded the handsome certificate of the Red Cross Society and the Order of St. John of Jerusalem, for her war-time services to the country. At the outbreak of hostilities, Mrs Fish (then Miss Norah Whitten) came home from Russia, and volunteered her services with the Red Cross. She was first sent to Malta, where she was engaged in picking up wounded soldiers. By strange coincidence one of the first soldiers to come under her care was her own brother. Later her knowledge of languages led to her transfer to the Intelligence Department, where she performed valuable work.
>
> The certificate bears the emblems of the two, organisations, and is signed by Queen Alexandra, president of the Red Cross Society, and the Duke of Connaught, Grand Prior of the Order of St John of Jerusalem, and officers of the joint committee. The text of the award, which is carried out in ornamental lettering, is as follows: Presented by the Joint Committee of the British Red Cross Society and the Order of St John of Jerusalem in England to Norah N. Whitten in recognition of valuable services rendered during the war."
>
> The Certificate is being despatched to Mrs Fish in New Zealand.

This Certificate of Service was awarded to Cecilia Matthews of Wanstead. © Redbridge Museum and Heritage Centre.1996.277

Cecilia Matthews lived at 36 Cowley Road, Wanstead. She was a 22 years old insurance clerk when she became a Voluntary Aid Detachment nurse in December 1915.

The St John Ambulance Brigade Ilford

Appendix No 5 VAD Record for Ilford Members

St. John Ambulance VAD Record for Ilford

Unit	St John Ambulance VAD Ilford Ambulance Division St John Ambulance
Commandant	Mr William R Magnus. M.B.E
Supported	Ilford Emergency Hospital, Valentines Mansions Hospital, Oakwood Hospital, Chigwell. Also provided Support with Air Raid Stand By and Ambulance Conveys
Commission	Essex 27
Information	Courtesy of the British Red Cross VAD Records

Title	Christian Names	Surname	Address	Served From	Served to	Rank	Ilford Emergency	Valantines	Oakwood Red	Air Raid Stand By	Ambulance Convoy	Other Hospitals and Notes
Mr	Walter Richard	Aldridge	77, Northbrook Road, Ilford	00/05/1915	00/04/1918	Corpl	Y	Y		Y	Y	Valentine Mansion, Ilford. Assisted 27 Convoys wounded. Acted as storekeeper and stood by for Air Raid. Ilfords Emergency Hospital and Valentines Mansion Hospital.
Mr	James Richard	Andrews	38 Charlbury Gardens, Seven Kings	00/03/1917		Pte				Y	Y	Attended 34 Convoys and stood by for Air Raids duties.
Mr	Walter	Bradell	47, Meath Road, Ilford	00/06/1915	N/A	Pte	Y	Y		Y	Y	Attended 33 convoys and stood by for Air Raid duties
Mr	Charles Willian	Clark	24, Clements Road, Ilford	00/12/1917		Pte				Y	Y	Attended 28 Convoys and stood by for Air Raids
Mr	John Alfred	Collin	40, Charlbury Gardens, Seven Kings	00/07/1918		Pte					Y	Attended 11 Convoys
Mr	Thomas	Cooling	6, Mansfield Road, Ilford	00/02/1917	00/04/1919	Non Member					Y	Attended 24 Convoys
Mr	George Willian	Dunster	43, Wards Road, Seven Kings	00/05/1915	00/05/1918	Pte	Y	Y		Y	Y	Assisted 24 Convoys & stood by for Air Raid duties
Mr	William Harrell	Hale	93, Cobham Road, Seven Kings	00/07/1915		Pte	Y	Y		Y	Y	Attended 40 convoys and stood by for Air Raid duties. Ilford Emergency Hospital amd Valentines Mansion Hospital
Mr	Henry Edward	Hawdon	14, Cavendish Gardens, Ilford	00/07/1915		Pte	Y	Y		Y	Y	Attended 37 Convoys & stood by for Air Raids
Dr	Edmund King	Houchin	Cranbrook Road, Ilford	00/05/1915		Medical Officer					Y	Stood by for Air Raid duties & assisted 6 convoys of wounded
Mr	Henry Charles	Legg	36, Colombo Road, Ilford	00/07/1915	00/04/1919	Pte	Y	Y		Y	Y	Attended 34 Convoys and stood by for Air Raids duties. Ilford Emergency Hospital and Valentines Mansion Hospital

The St John Ambulance Brigade Ilford

Title	First Name	Surname	Address	Joined	Left	Rank					Notes
Mr	Arthur William	Leyland	44, Sackville Gardends	00/07/1915	00/12/1919	Pte	Y	Y	Y	Y	Attended 13 Convoys and stood by for Air Raids duties. Ilford Emergency Hospital and Valentines Mansion Hospital
Mr	William Robert	Magnus	51, Stanhope Gdns, Ilford	00/05/1915	Still Serving	Commandant	Y		Y	Y Y	Organised whole of Ambulance Transport in connection with Ilford Emergency Hospital, also assisted in connection with Oakwood Red Cross Hospital, Chigwell - a total of 84 Convoys - and 1500 soldiers. In addition 44 journeys were arranged to variouse London and provincial Hospitals with transfer cases, over 100 wounded were transfered involving journeys from 10 to 110 miles. Personally driven car 6000 miles, Air Raid duties of detachment arraged also.
Mr	Morrision Geo	Matthews	13, Bathurst Road, Ilford	00/05/1915	00/04/1919	Ambulance Officer			Y	Y	Stood by for Air Raid duties. Assisted at 30 Convoys wounded
Mr	Thomas James	Mitchell	3, Henley Road, Ilford	00/05/1915	00/03/1918	Pte					Attended 10 convoys wounded
Mr	Albert Victor	Pitcher	211, Mortlake Road, Ilford	00/05/1915		Sergt	Y	Y	Y	Y	Assisted 36 Convoys & stood by for Air Raid duties. Ilford Emergency Hospital & Valentines Mansions Hospital
Mr	John Edward	Pratt	52, St Awdrys Road, Barking	00/05/1915		Pte	Y	Y	Y	Y	Attended 15 Convoys & stood by for Air Raid duties. Ilford Emergency Hospital & Valentines Mansions Hospital
Mr	George Percy	Skelset	3, Mayfair Aveenue, Ilford	00/04/1916		Pte			Y	Y	Attended 34 Convoys and stood by for Air Raids duties.
Mr	Charles	Smith	99, Mortlake Road, Ilford	00/06/1917		Pte			Y	Y	Attended 26 Convoys and stood by for Air Raids duties.
Mr	Thomas Brogd	Waldron	192, Balfour Road, Ilford	00/08/1915	N/A	Pte	Y	Y	Y	Y	Attended 50 Convoys and stood by for Air Raids duties. Ilford Emergency Hospital and Valentines Mansion Hospital

The St John Ambulance Brigade Ilford

Unit St John Ambulance VAD Ilford Nurshing Division St John Ambulance
Commandant Mrs Maud B Magnus
Supported Ilford Emergency Hospital, Valentines Mansions Hospital.
Commission VAD Essex 114
Information Courtesy of the British Red Cross VAD Records

Title	Christian Names	Surname	Address	Served From	Served to	Rank	Ilford Emergency Hospital	Valantines Mansions, Ilford	Oakwood Red Cross Hospital	Air Raid Stand By Ambulance Convoy	Other Hospitals and Notes
Miss	Dorothy	Avery	55, Sackville Gardens, Ilford.	05/05/1918	Still Serving	Nursing Sister		Y			68 Hours
Miss	Jennie	Baker	100, Norfolk Road, Seven Kings	00/05/1915	00/12/1918	Nursing Sister	Y	Y			732 Hours Part time
Mrs	Charlotte	Barnard	48, Seymour Gardens, Cranbrook Park Road, Ilford	00/08/1916	00/12/1919	Nursing Sister	Y	Y			503 Hours
Miss	Marjorie	Bird	108, Aldborough Road, Seven Kings	00/07/1916	00/04/1918	Nursing Sister	Y				720 Hours Part Time. Ilford Emergency Hospital
Mrs	Hannah	Bowyer	23, Dalkeith Road, Ilford.	00/07/1918	Still Serving	Nursing Sister		Y			509 Hours Part time
Miss	Alice E	Bramwell	21, Argyle Road, Ilford	00/05/1917	Still Serving	Nursing Sister	Y	Y			1020 Hours Part time
Miss	Dorothy	Carr	27, Mansfield Road, Ilford	00/08/1915	00/01/1919	Nursing Sister	Y				Aug 1915 to May 1916 Part time Ilford Emergency Hospital. May 1916 to Sept 1916 whole time Shrewsbury. Oct 1916 to July 1918 Whole time Colliton House, Doncaster. Nov 1918 to Jan 1919 Whole time Grata Quies Bournmouth Voluntary all the time. Whole Time
Miss	Norah	Carr	27, Mansfield Road, Ilford	00/08/1915	00/01/1919	Nursing Sister	Y				Aug 1915 to May 1916 Part time Ilford Emergency Hospital. May 1916 to Sept 1916 whole time Shrewsbury. Oct 1916 to July 1918 Whole time Colliton House, Doncaster Voluntary all the time. Whole Time
Miss	Ethel L.	Cue	40, Melbourne Road, Ilford	00/08/1917	Still Serving	Nursing Sister	Y	Y			307 Hours Part Time
Miss	Breacha	Culling	24, Gordon Road, Ilford	00/07/1915	00/04/1917	Nursing Sister	Y				636 Hours

The St John Ambulance Brigade Ilford

Title	First Name	Surname	Address	From	To	Role			Notes
Mrs	Charlotte	Davies	60, Clarendon Gdns, Ilford	00/01/1915	Still Serving	Nursing Sister	Y		680 Hours Attended meetings for the preparation of bandages ect. Ilford Emmergency Hospital and Valentines Mansions Military Hospital, East Ham Town Hall Needlework Depot.
Mrs	Marion	Drury	56, Kinfauns Road, Goodmayes	00/07/1916	Still Serving	Nursing Sister	Y	Y	920 Hours Ilford Hospital and Valentines Mansion Mil
Mrs	Ada M.	Erwood	69 Wards Road, Seven Kings	00/02/1918	Still Serving	Nursing Sister	Y		[Card No 1] Nursing Ilford Emergency Hospital, Valentines Mansions Hospital. Part time 896 hrs
Mrs	Ada Merion	Erwood	69 Wards Road, Seven Kings	00/04/1918	Still Serving	Nursing Sister	Y		[Card No 2] Nursing Valentines Hospital Ilford. Part time 389 hrs
Miss	Fanny G.	Gibson	Gants Hil Cottage, Cranbrook Road, Barkingside	00/05/1917	00/12/1918	Nursing Sister	Y	Y	Nursing Ilford Emergency Hospital, Valentines Mansions Hospital. 2705 hrs
Mrs	Katherine M	Goodes	106, Aldborough Rd, Seven Kings	00/09/1916	00/12/1918	Nursing Sister	Y		Nursing Ilford Emergency Hospital, Part Time 370 hrs
Miss	Ethel Clarice	Haslam	68. Cranbrook Park, Ilford	00/09/1916	Still Serving	Nursing Sister	Y		Nursing Ilford Emergency Hospital, Valentines Mansions Hospital. 2698 hrs
Miss	Elsie G	Jenks	16, Richmond Road, Ilford	00/05/1917	Still Serving	Nursing Sister	Y	Y	Nursing Ilford Emergency Hospital, Valentines Mansions Hospital. Part time 3354 hrs
Miss	Doris	Joy	7, Glencoe Avenue, Seven Kings	00/05/1918	Still Serving	Nursing Sister	Y		Nursing Valentines Mansions Ilford. Part time 237 hrs
Miss	Annie	King	147, Coventry Road, Ilford	00/08/1918	Still Serving	Nursing Sister	Y		Nursing. Part time 322 hrs Valentines Mansion Mil Hosp. Ilford
Miss	Mary	Lance	"Roseville" High Road, Ilford	00/03/1917	Still Serving	Nursing Duties	Y	Y	Nursing at Valentines Mansions Hospital. Ilford Emergency Hospital 1123 hrs
Mrs	Annie H	Law	129, Auckland Road, Ilford	03/05/1915	Still Serving	Quarter Master	Y	Y	Nursing at Ilford Emergency Hospital & Valentines Mansions Ilford. Part time 2800 hrs
Miss	Margery D	Lobb	202, Thorold Rd, Ilford	26/05/1915	10/09/1916	Nursing Sister	Y		Nursing Part time 208 hours. Ilford Emergency Hospital

The St John Ambulance Brigade Ilford

Title	First Name	Surname	Address	Start Date	End Date	Role			Notes
Mrs	Maud Beatrice	Magnus	51, Stanhope Gdns, Cranbrook Pk, Ilford	03/05/1915	Still Serving	Commandant		Y	9106 [Hours] Equipped first 20 beds for Military. Organised all the Voluntary Nursing Staff work at Ilford Emergency Hospital & did a considerable amount of night and day duty myself 9106 hours. From July 1918 prepared Valentines Mansions, Ilford for Military & and had sole charge of same until demobilsed March 1919. Served for over a year on the Executive
Miss	Rose A.	Newstead	11, Coventry Road, Ilford	00/11/1916	00/12/1918	Nursing Sister	Y	Y	Nursing Part Time 412 hours. Ilford Emergency Hospital, Valentines Mansions Military Hospital
Mrs	Ethel F.	Oxer	78, Cowley Road, Ilford	00/08/1918	00/12/1918	Nursing Sister		Y	Nursing Valentines Mansions, Ilford. [part time] 115 hrs
Miss	Nellie A	Oxer	78, Cowley Road, Ilford	00/04/1918	Still Serving	N/A		Y	Nursing Valentines Mansions, Ilford. [part time] 387 hrs
Miss	Elizabeth	Robinson	70, Elgin Road, Seven Kings	00/06/1916	Still Serving	Nursing Sister	Y	Y	Nursing at Ilford Emergency Hospital & Valentines Mansions Ilford. Part time 2690 hrs
Miss	Hilda M.	Rowe	9, Kildowan Rd, Goodmayes	00/06/1915	Still Serving	Nursing Sister		Y	Usual rate of pay. June 1915 to July 1916 Part time Ilford Emergency Hospital. July 1916 Whole time 1st London General Hospital Camberwell. Transferred April 1917 14 Stationary Hosp B.E.F. Feb 21st 1919 Returned sick to England.
Miss	Doris	Russell	52, Auckland Road, Ilford	00/06/1918	Still Serving	Nursing Sister		Y	Nursing Valentines Mansion, Ilford Part time 188 hrs. also about 500 hrs Nursing Romford Military Hosp while serving with Women's Volunteer Reserve.
Mrs	Edith S.	Rymer	62, Grosvenor Raod, Ilford	00/08/1916	Still Serving	Nursing Sister	Y	Y	Nursing at Ilford Emergency Hospital & Valentines Mansions Ilford. Part time 400 hrs
Miss	Annie. J	Rymes	8, Belmont Road, Ilford	03/05/1915	Still Serving	Nursing Sister	Y	Y	Nursing at Ilford Emergency Hospital & Valentines Mansions Ilford. Part time 3,500 hrs

The St John Ambulance Brigade Ilford

Title	First Name	Surname	Address	Date Joined	Date Left	Rank			Service
Miss	Doris P. S	Skinner	58, Kimberley Ave, Seven Kings	00/09/1918	Still Serving	Nursing Sister		Y	Nursing at Valentines Mansions Hospital. 144 hrs
Miss	Ellen E.	Smith	24, Belgrave Road, Ilford	00/12/1917		Nursing Sister	Y	Y	Nursing, Ilford Emergency Hospital, Valentines Hospital Part time 380 hrs. Munition Works Supervision Canteen, Woolwich Arsenal One 1/2 day a week from March 1917 to May 1918.
Miss	Rose S.	Smith	19, Wellesley Road, Ilford	00/05/1917	Still Serving	Nursing Sister	Y	Y	Nursing at Ilford Emergency Hospital & Valentines Mansions Ilford. Part time 1344 hrs Munitions Work London and Scottish En.Co Magnet Wharf, Bow Bridge, Stratford, March 31, 1916 to May 27, 1916. Hackney Marshes
Miss	Eva	Stenning	16, Norfolk Road, Seven Kings	00/07/1918	Still Serving	Nursing Sister		Y	Nursing and Needlework, Valentines Mansion, Ilford. Part time 400 hours.
Miss	Kathleen E.	Symonds	29, Wellsley Road, Ilford	00/07/1918	Still Serving	Nursing Sister		Y	Nursing, Valentines Mansion, Ilf Works YMCA Two 1/2 days a week from May 1916 to Nov 1918
Miss	Helena M.	Thirsk	20, Balfour Road, Ilford	00/07/1918	Still Serving	Nursing Sister		Y	Nursing, Valentines Mansion, Ilford. Part time 354 hours.
Miss	Rose A.	Vaughan	99, Henley Road, Ilford	00/05/1915	Still Serving	Nursing Sister	Y	Y	Nursing at Ilford Emergency Hospital & Valentines Mansions Ilford. Part time 2957 hrs
Mrs	Alice M	Waldron	192, Balfour Road, Ilford	03/05/1915	Still Serving	Nursing Sister	Y	Y	Nursing at Ilford Emergency Hospital & Valentines Mansions Ilford. Part time 3786 hrs
Miss	Murial D.	Webb	Hatley House, Cranbrook Rd, Barkingside	05/05/1917	03/03/1918	Nursing Sister		Y	Nursing Part time 720 hours. Ilford Emergency Hospital
Miss	Alice R.	White	84 Kensington Gdns, Cranbrook Park, Ilford	00/05/1915	Still Serving	Nursing Sister	Y	Y	Nursing at Ilford Emergency Hospital & Valentines Mansions Ilford. Part time 937 hrs
Miss	Ethel M.	White	84 Kensington Gdns, Cranbrook Park, Ilford	03/05/1915	10/09/1916	Nursing Sister		Y	Nursing. Milford Emergency Hospital. Part time 888 hours. Resigned to take up nursing as a profession at the Ilford Emergency Hospital (Military)
Miss	Cecile M.	Wilkins	9, Cavendish Gardens, Cranbrook Park, Ilford	00/08/1918	Still Serving	Nursing Sister		Y	Nursing Valentines Mansions Ilford. Part time 736 hrs
Miss	Ada. A	Willmott	43, Wanstead Park Road, Ilford	30/05/1915	30/12/1918	Nursing Sister	Y	Y	Nursing. Ilford Emergency Hospital & Valentines Mansions Ilford. Part time 888 hrs

The St John Ambulance Brigade Ilford

	Unit	Mixed Detachments
	Supported	Ilford Emergency Hospital, Valentines Mansions Hospital, Oakwood Hospital, Chigwell. Also provided Support with Air Raid Stand By and Ambulance Convoys.
	Information	Courtesy of the British Red Cross VAD Records
	Commissions	Mixed Detachments

Title	Christian Names	Surname	Address	Served From	Served to	Rank	Ilford Emergency	Valantines Mansions, Oakwood Red Cross	Air Raid Stand By Ambulance Convoy	Other Hospitals and Notes
Miss	Phyllis	Abbott	Torrington, Manor Road, West Worthing	00/02/1915	00/07/1918	Member/ Nursing			Y	Essex 1821 -Nursing at Oakwood VAD Hospital Chigwell Now training for Massage. Previouse SS member at Plymonth Hosp and 4th London General Hospital
Mrs	Constance	Allen	Barrington Lodge, Chigwell Row	00/06/1915	00/03/1919	Member/ Nursing & Orderley			Y	Essex 1821 Nursing & Orderely at Oakwood Hosp Chigwell
Mrs	Constance	Allen	Barrington Lodge, Chigwell Row	00/02/1916	00/11/1916	Member			Y	Essex [Card No 2] Oakwood VAD Hospital Chigwell - Nursing at Oakwood Hospital Chigwell. Member Chigwell Work Part - This member worked at home
Miss	Elsie May	Aslet	49, Eastwod Road, Goodmayes	00/01/1917	00/01/1919	Ordinary Member	Y			London 160 Stormont House VAD Hospital, Downs Park Road, Clapton & Darell Hospital Ward Work at IEH Kitchen Work at Stormont and Pantry Work at Darell
Mrs		Bass	Montfort House, Chigwell Row	00/00/1915	00/00/1919				Y	Essex Worker at Chigwell Row War Hospital, Supply Depot at Theydon Bois - Attended Depot Occassionally
Miss	Hilda	Bastard	The Friars, Chigwell Row	00/02/1915	00/13/1919	Quarter M			Y	Essex 82 Nursing and Q.M at Oakwood Hosp. Chigwell. Hours 8.30 am to 7.30 pm daily per week. On duty ever 4th week from 1917 3 hrs daily as q.master during period. Honours Awarded Blue Strip.
Miss	Nancy Littlewood	Bastard	The Tresco, Chigwell Row	00/06/1915	00/02/1918	Member			Y	Essex 1821 Oakwood VAD Hospital Chigwell Hours occasional duty as nurse during period. 1918 joined the W.A.A.C Serving in France.
Miss	Florence	Boddington	The Friars, Chigwell Row	00/02/1915	00/02/1918	VAM Member			Y	Essex 1821 Nursing at Oakwood Hospital Chigwell. Hours 8.30 am to 7.30 pm daily per week. On duty evey 4th week during claim.
Mr	Francis Arthur	Brown	5 Norfolk Rd, Seven Kings	21/12/1916	Armistce Still Serving	Orderly			Y	London Part time 1400 [Hours] Air Raid Duty 1040 Training 400 Commendable service
Miss	Muriel	Butters	37 Blythwood Rd, Seven Kings	00/09/1918	Still Serving	G.S.S	Y			Essex 130 (One years work at Miss McCauls Hospital hours 576) July 1917 to July 1918 Total 801 Gives out stores and assists pantry work. Part time 225 1/2 Ilford Emergency Hospital (Mil)
Mr	Archibald	Campbell	142 Elgin Road, Seven Kings	00/08/1918	Still Serving	Stretcher Bearer				City of London BRCS Branch Ambulance Colume London District

The St John Ambulance Brigade Ilford

Title	First Name	Surname	Address	From	To	Rank					Notes
Mrs	Clara	Church	Oakland Terrace, Chigwell	00/06/1916	00/03/1919	VAD G.S Memebr				Y	Essex 82 2nd Cook at Oakwood Hosp Chigwell. Hours 9 to 2.30 daily during period
Mrs	Hilda Muriel	Coker	Alderborough Rd, Ilford	01/02/1918	08/09/1918	Nurse					J.W.V.A.D Essex Res. Pavillion Mil Hosp Brighton
Miss	May Beatrice Adelai	Collinschon	50 Rosslyn Gardens, Seven Kings Road, Seven Kings	04/01/1915	23/07/1917	Private					City of London Red Cross Hospital, Finsbury Square EC2, City of London Hospital for Officers, Fishmongers' Hall, EC2 04/10/1915 to 1/11/1915 at Finsbury. 22/01/1917 to 23/07/1917 at Fishmongers Hall. Hospital Panty Duties and cooking
Mrs	Onyx	Cooke	33, Palmerston Rd, Dublin, Ireland	00/05/1915	00/02/1918	Trained Nurse				Y	Chigwell Previous Engagement Lady Balcarres Hospital and other Red Cross Hospitals. Sister in charge of Nursing at Oakwood Hospital, Chigwell. Whole time Honours Awarded Royal Red
	Ada	Daniels	Flint Cottage, Chigwell	00/12/1915	00/03/1919	VAD Member				Y	Essex 82 Oakwood VAD Hospital. Nursing at Oakwood Hosp. Chigwell. Occasional duty Saturday and Sunday. Whole weeks duty in holiday time (Teacher)
Miss	Lynette	Daniels	Flint Cottage, Chigwell	00/02/1915	00/03/1919	VAD Member				Y	Essex 82 Oakwood VAD Hospital. Nursing at Oakwood Hosp. Chigwell. Occasional duty Saturday and Sunday. Whole weeks duty in holiday time (Teacher)
Mr	Stanley George	Davis	38, Ladtsmith Avenue, Seven Kings, Ilford	00/05/1915	Still Serving	Stretcher Bearer					Ambulance Colume 56 hrs per week The British Red Cross Sociaty City of London Brance
Mr	Frederick George	Drayson	56, Emperess Avenue, Ilford	00/05/1915	Still Serving	Ambulance Officer	Y	Y	Y	Y	Essex Assisted in transport in connection with Ilford Emergency & Oakwood Red Cross Hospital Chigwell, a total of 84 convoysand 1500 wounded. Assisted in transfer of 100 wounded to variouse London and Provincial Hospitals. Personally driven car 1000 miles & acted as attendant for 4000 miles. Stood by for Air Raid duties.
Miss	Agnus	Durell	Forest View, Poppleton Road, Leytonstone	00/10/1915	00/12/1918	VAD	Y				Essex Ward Duties 1891 [Hours] Ilford Military Hospital, Livingston Military Hospital, Whipp Cross Military Hospital.
Mrs	Nellie	Finch	Forge House, Chigwell	00/06/1918	00/03/1919	VAD G.S Member				Y	Essex 82 Oakwood VAD Hospital, Chigwell. Kitchen Helper at Oakwood Hosp, Chigwell. Two half days per week kitchen work.
Mr	Oliver George	Firmin	39, Selbourne Road, Ilford	20/12/1916	Still Serving	Pte			Y	Y	VAD Essex 31 Part time Dealing with convoys of wounded for Local Hospitals. Organised Air Raid Duties.
Mrs	Ellen M	Fish	Millbrook, Chigwell	00/00/1915	00/00/1919	Asst Quartermaster				Y	Oakwood Hospital, Chigwell. Organiser of working party, Chigwell. Average 56 hours quarterly. Attended Work Party once a week during period.
Mrs	Ellen M	Fish	Millbrook, Grange Hill, Chigwell	00/01/1916	00/03/1919	Quarter M				Y	Essex 82 [Card No 2] Oakwood VAD Hospital Chigwell - Quartermaster's duties at Oakwood Hospital Chigwell. Hours 5 half days per week during period.

The St John Ambulance Brigade Ilford

Title	First Name	Surname	Address	From	To	Role	Y/N	Notes
Mrs	Ellen M	Fish	Millbrook, Chigwell	00/02/1916	00/11/1916	Quarter-master	Y	Essex [Card 3] Oakwood VAD Hospital. Quartermaster at Oakwood Hospiutal, Chigwell. Member of Chigwell Work Part. Attendance at Work Party one afternoon weekly during period.
Miss	Gertrude	Gadsdon	93. Elliscombe Rd, Charleton, S.E.9	00/06/1916	00/09/1918	VAD G.S Member	Y	Essex 82 Oakwood VAD Hospital, Chigwell. Ward Maids at Oakwood Hosp, Chigwell. Two half days per week kitchen work.
Miss	Louisa	Garrett	Bifrons, Aldeburgh.	00/10/1915	00/03/1919	VAD Member	Y	Essex 1821 Nursing at Oakwood VAD Hospital, Chigwell. At Warwick House Hosp, Aldeburgh. Seamans Hospital, Greewich.
Miis	Louisa Littlewood	Garrett	Bifrons, Aldeburgh.	01/01/1915	01/03/1919	Nurse	Y	House Aldeburgh Jan 1915 to March 1917 (part time). Dreadnought Seaman's Hos. Greenwich to Nov 1915 whole time. Night Nurse Whole timw from 8/4/18 to 1/3/1919 Chigwell Red Cross Hospital, Essex.
Mr	Henry Valintine	Geary M.B.E	62, Elgin Road, Seven Kings	04/01/1915		Accountant		Chief Accountant - Character Excellent - Accountants - Asst to the Chief Accountant Messrs
Miss	Ada Pethick	Glanvill	48, Mansfield Road, Ilford	21/08/1918	Still Serving	Ward Maid		L.328 Part time about 280 hours Miss Glanvill at the Habon Hospital on Saturdays and Sundays from Sept tp xmas and since Xmas on Sundays only. Imitial A. P written of front [of Card]
Miss	Beatrice Mary	Gould	Chigwell Lodge, Chigwell	00/02/1915	00/03/1919	VAD then Asst Commandant	Y	Essex 1821 Oakwood VAD Hospital Chigwell. Nursing and Assist Commdt at Oakwood Hosp, Chigwell. Hours 8.30 am to 7.30 pm daily per week. On duty every 4th week intil June 1916 after that Assist Commdt Whole time
Mirs	Emily	Gould	115 The Grove, Ealing West	00/06/1916	00/03/1919	VAD Member	Y	Essex Oakwood VAD Hospital Chigwell; Overcliff Hospital. Westcliff on Sea. Nursing at Oakwood Hosp. Chigwell. Hours half day daily at Overcliff Hospital for two years. Occasional duty at Oakwood Hospital
Miss	Isabel Lucy	Gould	Chigwell Lodge, Chigwell	00/02/1915	00/03/1919	Local Secretary B.R.C.S at Chigwell / Commdt	Y	Essex 1821 Oakwood VAD Hospital Chigwell. Local Secretary B.R.C.S at Chigwell. Administration of Oakwood Hospital, Chigwell
Mr	James Albet	Gould	67, Spencer Road, Seven Kings	29/10/1917	05/07/1918	Driver		Motor Ambulance. Previouse Engagement Boulogne Motor Ambulance Cert 14564
Miss	Dorothy	Hambridge	The Willows, Chigwell Row	00/06/1915	00/03/1918	VAD	Y	Essex 82 Cooking at Oakwood Hospital, Chigwell. Hours half a day weekly 2nd Cook during period
Miis	Laura	Hambridge	The Willows, Chigwell Row	00/06/1915	Still Serving	VAD Member	Y	Essex [1]821 Nursing at Oakwood Hosp Chigwell Whole time. Previouse Member still serving at War Hosp Napsbury, St. Albans. Honours Awards Two Red Strips
Miss	Muriel	Hambridge	The Willows, Chigwell Row	00/06/1915	00/03/1919	VAD Member	Y	Essex 82 Oakwood VAD Hospital Chigwell/ Nursing at Oakwood Hosp, Chigwell. Hours 8.30 am to 7.30pm daily per week. On duty every 3rd week during period

The St John Ambulance Brigade Ilford

Title	First Name	Surname	Address	Start	End	Role	Col1	Col2	Notes
Miss	Eva	Hamilton	The Acorns, Chigwell Road	00/02/1915	00/03/1919	VAD Member		Y	Essex 82 Oakwood VAD Hospital Chigwell. Nursing at Oakwood Hospital Hours 8.30 am to 7.30pm daily per week. On duty every 3rd week during period
Miss	Hilda	Hanbury-Tracy	62, Eaton Terrace, Londo, SW1	00/03/1915	00/12/1918	VAD Member		Y	Oakwood VAD Hospital Chigwell. Nursing at Oakwood Hospital Hours 8.30 am to 7.30pm daily per week. On duty every 4th week during period
Mr	A. W	Hare	Emergency Hospital, Ilford				Yes		Wounded are missing. No more Information - Searcher
Mrs	Florence	Hawker	Elces, Chigwell	00/05/1917	00/03/1919	VAD G.S Member		Y	Essex 82 Oakwood VAD Hospital, Chigwell. Kitchen Helper at Oakwood Hosp, Chigwell. One half day per week getting tea etc.
Miss	Florence	Hean	176. Uphall Rd, Ilford	00/05/1918	Still Serving	Nurse	Yes		Essex 130 At Ilford Emg Host (Military) Part time 201 [Hours]
Miss	Rosa	Heard	High Rd, Chigwell	00/06/1915	00/03/1919	VAD Member		Y	Essex 82 Oakwood VAD Hospital Chigwell. Nursing at Oakwood Hosp, Chigwell. Hours Occasional duty on Sunday. In bisiness.
Miss	Mary Chapman	Hewitt	Old Rectory, Tewin	00/06/1917	00/03/1919	Nurse	Y	Y	Essex 130 Took exams while at school was to commence service at earlist chance; Arsenal canteen 1918 Part Time 1319 [Hours]. A worker at Forest Gate War Hospital. Supply & Red X Centre from 1915. Organised Concert on behalf of same. Served at Hospital afterSilvertown Explosion. Attended Air Raid Dressing Station, on each occassion of raids, sometimes going there while danger was imminent. Served at
N/A	Rosalie Mary Blyth	Hill	34, Selbourne Road, Ilford	00/05/1915	00/03/1919	Concert Organiser	Y		Essex Organised 1800 concerts at Ilford Emergency Hosptal
Miss	Edith Mary	Hillyer	58, Browning Road, Leytonstone, E11	00/01/1915	00/10/1918	Assisting Nurses	Y		Essex Livingston College Hospital, Leyton, Ilford Emergencey Hospital, Whipps Cross infirmary, Leytonstone.
Mrs	Margaret Ann	Holmes M.B.E	33, Sackville Gardens, Ilford	01/01/1916	22/03/1916	Quartermaster Housekeeping			Hants,The St John Hospital Regents Park, Southampton Serving Sister Order of St John Aug, 6th 1914 to Nov 4 -St John Warehouse, Clerkenwell. Nov 4, 1914 to Dec 18 - Queen Mary's Hospital Southend. Nirse Jan 10th 1916 to 31 Dec 1916. St John Warehouse Apr 1916 to Oct 5 1916. Deveonshire House, London Oct 5 1916 to July 18 1917. Rouen France Sept 1917 to Dec 1918. St John Depot Belgrave Square. W Quartermaster

The St John Ambulance Brigade Ilford

Miss	Doris	Hughes	54, Colenso Rd, Seven Kings	00/05/1918	Still Serving	Nurse	Y	Essex 130 Night and Evening duties. Part time 400 [Hours]
Mrs	Mabelle	Ingram	Fairlight, Chigwell Row	00/02/1916	00/11/1916	VAD Member	Y	Essex Oakwood VAD Hospital Chigwell. Nursing at Oakwood Hosp, Chigwell. Member of Chigwell Working Party. Attendance at Works Party one afternoon nearley each week during period (Note on card, returned gone away, 7/9/21)
Mrs	Mabelle	Ingram	Fairlight, Chigwell Row	00/06/1915	00/03/1919	VAD Member	Y	Essex 82 [Card No2] Oakwood VAD Hospital Chigwell. Nursing at Oakwood Hospital Hours 8.30 am to 7.30pm daily per week. On duty every 4th week during period
Mrs	Clara Elzabeth	Ireland	The Vicarage E. Molesey	22/01/1918	02/08/1918	Nurse	Y	J.W.V.A.D Surrey 94 Silwood Park Auxillary Hospital, Sunninghill: Oakwood VAD Hospital, Chigwell. 22.01.1918 - 06.03.1918 Aux Hos Oakwood Chigwell 12.03.1918 - 02.08.1918 Aux Hos Windlesham Court,Sunningdale
Mrs	Clara Elzabeth	Ireland	The Vicarage E. Molesey	00/05/1917	00/08/1918	Nurse	Y	Surrey 94 Petersfield, Chigwell, Windlesham. Nursing Whole time Petersfield May - October, Chigwell January - March Windlesham March - October
Mrs	Margaret	Keaney		22/10/1917	11/02/1918	Trained		Devon Seaton and Districe V.A Hospital, Ryall Court, Seaton. Barry Docks, Chigwell, Southend-on-Sea. Rugby Non-V.A Der Member Service rendered at V.A Hospital Seaton 22nd Oct 1917 - 11th Feb 1918
Mrs	Mary Frances	Knight	Carbes, 29 Kendrick Road, Reading	00/05/1917	00/03/1919	VAD G.S Member	Y	Oakwood VAD Hospital Chigwell; Auxillary Hospital, East Colne Previouse Red Cros Hospital Earl's Colne, Essex. Head Cook at Oakwood Hospital, Chigwell Whole time
Miss	Gwendoline	Knowles	Gaemar, Hainault Road, Chigwell	00/04/1918	00/03/1919	VAD Member	Y	Essex 82 Oakwood VAD Hospital Chigwell. Nursery at Oakwood Hosp Chigwell Hospital Hours 8.30 am to 7.30pm daily per week. On duty alternate weeks during period. every 3rd week during period
Mrs	Florence	Lambert	5, Whitta Rd, Manor Park, Ilford	00/02/1915	00/03/1919	VAD Member	Y	Essex 1821 Oakwood VAD Hospital Chigwell. Nursing at Oakwood Hospital Hours 8.30 am to 7.30pm daily per week. On duty every 4th week during period
Mrs	Louise	Lambeth	Lynton, Woodford Bridge	00/06/1916	00/13/1919	VAD Member	Y	essex 1821 Ward Maid and Nursing at Oakwood Hosp Chigwell. Hours 8.30 am to 7.30 pm daily per week. On duty ever 3rd week during period.

The St John Ambulance Brigade Ilford

Title	First Name	Surname	Address	From	To	Rank		Notes
Miss	Ivy	Lewis	Stondon Massy, Brentwood	00/09/1916	00/01/1919	Member		Essex 32 Worked at Chigwell Red Cross Hospital VAD October 14 till June 1916. VAD Nurse Ongar Hospital Part time 1283 Hours. Budworth Haal Red Cross Hospital, Ongar, Essex 32
	Minnie Russel	Lloyd	Theydon Garnon Rectory	00/06/1915	00/10/1915		Y	Essex Oakwood VAD Hospital Chigwell, Worker War Hospital, Supply Depot, Theydon Bois One day weekly during period.
Miss	Russel	Lloyd	Chigwell Lodge, Chigwell	00/06/1917	00/06/1918	Member	Y	Essex 82 Oakwood VAD Hospital Chigwell. Nursing at Oakwood Hospital Hours 8.30 am to 7.30pm daily per week. On duty every 4th week during period
Miss	Mary	Mooney	1, Khedive Rd, Forest Gate, E7	00/04/1918	00/03/1919	Nurse	Y	Essex 130 Night Duties 290 [Hours]
Mrs	A. Maud. M	Morgan	Homleigh, Oatlands Drive, Weybridge	03/07/1916	30/10/1916	Nurse	Y	J.W.V.A.D London 200 Oakwood VAD Hospital Chigwell. Nursing at Oakwood Hosp, Chigwell. Hours Occasional duty on Sunday. In bisiness.
Miss	Winifred	Moseley	North View, Chigwell	00/02/1915	00/06/1916	VAD Member	Y	Essex Oakwood VAD Hospital Chigwell. Nursing at Oakwood Hospital Hours 8.30 am to 7.30pm daily per week. On duty every 4th week during period
Miss	Winifred	Moseley	North View, Chigwell	00/02/1915	00/11/1916		Y	Essex [Card No 2]Oakwood VAD Hospital Chigwell. Nursing at Oakwood Hospital. Member of Chigwell Work Party. This Member did a lot of work at home as she could not attend the Work Paty.
Miss	Constance	Nobel	Savill Cottages, Chigwell	00/11/1918	00/03/1919	VAD G.S Member	Y	Essex 82 Oakwood VAD Hospital Chigwell Ward Maid at Oakwood Hosp Chigwell. Hours 6.30 am to 8 am every day weekly altenate weeks.
Miss	Lily	Osborne	High Rd, Chigwell	00/06/1916	00/03/1919	VAD G.S Member	Y	Essex 82 Oakwood VAD Hospital Chigwell 2nd Cook at Oakwood Hosp Chigwell. Hours Half day every Sunday and othe occasional days during period.
Miss	Constance	Paget	Moorabin, Buckhurst Hill, Essex	00/06/1915	00/03/1919	VAD Member	Y	Essex 82 Oakwood VAD Hospital Chigwell Nursing at Oakwood Hosp Chigwell. Hours 8.30 am to 7.30 pm daily per week. On duty only 3rd week during period
Miss	Kate Ethel	Paget	Moorabin, Buckhurst Hill, Essex	00/06/1915	00/03/1919	VAD Member	Y	Essex 1821 Oakwood VAD Hospital Chigwell Nursing at Oakwood Hosp Chigwell. Hours 8.30 am to 7.30 pm daily per week. On duty every 3rd week during period
Mrs	Frances	Pain	1, Maybank Rd, George Lane, South Woodford	00/02/1915	00/03/1919	VAD Member	Y	Essex 82 Oakwood VAD Hospital Chigwell Nursing at Oakwood Hosp Chigwell. Hours 8.30 am to 7.30 pm daily per week. On duty every 4th week during period
Miss	Dorothy	Parker	23, Vernon Gardens, Ilford	00/10/1916	Still Serving	Nurse	Y	Essex 130 Manor House Hosp, West Ham & Ilford Emergency Hospital.Part time-582 Hours

The St John Ambulance Brigade Ilford

Title	First Name	Surname	Address	From	To	Role	Y	Notes
Miss	Charlotte C	Plowden	745 Eccleston Square, SW1	00/10/1916	00/03/1919	Member	Y	London 198 Oakwood VAD Hospital Chigwell. Nurse at Chigwell Aug-Sept 1915. West Park Mil Hosp Dec 15 -Sept 1916 whole time. Posted Nurse by Devonshire House, France Whole time 31.05.15 Honours Awarded 1 Red Stripe
Miss	Nellie	Polglase	Braeside, Theydon Bois.	00/02/1915	00/03/1919	VAD Member	Y	Essex 82 Oakwood VAD Hospital Chigwell Nursing at Oakwood Hospital Chigwell. Occassional Nurse chiefly night duty.
Miss	Nellie	Polglase	Braeside, Theydon Bois.	00/00/1915	00/00/1919	VAD Member	Y	[Card No 2] Oakwood VAD Hospital Chigwell Nursing at Oakwood Hospital Chigwell. Worker at War Hosp, Supply Depot, Theydon Bois. Attended Depot occasionally during period.
Miss	Constance	Poulter	243, High Rd, Ilford	13/05/1917	17/03/1919	Nurse	Y	Essex 130 Night & day duties as required 3598 [Hours] Still serving. Now at St. Dunstans. At Ilford Emergency Hospital. 1st Year service bars
Mrs	Constance	Power	202 Portsdown Rd, Maida Vale. W	00/02/1915	00/07/1918	VAD Member	Y	Essex 1821Oakwood VAD Hospital Chigwell Nursing at Oakwood Hosp Chigwell. Hours 8.30 am to 7.30 pm daily per week. On duty every 5th week during period
Mrs	Olive Lydell	Pratt	The Haylands, Chigwell	00/02/1915	00/01/1917	Quarter M	Y	Essex Oakwood VAD Hospital Chigwell Quartermaster Hours 8.30 am to 7.30pm daily per week. Onduty every 4th week until end of 1915 after that daily for 2 hours as Quartermaster during period.
Miss	Daisy	Price	32 Belchford Rd, Seven Kings	00/05/1918	Still Serving	Nurse	Y	Essex 130 Night and Evening duties. Part time 50 [Hours] Ilford Emergency Hosp
Miss	Dorothy Annie	Pugh	15, Sunnyside Rd, Ilford	01/11/1915	00/03/1919	Nurse Probationer	Y	Essex 130 Norfolk War Hospital and Ilford Emergency Hospital. Probationer 01/11/1915 £20 per ann to 09/1917 . Night or Day as required. Part time 342 [Hours].Will continue to serve when need among civillians.
Miss	Ruby	Rapkin	Sr. Elms, Valentines Rd, Ilford	14/01/1919	Still Serving	Nurse	Y	Ilford Emergency Hospital + Surbiton & Kingston Auxillary Hosp Aug 1918 to Oct 1918, about 100 hours.
Miss	Emily	Reynolds	Percival House, Maybank Rd, South Wodford	00/06/1918	00/03/1919	VAD Member	Y	Essex 1821 Oakwood VAD Hospital Chigwell Nursing at Oakwood Hosp Chigwell. Hours 8.30 am to 7.30 pm daily per week. On duty every 4th week during period
Mr	Herbert Charles	Roberts	55, Oakfield Road, Ilford	04/04/1917	18/01/1919	In Charge of Depot		Stores. Pay 41/- [41 Shillings = £2.05p]

The St John Ambulance Brigade Ilford

Title	First Name	Surname	Address	From	To	Rank		Details
Mrs	Mildred	Savill	Whitehall, Chigwell Row	00/06/1915	00/03/1919	VAD Member	Y	Essex 1821 Oakwood VAD Hospital Chigwell. Nursing Motor transport at Oakwood Hospital, Chigwell. Hours ocassional duty as nurse. Principally as motor transport 3 times a week during period
Mrs	Renee	Savill	Brimstones Chigwell	00/02/1915	00/11/1918	VAD G.S Member	Y	Essex 1821 Oakwood VAD Hospital Cooking at Oakwood Hospital Chigwell. One half day per week during period.
Mrs	Renee	Savill	Brainstone Chigwell	00/02/1915	00/11/1916	VAD G.S Member	Y	Essex [Card No 2] Oakwood VAD Hospital Member at Chigwell Work Oarty. Attendent at Work Party One Afternoon each week during period.
Miss	Winifred Lydall	Savill	Woodlands, Chigwell Row	00/02/1915	00/03/1919	VAD Member	Y	Essex 1821 Oakwood VAD Hospital. Nursery at Oakwood Hosp. Chigwell. Hours 8.30 am to 7.30 pm daily per week. On dity every 4 weeks during period.
Miss	Violet	Sendell	The Grove, Chighwell Row	00/03/1915	00/02/1916	VAD Member	Y	Essex 1821 Oakwood VAD Hospital. Nursing at Oakwood Hosp. Chigwell. Hours 8.30 am to 7.30 pm daily per week. On dity every 4 weeks during period.
Miss	Mary Vivian	Smith	Rolls Park, Chigwell	00/10/1918	00/03/1919	VAD G.S Member	Y	Essex 182 Oakwood VAD Hospital Ward Maid at Oak. Oakwood,Hosp Chigwell. 5 half days per week during period.
Lady	Sybil	Smith	Rolls Park, Chigwell	00/04/1917	00/03/1919	VAD G.S Member	Y	Essex 1821 Oakwood VAD Hospital, Chigwell. Kitchen Helper at Oakhurst Hosp, Chigwell. Two half days per week kitchen work. Cert ret Gone Away 21/11/21
Mrs	Maud	Swann	18 Edith Grose, Chelsea, S.W	00/10/1918	00/03/1919	Trained Nurse	Y	Essex Oakwood VAD Hospital Chigwell Previous Engagement France and England, Sister in charge of Oakwood Hosp. Chigwell Red Cross Hospitals. Sister in charge of Nursing at Oakwood Hospital, Chigwell. Whole time.
Mrs	Maud Ellen Constan	Swann	6 Matheson Road, W. Kensington. London S.W	00/09/1914	Still Serving	Sister / Matron	Y	BRCS Sessex 40 Racecourse, Presbury, Cheltenham; The Priory, Ware; Oakwood VAD Hospital Chigwell. Sister and Matron Wholetime. The Red Cross Hospital 1914 to 6 Third Avenue Ware May 1915. (Invilid home for Typhoid) Anglo French Hospital Matron 1917. Palavas France Race Course Hospital Feb 1918. Cheltenham Sept 1918. Oakwood VAD Hospital now Matron 1919

The St John Ambulance Brigade Ilford

Mrs	Evelyn	Todd	St Breock, Woodford Bridge	00/06/1916	00/03/1919	VAD G.S Member		Y	Essex 82 Oakwood VAD Hospital, Chigwell. Kitchen Helper at Oakwood Hosp, Chigwell. One half days per week kitchen work.
Mrs	Mabel	Underwood	10 Eglington Gardens, Chingford	00/02/1915	00/01/1917	VAD Member		Y	Essex 82 Oakwood VAD Hospital Chigwell. Nursing at Oakwood Hospital Hours 8.30 am to 7.30pm daily per week. On duty every 4th week during period
Mrs	Lucy	Wait	Ellborough, Chigwell Row	00/06/1915	00/03/1919	VAD Member		Y	Essex 1821 Oakwood VAD Hospital Chigwell; Nursing at Oakwood Hosp, Chigwell. Hours Occassional duty as Nurse and G.S. Member Health prevented reqular time
Mrs	Ethel	Walde	The Grammer School, Chigwell	00/02/1916	00/11/1916	Member			Essex Member of Chigwell Work Party. Full attendanceweekly at Work Party held at Mrs. Walde's house.
Mr	Albert Tom	Waters	46 Ranelagh Gardens, Ilford	00/04/1916	N/A	Pte		Y Y	Essex 24 Attended 28 Convoys and stood by for Air Raids duties.
Mrs	Eva	Watson	40 Clarendon Gdns, Ilford	00/10/1914	Still Serving	Concert Organiser		Y	organised. Concerts arranged at Ilford Emergency Hospital, Brook War Hospital, Royal Herbert Hospital, Metropolitan Hospital, Kingsland Rd, Mile End Hospital, Epping Military Hospital, Woodford and Wanstead Military Hospital, Whips Cross Hospital, The Anzac con: Camp Purfleet Mil
Miss	May	Whiteman	48 Rosedale Rd, Forest Gate, E7	00/10/1914	Still Serving	Nurse		Y Y	Kent & Essex Whole Time. All military Oct 1914 to Nov 1915. Sea Bathing Hospital Margate (Nurse) April 1916 to Sept 1917. Ilford Emergency Hospital (Night Charge) August 1918 to March 1919. Valentines Mansion (Sister in charge)
Mrs	Margaret	Whittal	The Laurels, Boxmoor	06/11/1916	27/11/1917	Nurse		Y	J.W.V.A.D Herts 16 Oakwood VAD Hospital, Chigwell - Oakwood Chigwell Auxillary
Mrs	Sarah	Whittall	1, Soho Square, London. W.1	00/11/1916	00/01/1918	VAD Member		Y	Essex Oakwood VAD Hospital, Chigwell - Night nurse at Oakwood Hosp Chigwell
Mrs	Rose	Woodley	Afton Villa, Woodford Brige	00/06/1916	00/01/1918	VAD G.S Member		Y	Essex 1821 Oakwood VAD Hospital Chigwell Ward Pantry and Kitchen helper Oakwood, Hospl Chigwell. One half day per week during period.

All records courtesy of the British Red Cross online archive of Voluntary Aid Detachment Records 1914 -1919 access May 2022.

E & O.E.

The St John Ambulance Brigade Ilford

Appendix No 6 County Directors and VAD Working Parties in Ilford[126]

Appendix II

Roll of County Directors for Essex

Lieut- Col. Colvin, CBE   Appointed by BRCS
E. J. Wythes, Esq., CBE Appointed by BRCS

Appendix V

Members Registrations Number and Working Locations

Central Work Rooms. 1001 – 1999
      "   "   "   4000 – 5000
Burlington House.   1 - 1000
Home Workers   2000 – 3999

The Ilford Working Party Members are listed as follows for the Ilford area

Central Work Rooms 1796   Chigwell. Mrs Wade, Chigwell School

Central Work Rooms 1912   Ilford. Mrs Bell, Mrs Evdon. Parish Church W.W Party

Central Work Rooms   4165   Ilford. Mrs Durrant 36, The Mill

Central Work Rooms[127] 5770 Ilford. Mrs Carrell, 34, The Drive

---

[126] Reports by the Joint War Committee and Joint War Finance Committee of the British Red Cross Society and the Order of St. John of Jerusalem on England on Voluntary Aid rendered to the sick and wounded at Home and Abroad and to British Prisoners of War, 1914 - 1919.

[127] Index for location finishes at 5,000. However, members are recorded with number that exceed this.

Appendix No 7 Royal Red Cross – Ilford

The Royal Red Cross medal (or more accurately decoration) was introduced to Military Nursing by Royal Warrant by Queen Victoria on 23 April 1883, St George's Day, and it was announced in the *London Gazette* on 27 April 1883.

The Royal Warrant said that it be given:
> upon any ladies, whether subjects or foreign persons, who may be recommended by Our Secretary of State for War for special exertions in providing for the nursing of sick and wounded soldiers and sailors of Our Army and Navy.

The second class Associate Royal Red Cross grade was added during the First World War in November 1915 with bars to the first class RRC being introduced in 1917. Bars are awarded in both classes to those nurses who perform further acts of devotion or bravery.

Whilst not an inclusive list, those below have, through the *London Gazette*, press information and the Register of the Royal Red Cross (1883-1994) have a directed attribution to Ilford Emergency Hospital or Oakwood Auxiliary Hospital, Chigwell.

Francis Mary Cooke, Mrs – Matron Oakwood Auxiliary Hospital, Chigwell.
Awarded Royal Red Cross Second Class. *London Gazette* 24 October 1917.
Decorated by the King at Buckingham Palace 5 December 1917.

Letitia Emma Green, Miss – Matron Ilford Emergency Hospital, Ilford.
Awarded Royal Red Cross Second Class. *London Gazette* 21 June 1918.
Decorated by the King at Buckingham Palace 12 April 1919.

Annie Gertrude Duxfield – Sister Ilford Emergency Hospital.
Awarded Royal Red Cross Second Class. *London Gazette* 31 July 1919. Royal Red Cross sent to Seamen's Hospital Society (Dreadnought) Greenwich, London, SE10 13 August 1920.

All the awards mentioned refer to the following decoration the Royal Red Cross Second Class or known more commonly as Associated Royal Red Cross

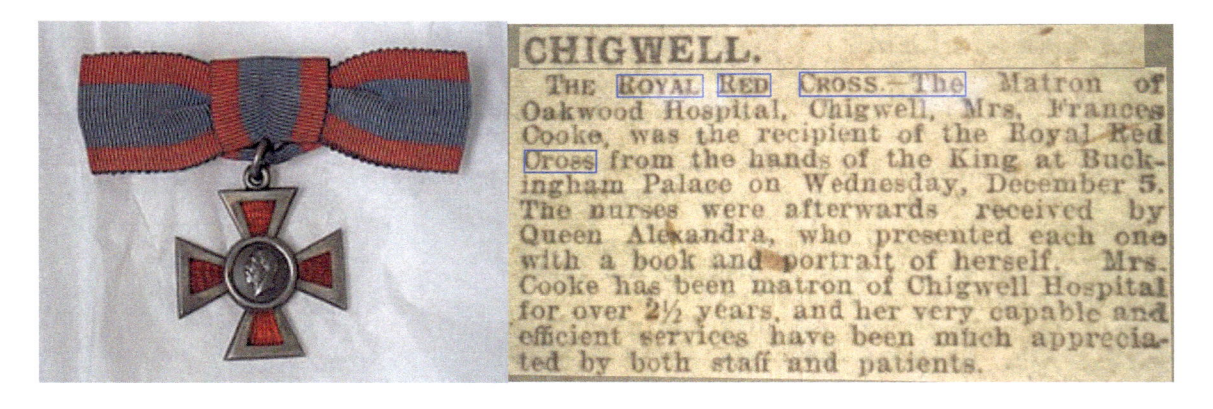

Badge of Royal Red Cross Second Class.

CHIGWELL.
THE ROYAL RED CROSS.—The Matron of Oakwood Hospital, Chigwell, Mrs. Frances Cooke, was the recipient of the Royal Red Cross from the hands of the King at Buckingham Palace on Wednesday, December 5. The nurses were afterwards received by Queen Alexandra, who presented each one with a book and portrait of herself. Mrs. Cooke has been matron of Chigwell Hospital for over 2½ years, and her very capable and efficient services have been much appreciated by both staff and patients.

Chelmsford Chronicle 14 December 1917

The St John Ambulance Brigade Ilford

Appendix No 8 'B' Mention in Dispatches for Ilford

Joint War Committee of the Red Cross - valuable service via a VAD or Hospital in connection with the war.

At several occasions from 1917 to 1920, the chairman of the Joint War Committee of the Red Cross brought to the notice of the Secretary of State for War the names of ladies and gentleman who had rendered valuable service via a VAD or Hospital in connection with the war.

3rd March 1917
Green, L.E   Matron, Ilford Emergency Hospital

18th October 1917[128]
Miss H Bastard,   Quartermaster of Oakwood Aux Hospital, Chigwell, Essex
Miss I Gould   Comdt [Commandant], Oakwood Aux Hospital, Chigwell, Essex

12th March 1918
Magnus Mrs B M   Comdt, VAD Ilford Emergency Hospital, Ilford Newbury Park, Essex.

Waldron Mrs A M   Nursing Sister Ilford Emergency Hospital, Newbury Park, Ilford

10th August 1918
Duxfield Miss A G   Sister Ilford Emergency Hospital, Ilford

8th April 1919
Magnus Mrs M. B   Ilford

19th August 1919
Baker, Miss F   S/Nurse TFNS[129], Ilford Emergency Hospital, Ilford

21st April 1920
Magnus Mr W R   Ilford

7 May 1920
Miss I L Gould   Comdt, VAD Oakwood Aux Hospital, Chigwell, Essex

E & O.E

---

[128] Miss V Gotch, had a 'B' mention and was shown in one paper as a Nurse at Oakwood, Chigwell. This was incorrected and later amended to read "Probationer, Kensington `Aux. Hosp, Weir, Surrey" as per the War Office Communique.

[129] Territorial Forces Nursing Service

Appendix No 9 Silver War Badges – Ilford

The following is a short transcription of names on the Silver War Badge Roll for Nurses held at The National Archives (WO329/3253). Only names and address are included here; the full roll also includes the badge number, date of issue, and 'rank' for trained nurses, i.e. either Matron, Sister or Staff Nurse. There is no reference in the roll to medical conditions or actual cause of discharge.

TURNEY, E., V.A.D., 34A Clarendon Gardens, Ilford, Essex

Around the rim of a Silver War Badge is "For King and Empire; Services Rendered"

Appendix No 10 Valentines Mansion Correspondence

The following is an exchange of correspondence between 12 June 1918 and 15 August which relates to No 15 Ilford Nursing Division (Voluntary Aid Detachment Essex114) taking over the running of Valentines Mansion as an Auxiliary Hospital to the Ilford Emergency Hospital.

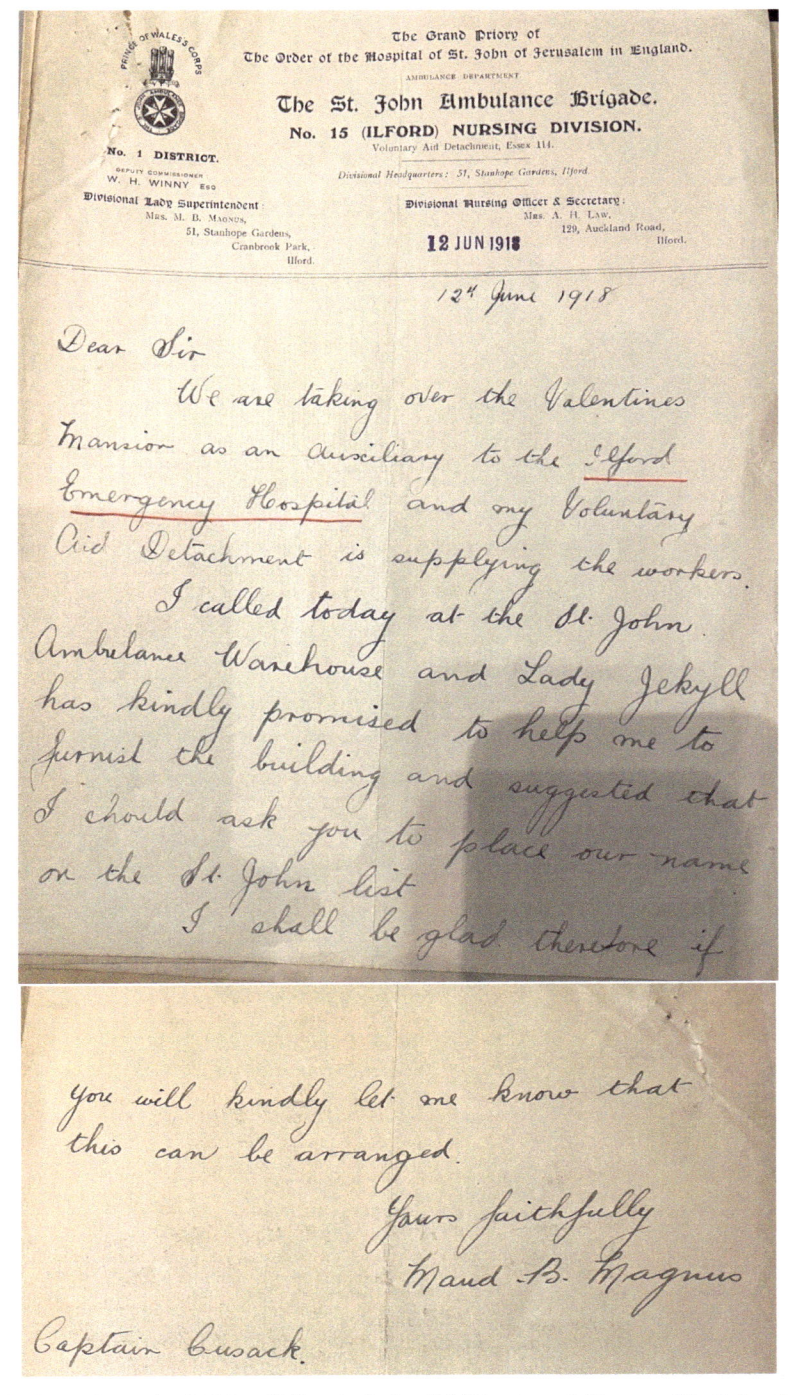

> 12th June 1918
>
> Dear Sir
>
> We are taking over the Valentines Mansion as an auxiliary to the Ilford Emergency Hospital and my Voluntary Aid Detachment is supplying the workers.
>
> I called today at the St John Ambulance Warehouse and Lady Jekyll has kindly promised to help me to furnish the building and suggested that I should ask you to place our name on the St John list
>
> I shall be glad therefore if you will kindly let me know that this can be arranged.
>
> Yours faithfully
> Maud B. Magnus
>
> Captain Cusack.

Mrs M. B Magnus Letter dated 12 June 1918 to the Acting Chief Secretary. © Museum of the Order of St John

The St John Ambulance Brigade Ilford

> The A.M.D. 2.
> War Office,
> Adastral House,
> Victoria Embankment.
>
> 19th June, 1918.
>
> Dear Sir,
>
> I enclose herewith a form of registration for the Valentine's Mansions which is an Annexe to the Ilford Emergency Hospital. Would you kindly add this to the list of St. John Hospitals and return the form in due course.
>
> Yours faithfully,

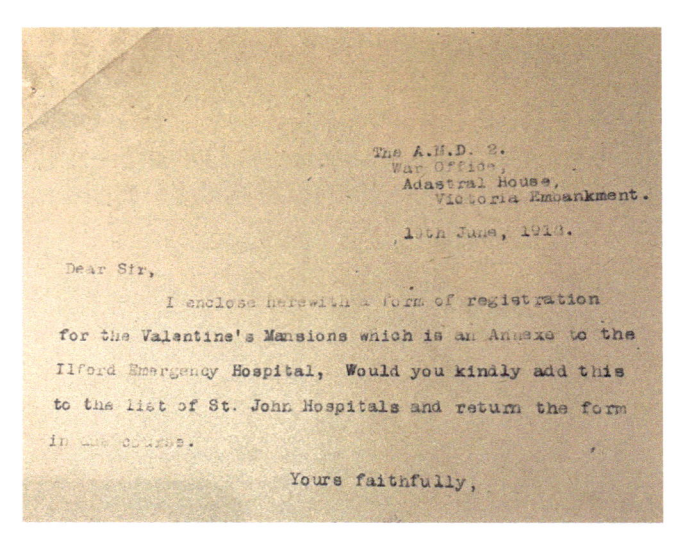

Letter from Chief Secretary to Army Medical Department at the War Office dated 19 June 1918. © Museum of the Order of St John

> COPY.
>
> Name of Hospital. - Valentine Mansions, Ilford,
> (Annexe to the Ilford Emergency Hospital, Ilford.)
>
> 1. Number of Beds: 60
>   Whether for Officers only..........
>   Whether for Officers and Rank & File..........
>   Stating numbers of each..........
>   Whether for Rank & File alone. Rank & File 60 beds.
>
> 2. Staff provided
>   Number of Medical Men available. Medical Staff Ilford Emergency Hospital,
>   " " Nurses fully trained One at present contemplated.
>
> 3. Whether full provision of
>   a) Beds, &c.... The Governors of the Ilford Emergency Hospital are hoping that
>   b) Hospital Stores & Drugs. the expenses of bedsteads, bedding, etc. will be met by public
>   c) Food.......... subscription.
>
> 4. Are you prepared to undertake the whole cost of maintenance, including pay of entire staff, if so, for how long?... Paid for out of Government Grant by Committee of Ilford Em. Hosp.
>   If not, state definitely what financial aid is required....... Not any.
>
> Maud H. Magnus,
> Essex 114.
> Commandant.

The Registration Form Completed by Mrs Magnus © Museum of the Order of St John

IB.

Mrs. Magnus,
51, Stanhope Gardens,
Cranbrook Park,
Ilford.

Dear Madam,

I regret that I omitted to acknowledge the receipt of your letter dated the 13th instant forwarding the form of registration for Valentine Mansions. This form has been sent to the War Office.

Yours faithfully,

Undated Letter to Mrs Magnus from the Chief Secretary acknowledging receipt of the Registration form.

© Museum of the Order of St John

ILFORD EMERGENCY HOSPITAL (Incorporated).

VALENTINES MANSION.

NOTE.—All communications and goods should be addressed to Valentines Mansion, Cranbrook Road, Ilford.

'Phone: Ilford 349.

Valentines Mansion,
Cranbrook Road,
Ilford.

7 AUG 1918

4th August 1918.

Dear Sir,

In reference to my letter of June 12th & again in July, could you let me know whether we shall receive the articles asked for, from our St. John warehouse, for the Hospital at Valentines Mansion, of which I am Commandant.

We expect to open very shortly, & if you cannot help us, I must think of other ways & means of obtaining these very necessary articles, although I understood that the Warehouse was for the help of Hospitals where St. John Voluntary Aid Detachments were working.

Yours faithfully
Maud B. Magnus

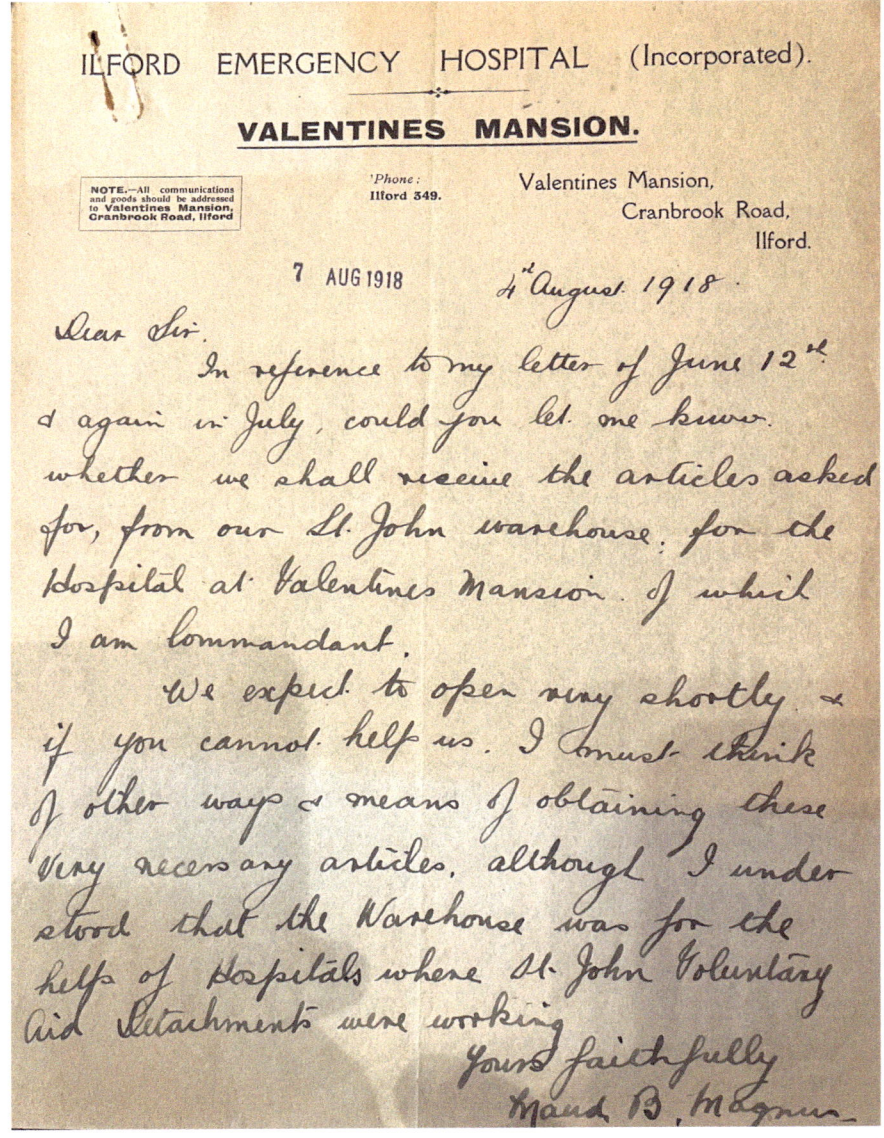

Letter from Mrs Magnus on a Ilford Emergency Hospital, Valentines Mansion Letterheading to the Chief Secretary, dated 4 August 1918

© Museum of the Order of St John

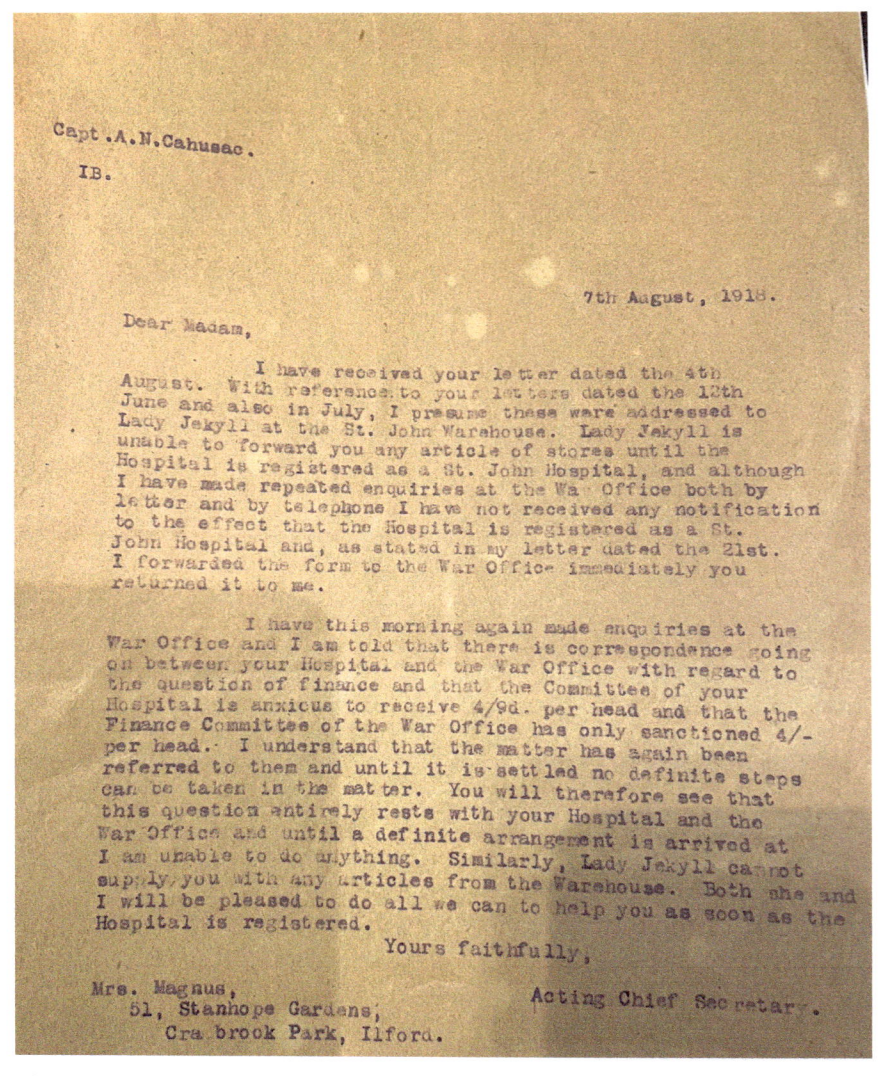

The St John Ambulance Brigade Ilford

Capt. A.N.Cahusac.
IB.

7th August, 1918.

Dear Madam,

I have received your letter dated the 4th August. With reference to your letters dated the 12th June and also in July, I presume these were addressed to Lady Jekyll at the St. John Warehouse. Lady Jekyll is unable to forward you any article of stores until the Hospital is registered as a St. John Hospital, and although I have made repeated enquiries at the War Office both by letter and by telephone I have not received any notification to the effect that the Hospital is registered as a St. John Hospital and, as stated in my letter dated the 21st. I forwarded the form to the War Office immediately you returned it to me.

I have this morning again made enquiries at the War Office and I am told that there is correspondence going on between your Hospital and the War Office with regard to the question of finance and that the Committee of your Hospital is anxious to receive 4/9d. per head and that the Finance Committee of the War Office has only sanctioned 4/- per head. I understand that the matter has again been referred to them and until it is settled no definite steps can be taken in the matter. You will therefore see that this question entirely rests with your Hospital and the War Office and until a definite arrangement is arrived at I am unable to do anything. Similarly, Lady Jekyll cannot supply you with any articles from the Warehouse. Both she and I will be pleased to do all we can to help you as soon as the Hospital is registered.

Yours faithfully,

Mrs. Magnus,
51, Stanhope Gardens,
Cranbrook Park, Ilford.

Acting Chief Secretary.

Reply to Mrs Magnus from Acting Chief Secretary dated 7 August 1918 © Museum of the Order of St John

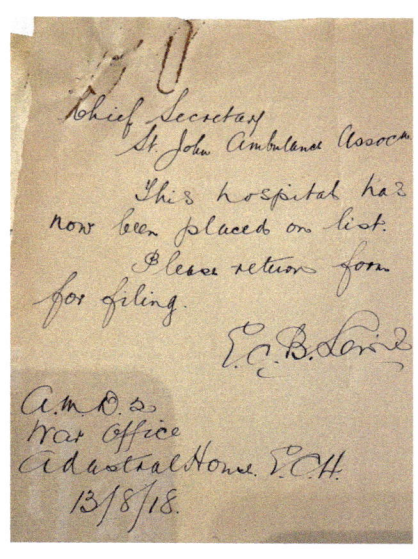

Chief Secretary
St John Ambulance Association

This hospital has now been placed on list. Please return form for filing.

E.C.B. Levine

A.M.D.2
War Office
Adastral House, E.C.4.
13/8/18.

Note from Army Medical Department 2, War Office to Chief Secretary, St John Ambulance © Museum of the Order of St John

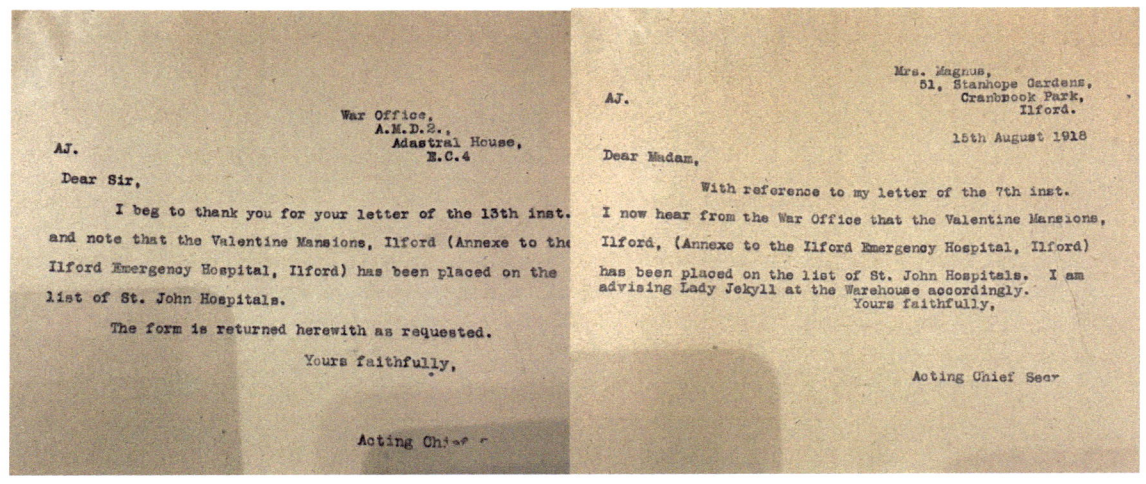

Letter of acknowledgment from Chief Secretary to War Office and a letter to Mrs Magnus from Chief Secretary date 15 August 1918
© Museum of the Order of St John

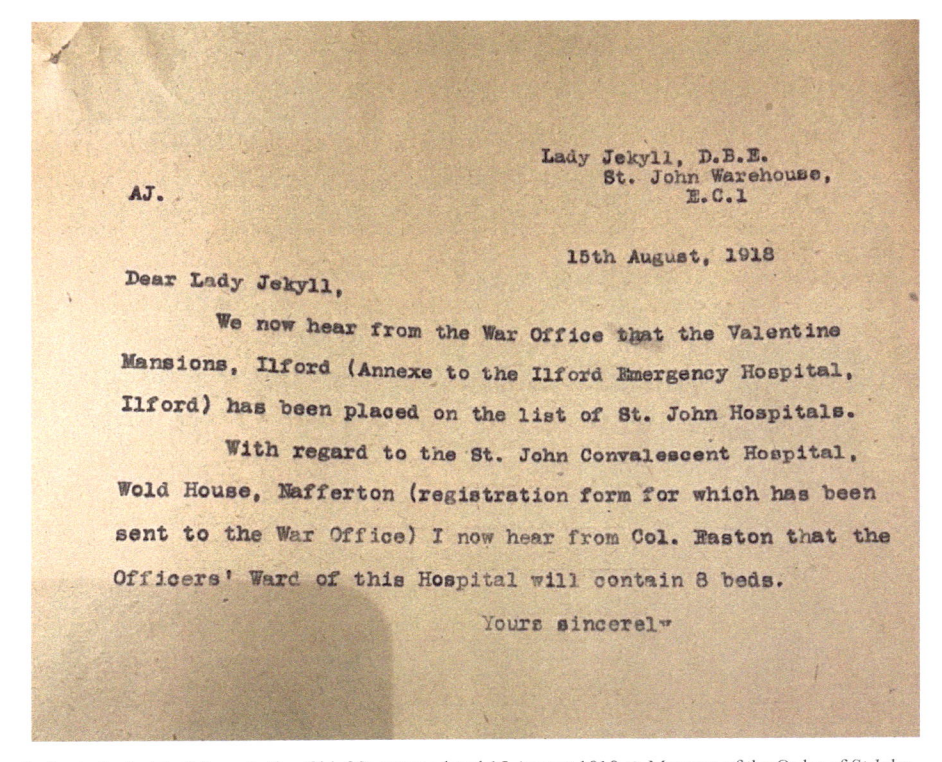

Letter to Lady Jekyll from Acting Chief Secretary dated 15 August 1918 © Museum of the Order of St John.

This was the final letter in the file. The Mansion ceased to be an auxiliary military hospital in March 1919.

After the war, Ilford Borough Council bought the remainder of the land (which had been used for farming) and created a public park - Valentines Park.

The Mansion is now a Grade I* listed building and it was restored in 2007 and is now a venue for community activities, such as exhibitions, talks and tours.

Appendix 11 Miss Alice White 1880- 1963 A Founder Member.

The Recorder on the 19 October 1961 carried the story of Miss Alice White a founder member of the No 15 Ilford Nursing Division under the headline *"She helped to form St John's – 50 years ago."* The article read -

> Among those present at the golden jubilee celebrations of the 15th (Ilford) Nursing Division of the St John Ambulance Brigade, held at the seven Kings Hotel last week, was a founder-member of the division. With 35 years' service to her credit.
>
> She was 82 year-old Miss Alice White, who lives at 84 Kensington-gardens, Ilford. Miss White who since her retirement has been a Serving Sister of the Order of St John, was one of 12 women who formed the 15th Division in 1911. Their first duty, Miss White told the recorder was to set up a tent in Valentines Park and treat the many casualties, many cuts and bruises that came to them.
>
> Miss White gave a record number of years of service to the division, treating the wounded during both wars, when an emergency ward was set up in King George Hospital.
>
> At her home this Miss White sat treasuring photographs of her early nursing year days and recalled her first inspection in Hyde Park "It was terrifying," she declared.
>
> What does Miss White do now? "Housework takes up all my time now," she said.

Miss White[130] retired from the division in 1947.

Nursing Sister Miss Alice R White

Miss White's, service record during WWI is recorded in Appendix 4. This shows she served in the Emergency Hospital & Valentines Mansion, Ilford, on a part time basis and performed 937 hours.

---

[130] Died 1963 in Poplar.

The St John Ambulance Brigade Ilford

Appendix 12 Joseph Charles Raith. 1894 - 1984

Charles was born in Ilford Essex on 12 April 1884 by occupation he was a butcher. He joined the Navy at Chatham on 31 January 1913 and he served until 21 May 1920. He then joined the Royal Fleet Auxiliary 22 May 1920. His service record is given below. He was a member of Ilford Division St John Ambulance up to the 1930's.

On the 1939 register he was living at 7 Railway Street, Redbridge, Essex

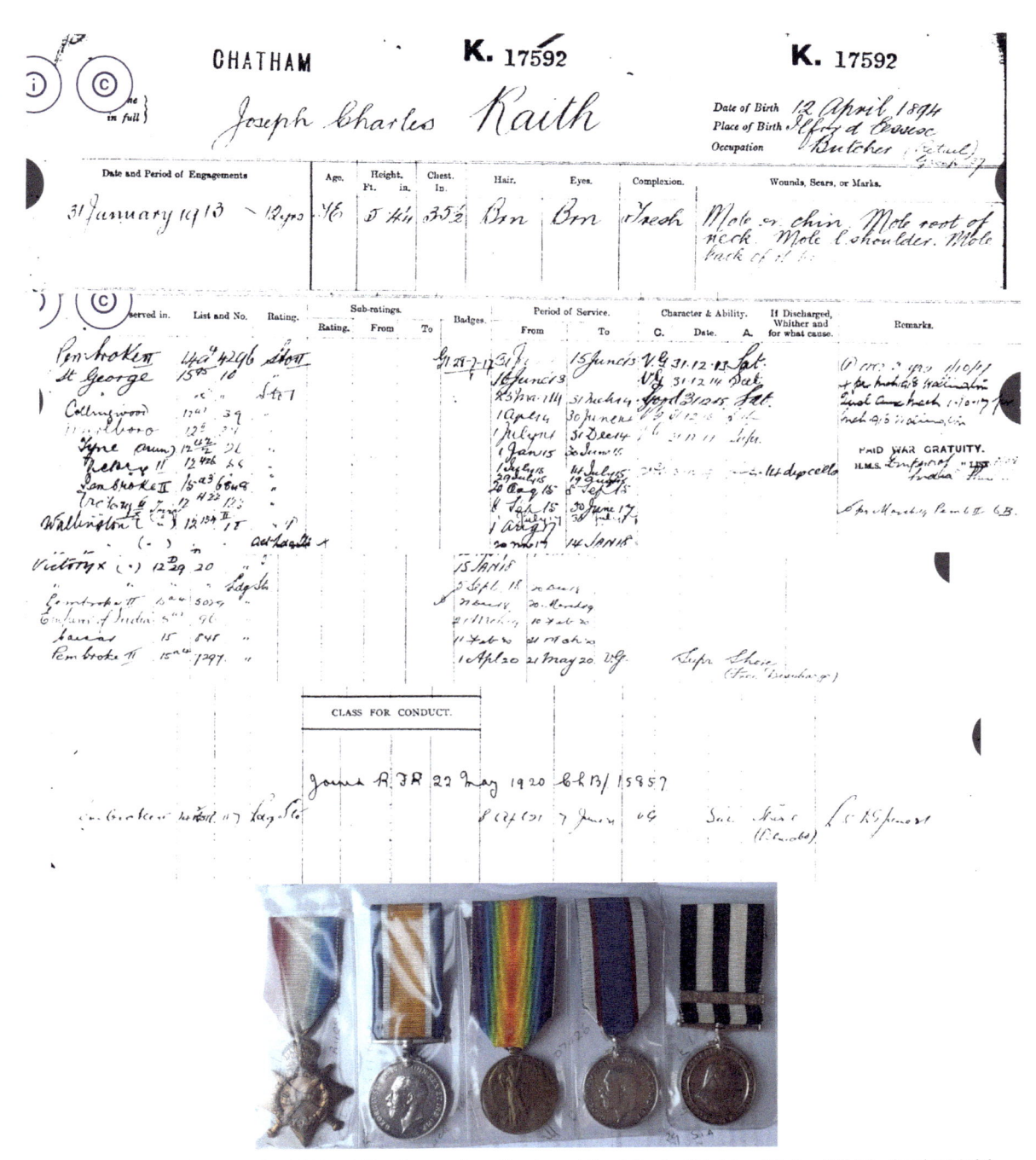

14/15 Star, War Medal, Victory Medal, Royal Fleet Reserve Long Service and Good Conduct Medal and Order of St John Service Medal and Bar (20 Year's). From the Collection of Mr Gary Coker and used with permission.

* * * * * *

Bibliography

Books Accessed

1. Imperial Gazetteer of England and Wales 1870 -1878 by John Marius
2. Annals of the Ambulance Department, by N. Corbet Fletcher, Second Edition 1947
3. The Ambulance Men of March by Alan J. Sharkey 2017 ISBN 978-1-905729-40-1
4. Potted History of Ilford by Norman Grunby Privately published in 1997
5. The Annual Report of the Order of St John 1905 - No 15 (East Ham) Ambulance Division
6. The Annual Report of the Order of St John 1907 No 46 (Ilford) Ambulance Division.
7. United Grand Lodge of England Freemason's Membership Registers of 1751-1921
8. The Medical Register 1915
9. War Diary of 29th Casualty Clearing Station at Gezaincourt National Archives WO95/415
10. War Diary: Matron-in-Chief, British Expeditionary Force, France and Flanders The National Archives WO95/3988-91
11. Hired to Kill by John Morris. Publisher: Rupert Hart-Davis, London. 1960
12. Behind the Blue Lamp by P.Kension & D. Swinson Publisher Coppermill Press 2003 ISBN 0-9546534-0-8
13. The German Air Raid in Great Britain 1914-1918 by J. Morris. First Published in 1925 by Sampson Low, Marston & Co. Ltd. (Managing Director Fred J Rymer, a member of Ilford Division)
14. Reports by the Joint War Committee and Joint War Finance Committee of the British Red Cross Society and the Order of St. John of Jerusalem on England on Voluntary Aid rendered to the sick and wounded at Home and Abroad and to British Prisoners of War, 1914 -1919.

The "B" Mention in Dispatches Published by The Naval & Military Press Ltd Facsimile from Original

1. War Office Communique B' Mention in Dispatches 3rd March 1917
2. War Office Communique B' Mention in Dispatches 18th October 1917
3. War Office Communique B' Mention in Dispatches 12th March 1918
4. War Office Communique B' Mention in Dispatches 10th August 1918
5. War Office Communique B' Mention in Dispatches 8th April 1919

6. War Office Communique B' Mention in Dispatches 19th August 1919
7. War Office Communique B' Mention in Dispatches 21st April 1920
8. War Office Communique B' Mention in Dispatches 7th May 1920

Registers and Roll of The Order of St John

1. The Medical Register 1923
2. Roll of the Order of The Order of St John 18 February 1927
3. The Medical Register 1935
4. Probate Register Norwich 1934
5. Probate Register Norwich 1962
6. Probate Register Norwich 1985

Files accessed through the National Newspaper Archives in Chronological Order

1. The Chelmsford Chronicle 17 December 1875
2. The London Evening Standard 11 December 1875
3. Tower Hamlets Independent on 19 January 1884.
4. The Standard of 8 February 1884
5. London Gazette 9 November 1886
6. The Times 17 February 1891
7. The Standard 30 April 1892
8. The Essex Herald 11 July 1893
9. The Forres, Elgin and Nairn Gazette of 12 July 1893,
10. The East London Observer 5 August 1893
11. The East London Advertiser 10 March 1894
12. The Advertiser of Somerset 22 March 1894
13. The Thetford and Watton Times 10 November 1894.
14. The Herald 8 August 1896.
15. The Tower Hamlets Independent and East End Local Advertiser 10 April 1897
16. The West Ham and South Essex Mail 10 April 1897
17. The Essex Herald 18 May 1897
18. The Herald 29 May 1897
19. Essex County Chronicle on 4 June 1897.
20. The West Ham and South Essex Mail 9 April 1898
21. Morning Post 13 May 1898
22. Bury Free Press, Bury St Edmunds 14 May 1898
23. The Eastern 7 December 1898
24. The Essex County Standard 29 April 1899
25. The Diss Express 12 May 1899
26. The Monmouth Beacon 17 November 1899
27. East London Advertiser 25 November 1899
28. The West Ham and South Essex Mail 24 February 1900
29. The Eastern Counties Times 10 August 1901

30. The Eastern Counties Times 7 September 1901
31. The Essex Guardian 19 October 1901
32. The Recorder 14 February 1902
33. The Essex Newsman 12 April 1902
34. The Essex Newsman 06 December 1902
35. The Essex Newsman 12 April 1902
36. The Leominster News 17 July 1903
37. Essex County Chronicle 24 July 1903
38. Evening Post 31 July, 1903.
39. Ilford Guardian 29 August 1903
40. The Barking, East Ham and Ilford Advertiser 5 September 1903
41. The Recorder on 29 July, 1904
42. The Recorder on 2 December 1904
43. East Ham Echo 27 November 1904
44. The Recorder 30 December, 1904
45. The East London Advertiser 10 June 1905
46. The Recorder 4 August, 1905.
47. The Essex Chronicle On 20 July 1906
48. The Eastern Counties' Times 12 October 1906
49. The Shipping Gazette and Lloyds List 23 March, 1907
50. The Berks and Oxon Advertiser 31 May 1907
51. The Eastern Counties' Times 21 June 1907
52. The Essex Guardian June 22, 1907
53. East London Advertiser 13 June 1908.
54. The Essex Guardian 8 July 1908
55. The Eastern Counties News 22 October, 1909
56. The Barking, East Ham and Ilford Advertiser 4 December,1909
57. The Essex Times 16 October 1910
58. The Recorder 2 June,1911
59. The Recorder 23 June 1911
60. The Recorder 30 June 1911
61. The Recorder 7 July 1911
62. The Daily News 12 July 1911
63. The Recorder 28 July 1911
64. Eastern Counties' Times London 22 September 1911
65. The Recorder 29 September 1911
66. The Recorder 13 October 1911
67. The Recorder 17 November 1911
68. The Recorder 1 December 1911
69. The Barking East Ham and Ilford Advertiser 27 January 1912

70. The Recorder 7 June 1912
71. The Recorder 28 June 1912
72. The Recorder 12 July 1912
73. The Daily Mirror 24 July 1912
74. The Recorder 8 November 1912
75. The Recorder 8 May 1914
76. The Recorder 26 June 1914
77. The Recorder 11 September 1914
78. The Recorder 21 May 1915
79. The Recorder 11 September 1914
80. The Recorder 9 October 1914
81. The Recorder 6 November 1914
82. The Globe 1 January 1915
83. The Westminster Gazette 1 January, 1915
84. The Standard 2 January 1915
85. The Loughborough Newspaper 08 January, 1915
86. The Recorder 8 January 1915
87. The Recorder 15 January 1915.
88. Essex County Chronicle 15 January 1915
89. Framlingham Weekly News 30 January 1915
90. Birmingham Mail 27 January 1915
91. The Recorder 2 April 1915
92. The Recorder 7 May 1915
93. Sheffield Telegraph 13 May 1915
94. The Recorder 14 May 1915
95. The Recorder 21 May 1915
96. The Evening Standard 13 May 1915
97. Chelmsford Chronicle 17 May 1915
98. The Recorder dated 28 May 1915
99. The Recorder on 18 June 1915
100. The Recorder 30 July 1915
101. Eastern Counties Times 26 March 1915
102. The Recorder 30 April 1915
103. Stratford Express 15 May 1915
104. The Recorder 22 October, 1915
105. The Recorder 26 November 1915
106. The Recorder March 3, 1916
107. Echo and Mail Friday 9 June 1916
108. Eastern Counties News 8 September 1916
109. The Northampton Daily Echo 20 December 1916
110. London Gazette New Year Honours 1 January 1917
111. The Recorder January 1917
112. London Gazette 1574 13 February 1917
113. The Scotsman 14 February 1917

114. The London Gazette 27 April 1917
115. The Recorder 1 June 1917
116. The Recorder 15 June 1917
117. The Recorder 15 June 1917
118. The Recorder 22 June 1917
119. The Recorder 29 June 1917
120. The Recorder 6 July 1917
121. The Globe 10 July 1917
122. The Recorder 17 August 1917
123. London Gazette 24 October 1917
124. London Gazette, 30453 Page 143, 1 January 1918
125. The Recorder 4 January 1918
126. The Kenilworth Advertiser 12 January 1918
127. Sunday Pictorial 6 January 1918
128. London Gazette 21 June 1918
129. The Illustrated Police News 8 August 1918
130. The Eastern Counties Newspaper 18 October, 1918
131. The Recorder dated 16 August 1918
132. The London Gazette Birthday Honours List 1918
133. London Gazette 31 July 1919.
134. The Recorder 5 March, 1920
135. The Recorder 26 March 1920
136. The Birmingham Gazette 25 March 1920,
137. The Recorder 30 April 1920.
138. The Recorder 30 July 1920
139. Eastern Counties News 27 August 1920
140. London Illustrated News 9 October 1920
141. The Recorder 15 October 1920
142. Leicester Daily 13 October 1920
143. The Pall Mall Gazette 4 November, 1920
144. The Daily News 7 October 1921
145. The Recorder 04 November 1921
146. The Recorder 31 March 1922
147. The Recorder 28 July 1922
148. The Recorder 11 August 1922
149. The Recorder 10 November 1922
150. The Recorder 30 March 1923.
151. The Recorder 18 April 1924
152. The Recorder 11 January 1924
153. The Eastern Counties News 11 January 1924
154. Chelmsford Chronicle 15 February 1924
155. The Recorder 12 September 1924
156. The Globe 1 October, 1926
157. The Globe 4 October 1926

158. The Eastern Counties News 31 August 1928
159. The Recorder 13 December 1929
160. Eastern Counties News 04 January 1929
161. The Essex Chronicle 6 May 1930
162. The Advertiser dated 6 June 1930
163. The Diss Express 20 March 1931
164. The Recorder 10 July 1931.
165. The Diss Express 17 March 1933
166. The Recorder 8 June 1933
167. The Recorder 12 October 1933
168. The East Ham Echo 19 January 1934
169. The Recorder 16 May 1935
170. The Recorder 14 June 1934
171. The Recorder 9 August 1934
172. The Essex Chronicle 21 June 1935
173. The Essex Newsman February 1936
174. Yarmouth Independent 01 February 1936
175. Yarmouth Independent 29 January 1938
176. The Advertiser dated 11 February 1938
177. Portsmouth Evening News 14 October 1940
178. London Gazette 27 June 1941 issue 35203 page 3674
179. The Rugby Advertiser 20 January 1948 informed its
180. Leicester Evening Mail 21 February 1953.
181. The Rugby Advertiser 27 February 1953
182. The Rugby Advertiser 6 February 1959
183. Coventry Evening Telegraph 3 March 1965.
184. The Recorder 12 October 1961
185. The Recorder 19 October 1961

Professional Journals Accessed

1. The British Medical Journal 21 August 1897
2. Great Eastern Railway Magazine Volume 3 September 1913 No 33
3. The Railway News 09 April 1898
4. Royal Army Medical Corp Journal February 1919
5. Army and Navy News Orders (Order No 161) dated 10 June 1911.
6. First Aid Journal April 1914
7. First Aid Journal July 1914.
8. The Engineer 8 January 1915.
9. Great Eastern Railway Magazine Volume 5 May 1915 No 53
10. Board of Trade Report by Lieutenant-Colonel Pelham George von Donop On the Ilford Train Crash published 16 February 1915.
11. First Aid Journal August 1915

12. St Bartholomew's Hospital Journal April 1918 Copyright Bart's Health NHS Trust
13. First Aid Journal January 1917
14. First Aid Journal June 1918
15. First Aid Journal District Orders of November 1919.
16. Great Eastern Railway Magazine Volume 8 March 1918 Page No 46
17. The Railway News 15 June 1918
18. The Great Eastern Railway Magazine, 1920 Volume, Page 87
19. The London & North Eastern Railway Magazine March 1928
20. The London & North Eastern Railway Magazine June 1928
21. The London and North Eastern Railway Magazine May 1929
22. The London and North Eastern Railway Magazine November 1929
23. The London and North Eastern Railway Magazine Norwich Social Club October 1929
24. The Journal (Norwich Hospital Fund, Contributory Scheme Committee) 30 December 1933
25. The Journal 14 April 1934
26. The Journal 21 April 1934
27. The London & North Eastern Railway Magazine, March 1937 (Volume 26 No 3 page 617) Ilford Historical Society Newsletter, No.121 August 2016

Photographs

1. Ilford Bed Plaque photograph by Brian L Porter Courtesy of Redbridge Museum and Heritage Centre 17 June 2022
2. Liverpool Street Station Photograph of Ambulance Train Science Museum Group Collection February 1916
3. Lady Ethel Perrott RRC Photograph by Bassano Ltd 23 March 1920 – Photograph Courtesy NPG (x120383) License 24674 30 April 2022
4. Ilford Division Ambulance c1930. Location and Photographer not known. Courtesy of Redbridge Museum and Heritage Centre
5. Ilford Division and Ambulance c1930 at Hainault Forest Photographer Unknown Courtesy of Redbridge Museum and Heritage Centre
6. 1930 Ilford Division Evening Concert Programme and the Arterial Road Service Dressing Station. Courtesy of Redbridge Museum and Heritage Centre
7. Evening Concert programme, Capitol Cinema, Upminster 29 April 1934. Courtesy of Redbridge Museum and Heritage Centre
8. Snapshot Photograph Album of Ilford Emergency Hospital. Facebook page of "Remembering British women in WW1 – The Home Front and Overseas" 14 May 2019 - 27/02/2019,
9. Autograph Book Ruth Gillam, Ilford Emergency Hospital.

Census Records Accessed

1. Census for 1881 Battersea
2. Census for 1891 Lower Leyton, Essex.
3. Census for 1901 Ilford
4. Census for 1901 Manor Park
5. Census for 1901 Leyton Parish of West Ham District
6. Census for 1911 Ilford.
7. Census for 1911 Manor Park
8. Census for 1921 Maldon
9. The Register for 1939 Redbridge

Internet Sites visited

1. https://www.eastlondonhistory.co.uk/west-ham-conference-centre-ww2-photos/
2. www.geni.com/people/Lord-Claud-John-Hamilton/6000000003714066802)
3. https://blogs.ucl.ac.uk/survey-of-london/tag/portman-rooms
4. https://www.historyfiles.co.uk/ChurchesBritain/London/East_Newham14.htm
5. https://www.ancestry.co.uk
6. https://www.findmypast.co.uk
7. https://ezitis.myzen.co.uk/oakwoodmilitary.html
8. https://www.cwgc.org
9. http://www.ramc-ww1.com/profile.php?cPath=211_654&profile_id=5663
10. https://www.facebook.com/groups/1468972083412699/
11. https://www.gordonhighlanders.com
12. https://www.watfordobserver.co.uk/news/9996344.jack-the-ripper-suspect-buried-in-jewish-cemetery-in-east-ham-claim/.

Achieves Accessed

1. Order of St John Museum Archive
2. Redbridge Museum and Heritage Centre Achieve
3. Wellcome Collection First World War and Later Material Licence Attribution -Non-Commercial 4.0 International (CC BY-NC 4.0) Date1916-1920 Reference RAMC/446/17-26 4 Royal Army Medical Corps Muniments Collection
4. The British Red Cross online archive of Voluntary Aid Detachment Records 1914 - 1919 acc.
5. The National Archives (WO329/3253).